W9-BRG-835

Ladies' Vintage Accessories

Identification & Value Guide

LaRee Johnson Bruton

COLLECTOR BOOKS

A Division of Schroeder Publishing Co., Inc.

The current values of this book should be used only as a guide. They are not intended to set prices, which vary from one section of the country to another. Auction prices as well as dealer prices vary and are affected by condition as well as demand. Neither the author nor the publisher assumes responsibility for any losses that might be incurred as a result of consulting this guide.

Front cover:

Pink chenille hat with ostrich plume, "Beth Hat" label, dating to late 1930s, $65.00 – 75.00; ivory lace collar shown on page 71; pale blue gloves shown on page 117; petit point purse shown on page 243; metallic silver shoes shown on page 284; lovely background is silk shawl shown on page 68.

Cover photo: Chris Bryant, Paradise Productions
Cover design: Beth Summers
Book layout: Mary Ann Hudson
Book design: Ben Faust

Searching for a Publisher?

We are always looking for knowledgeable people considered to be experts within their fields. If you feel there is a real need for a book on your collectible subject and have a large comprehensive collection, contact Collector Books.

COLLECTOR BOOKS
P. O. Box 3009
Paducah, Kentucky 42002-3009
www.collectorbooks.com

Copyright © 2001 by LaRee Johnson Bruton
Values updated, 2003

All rights reserved. No part of this book may be reproduced, stored in any retrieval system, or transmitted in any form, or by any means including but not limited to electronic, mechanical, photocopy, recording, or otherwise, without the written consent of the author and publisher.

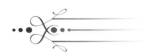  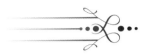

Contents

Photo Credit: © 2000 Chris Bryant

Acknowledgments

There are many people to acknowledge who have made this project so rewarding. Over the years of collecting I have met wonderful people who have supported and inspired me to follow my passion. *Hats off!* to the many vintage clothiers who have found marvelous pieces for my collection and the generous people who have trusted me with the stewardship of their treasured family heirlooms. I would especially like to say *Hats off!* to my parents, June and Lew Harman, who over the years have been on the look out for "old clothes" at auctions and estate sales. Mother has always loved hats. She gave me her own, plus any others she could find!

Hats off! to the many good friends who have contributed to this book. Rosetta Hurley, a long-time friend and well-respected vintage clothier, has supported this project by loaning me special pieces from Persona Vintage Clothing, as well as consenting to review the values from a retail perspective. Bette Belle, a licensed appraiser and long-time friend from Montana, has also been very generous with her professional evaluation of the accessories in this book. Chris Bryant, professional photographer, has added her artistic eye and talent to make this an aesthetic, as well as an informative book, with cover and chapter heading photos. My friends Beth, Joy, Jane, Jessie, and Anne have given me their support in loaning accessories from their collections, as well as envisioning a successful book that will be of benefit to other collectors. *Hats off!* to you all!

Hats off! to Lisa Stroup for trusting in my vision of this book, and for her guidance. Finally and most importantly, I would like to say *Hats off!* to my dear husband, Tim, who has been understanding of the time it has taken away from household responsibilities that he has willingly taken on (and I will soon have to resume) while the focus has been on writing. He has overlooked stacks of hat boxes waiting for a good day to photograph, piles of notes and quotes on the desk, and an array of old magazines waiting to be researched. *Hats off!* to him for agreeing to edit the final manuscript before it was sent off to the publisher.

Hats off! and my gratitude to you all!

LaRee Johnson Bruton

Photo credit: © 2000 Chris Bryant

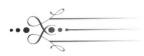  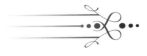

Preface

hy do we collect vintage accessories and garments? And what do we do with stacks of hat boxes, crinolines, corsets, parasols, and purses? As collectors, each of us has embarked upon a challenging path. In our care we have precious artifacts that blend social meaning with material beauty. I must admit it was that beauty that intrigued me at first, which set my course as a collector. The passion simply was to acquire as many beautiful accessories and fashion pieces as I could find and afford. A "holy greed," one collector called his obsession. In the beginning it was a quest for beautiful pieces that I could actually wear.

Many people have asked me over the years, "How did you start collecting old clothes?" My love for old clothes, fabric, and fashion began long before I found my first vintage dresses in an old trunk in the back of an antique shop in Missoula, Montana. It may have begun with my first home economics class in high school when I gained the knowledge of how to put the language of fabric and fashion together, creating style. Or maybe before then, at age 7, in a school program dressed in flowing fabric and glittering rhinestones, I dreamed of being a fairy princess.

In a letter to my Grandmother, my mother wrote, "LaRee really enjoys the nightgown you sent — she parades around in it like a fashion model." Whenever this passion for fashion began, "dress-up" was the name of the game.

The language of wool, linen, and lace is the language I speak. And I still like to play dress up! With care and caution, it's an opportunity to share treasured pieces of the past.

LaRee, at age 2, in the true fashion model pose.

LaRee, at age 7, fully accessorized to grant wishes.

LaRee, at a grown-up age, modeling a 1930 bias cut silk chiffon gown.

To Wear or Not to Wear

I was frequently asked to provide clothing and model in various fund-raising events. However, using antique or collectible garments and accessories presents many questions for consideration. How old is it? Is it of historical significance? Will cleaning destroy the fabric? Are the threads strong enough to hold the beads in place? Will there be irreversible damage if it is worn or carried? There are some pieces, because of their age, their history, or delicate fabric that would be best used for museum exhibits or even carefully framed and passed down to future generations to enjoy.

Most of us love these vintage treasures and would not intentionally destroy them. Yet, we need to use extreme care with regard to those pieces we choose to use in our daily lives. Wearing a pair of 1800s wedding slippers that belonged to your grandmother, inside a church for your own wedding day may be a special sentimental touch. If they are not unduly stressed and only worn on carpet for the 5 – 10 minutes of the ceremony, it may be worth the risk. However, it would not be wise to dance at your reception in these same shoes. Wearing a 1940s felt hat for a day in the city may add that bit of panache your ensemble needs and would usually be no problem. If the hat is a rare Lilly Dache design and it is pouring down rain, that would not be a wise choice. I must admit I have become more conservative over time. Whether it is a hat or purse or pair of shoes, we need to learn about the item before we take measures that could, over time, destroy that which we love.

Besides wearing our vintage accessories many of these items can be enjoyed in other ways, as wonderful accessories for the home. For instance, a group of 1950s box purses on a shelf can be an interesting focal point that others will enjoy. A silk shawl casually draped over a chair adds flair and color. Your grandmother's wedding hankie framed on moire taffeta for the bedroom is a sentimental romantic touch. Your collection should be enjoyed, with these cautions in mind:

- Rotate vintage accessories for display and avoid direct sunlight.
- Store items in acid-free tissue or wrap in washed cotton sheets.
- Keep your collection in a smoke-free environment.
- Maintain a stable temperature, no extremes of hot and cold.
- Monitor humidity with a dehumidifier or fan.
- Do not make irreversible alterations.
- Ask a professional for advice to maintain the historical integrity.

Documentation

As a good steward of these purses, parasols, hankies, and handbags, may I suggest that you consider documenting these treasures. Did Great Aunt Millie get married in those ivory silk shoes? Did your grandmother carry that mesh purse to a speakeasy in the 1920s? Did your mother wear that molded magenta felt hat during World War II?

Often the stories that accompany each bit of history are as fascinating as the fashion accessory itself. When you acquire a piece, whether a hat or hankie, parasol or purse, ask questions. As lovely and wonderful as the piece is, any history you can record makes it that much more significant. This is called the provenance — the place of origin, the source of the item, the date when it was used, who owned it, and any information that can be acquired from a family member or the original owner.

It is like an archeological dig. The shard of glass or bowl or bead is wonderful to find as you dig, but what does it tell you about the people and the times? Our fashion accessories have a story. Learn what you can at the time of acquisition, then write it all down. For instance, the shoes in the photo on page 11 are lovely, but who wore them? And where might she have gone?

This is the story I got from the daughter-in-law:

These ivory silk shoes and pale peach stockings were worn by Louise Vaughn of Springfield, Missouri. She was born in 1908, her father worked for the railroad. Louise was a well-traveled and independent young woman. She married twice and had one son. She was also a woman before her time and definitely not the traditional woman who was a mere shadow of a man. She probably cast her own shadow very well, thank you very much. Although she was a private person, love letters found after her death in 1997, reveal that she rendezvoused with a well-known movie star of the 1940s. When you look at her photo taken in the 1920s, you can only imagine what a coquette she must have been! The lace collar was packed with the shoes and stockings when I received the box. The family was kind enough to tell me the story and loan me the photo.

This information is documented and will remain with the shoes and stockings when my collection is passed on to someone else. The history of who wore the shoes and the personality behind the accessories, gives the shoes and stockings provenance, thereby making them more historically significant.

Determining Age

The exact age of an accessory is extremely difficult to determine, unless you have first-hand information, such as shoes that you wore when you were married. Or a photograph of your mother wearing that hat with a date on the back. Memory can even play tricks on us as time goes by. I've had people tell me one thing, with the best intentions, while indications are that the piece is from ten years earlier or much later. For instance, "It's really old, it belonged to my grandmother who wore it in the twenties." But it is made of polyester and has a zipper down the back!

A good example is the beaded purse, right. If it had been found in an antique shop it would be worth a certain amount of money because of the beaded scene, the frame, its condition, and its age. These are all factors we use in determining a dollar value. However, there is another value that we can attribute to an item, and that is its historical value. This purse is engraved with the original owner's name, Mrs. H. J. Droppers, the grandmother of a very good friend, Jane Audrey. The purse had been passed on to Jane from her mother, in the original T. A. Chapman Co. box. This knowledge allows us to more accurately date the purse to about 1910, when Jane's grandmother purchased it from the well-known department store in Milwaukee.

Determining the age of an accessory based on fashion pictures can be a challenge. A perfect example is the hat in the photograph on page 13. From all indications it looks like mid-twenties with the large sloping brim, deep crown, and wonderful

Cover of Pictorial Review, July 1925.

band detail, similar to the lovely *Pictorial Review* cover from July 1925. It is even lined, which is often a clue to the age of a hat. But look again, it has a new label, "Frederick & Nelson, Seattle," as well as a small rayon size "7" tag. It is a beautiful reproduction!

Just because a hat is old does not mean it was in good taste in its day or that it was considered the typical example of the era. A fashion faux pas most certainly existed in our grandmothers' time, as well as bad taste, just like today. We also fall into thinking that certain styles were the only style for that period; for example, the cloche of the 1920s. Other styles were worn in the 1920s, including broad brims. Many people mistake some of the 1960s-style hats for 1920s. Look at the finishing details for clues, as well as the labels. New labels are very different.

Studying the trends in the history of fashion is helpful, as well as studying the period fashion magazines of the times. Spending time in museums studying fashion accessories will help one distinguish the characteristics of a beaded bag from the 1920s versus the 1940s. Exposure to many items over time helps one recognize the "feel" of different eras. That is why trusting a dealer who specializes in the accessories you collect can be important when buying an accessory. Without firsthand information from the original owner, that dealer can give you an educated "guesstimate" because of his or her exposure to hundreds of beaded bags from many different eras.

What may have been on the cutting edge of style in New York in 1910 may not have reached Idaho or Washington until 1912 or 1913. Trends did seem to move from east to west, and from large cosmopolitan cities to rural areas. Even with years of experience, we have to know that there are some accessories that defy the fashion trends, just like today.

Front view of straw hat.

Side view of straw hat.

Inside view of lining and label.

How Much Is It Worth?

The question most collectors want to know is, "How much is it worth?" Updating values is tricky business. The market for vintage accessories has been up and down over the past few years, due in part, to the influence of online auctions such as ebay. Depending on who is bidding, a beaded purse, for example, may sell for many times what it is really worth, simply because one person has decided they have to have it! At first, the inflated prices seem like good news when you see a similar item in your collection or remember that your great aunt has "one exactly like that!" However, trying to re-create that market can be difficult.

There are many other factors that one must take into consideration when placing a monetary value on a fashion accessory. Let's take the example of an apron. Aprons were often found in yard sales or church rummage sales a few years ago for $.50 or less if you lived in certain parts of the country. They are becoming harder to find. You might be able to find the same apron in secondhand or thrift stores for $3.00–5.00. Perhaps that same apron could be found in a general antique store not specializing in textiles or clothing, with prices ranging from $10.00 to $15.00, or more. That same apron in good condition may be available in a vintage clothing store at a slightly higher price. A collector would rather pay a couple bucks, but how many yard sales and thrift stores would they have to visit to find the same quality item?

At the top price, what are you really paying for?
- Hours of searching, and often many miles traveling
- Expertise in recognizing authentic accessories, not copies
- Time to clean, repair, and mend
- Store overhead and the employees' salaries to make these accessories available
- Risk, that the right collector will come through the store to purchase the item
- Loss of merchandise due to theft or breakage
- Knowledge which can be passed on to the collector

What are the factors that increase the value of an accessory? Generally the older purse will be of greater value. A beaded purse from the turn of the century will usually have more value than a beaded purse from the 1950s. However, a beaded Judith Lieber designer purse may have more value than a plain 1900s gold beaded purse with no label or designer. A plain gold beaded purse from the turn of the century that is in mint condition with the original chain and lining will have more value than a more elaborate beaded purse that is in poor condition with bead loss and a replaced lining.

What are the factors that one should keep in mind when buying accessories?
- Condition, condition, condition.
- Does it have its original lining, chain, feathers, veil, buttons?
- Has it been altered or "prettied up?"
- Does it have a label or maker?
- Is there a provenance, information on the original owner?
- Is it an unusual example or common example?
- What part of the country are you searching?
- What is "hot" or in demand this year, thus increasing the price?

A value guide is just that, only a guide. Back to our original question, "How much is it worth?" The value of an accessory depends on many factors, as listed above. Often the value and the price are not the same. The accessory may have great sentimental value or great historical value, but can only be priced for a few dollars when trying to sell it. Likewise, someone may not place much value on "that old thing" and not realize how much someone would pay for it. In my early years of collecting, I was appalled to hear all too often, "Oh, if I had only known someone would have even wanted it, but we burned the trunk and everything in it out back." Alas!

In the end, an accessory is only worth what someone is willing to pay for it. Our real challenge is to educate people as to the historic value, and the fact that these beautiful accessories are fragile and are becoming more and more scarce in their original condition. It is significant to recognize our roles as caretakers of these fragile pieces of history. As a fellow collector, my hope is that you will find this book helpful and educational. And if this book inspires anyone to become a better caretaker of his or her collection, it will be worth it (and I will be applauding)!

****

Except where indicated, all accessories are from the private collection of the author.

At one time a woman's purpose may have been to be an accessory to her husband, showing his wealth or status in society, but that time is no more. The dictionary defines accessory as "a thing of secondary or subordinate importance" and "an object or device that adds to the beauty, convenience, or effectiveness of something else." The fashion accessory that is chosen will enhance the overall look and effectiveness of a particular dress or suit. If a Victorian bustle gown was worn with stiletto heels and a lucite purse, it would look bizarre. If you want to truly understand how the bustle gown would have looked, the appropriate accessories, including hat, shoes, gloves, etc., need to be worn with the gown.

In this book of accessories, the hope is that you will enjoy a part of fashion that is intrinsic to the look of an era. If a person were to wear a Civil War era hoop dress, with a modern hairstyle of today, lacking the proper foundation garments, without gloves or an appropriate hat, it will tell you nothing of the fashion during the Civil War period. To really understand the fashions of the past, they must be accompanied by the accessories of the past, and those accessories must be appropriate for the era, as well as the occasion. You may have a matching hat in regard to color, but is it appropriate to the period and the style of dress? If it is a sporting costume, or a casual costume it must have an appropriate casual hat, not a hat worn for dress occasions.

The styles for hats or shoes or purses have been in constant flux. The degree of change for accessories is small each year, and what was "in," is now "out." But, have no fear, it will be back. There are only two constants in fashion. One constant is change, year by year, season by season. The second constant is it will be back again. For instance, some of the close-fitting hats of the 1960s were similar in style to the cloche style hats of the 1920s. The difference was the way they were worn, as well as construction techniques and details.

> *"If you look good and dress well, you don't need a purpose in life."*
>
> Robert Dante

To begin the study of fashion trends for accessories, year by year, we see only small differences. Maybe an inch in the length of gloves or an ever-so-subtle change in the heel shape. We must stand back and look at the overall trend for that decade or that period. Fashion was slower to change in the 1800s than in modern times. Part of that tendency is set into motion by marketing and the desire for increased sales. Convince a woman she is out of style, and she will go shopping, unless she is a trend-setter herself, in which case she will pay no heed to the skillful media assault through magazines and TV.

Women were influenced in the past by what was the in fashion. There are many sources one can look to for the correct period accessories, starting with the fashion plates of the periodicals for the era you are interested in researching. Below is an 1861 hand-tinted fashion plate from a fashion source of the Victorian era, *Godey's Lady's Book*.

Fashion illustrations in the period magazines are helpful in showing the idealized shape and form for

The appropriate bonnets and headdresses for adults, as well as children, are shown in this fashion plate. The little girl is wearing a cape, and the lady in front is carrying a small parasol. Godey's Lady's Book, July 1860.

THE DELINEATOR

OCTOBER 1913

The Palm Court at the Ritz Carlton Hotel in New York
The "smartest" people in the world may be found here of an afternoon

FIFTEEN CENTS   THE BUTTERICK PUBLISHING COMPANY   NEW YORK $1.50 A YEAR

the era. Below is a good example of the small waist, small hands, and petite feet that were the ideal beauty of the Edwardian era. This illustration also shows the correct tip of the hat, the length of the gloves, and the shoes worn at this time.

Fashion illustration from The Delineator, October 1906.

about when and how accessories were worn in a specific era. On the back of this postcard is a note from Helen to Miss Grace Kern, postmarked May 27, 1911. Photographs could be printed on postcard forms and mailed to friends. This was very popular in the early 1900s.

The periodicals of the era often describe the times and the reason for the accessory. As illustrated on page 18 in the June 1918 issue of *The Ladies' Home Journal*, hats, parasols, and purses are described. The hat and matching purse on

Photograph of Mrs. Greenfield, circa 1910.

Accessories in old family photos are interesting to compare with the accessories you may have in your collection. Old photos that you find in flea markets or at the auction also show what people actually wore, not the idealized fashion. The photo, top right, is excellent to understand how the large hats were worn correctly. This photo of Mrs. Greenfield is a beautiful example of a woman wearing a tailored suit, large plumed hat, and carrying a crocheted purse.

The real photo postcards (right) are often dated on the back, which give us valuable clues

Postcard of two cheeky young ladies in casual attire with hats, dated May 27, 1911.

the left is designed "since yarn is denied us, twine has been requisitioned to take its place, with such stunning results as this crocheted hat and bag, threaded with green ribbon." Accessories in "The World of Lovely Things" are intended to aid "in these war and thrift days." Fashion was important to women in World War I.

The 1920s gave way to accessories for the liberated woman who was more active in sports, as shown in the fashion illustration on page 18. Paris says, "The sports mood is gayly expressed in the matched hat and scarf, or kerchief, in painted or printed silks and linens." "Belt buckles match

The World of Lovely Things

In These War and Thrift Days

Clothes for the Well-Earned Recreation

For in These War Times We Must Keep Ourselves in Working Condition

1. Hair braid and Chantilly lace combine to make this black hat, trimmed with ciré ribbon. Price, $10.

2. On a taffeta crown and narrow facing, superimposed on this droopy leghorn-brimmed hat, flowers of variegated colors are lightly arranged on top. Price, $15.

3. Since yarn is denied us, twine has been requisitioned to take its place, with such stunning results as this crocheted hat and bag, threaded with green ribbon. Set, $50.

9. The becomingness of line of a college mortar board is given to this straw and silk hat, with quills; $5.75.

7 and 8. Field flowers imprisoned by brown malines give color to this beige liséré poke; $8.50. To the patent-leather hat on the right are added red hemp flowers; $12.50.

10. A sailor collar, sash and pockets smarten this sleeveless white satin coat below; $8.90. Striped serge skirt in green and brown. Price, $6.75.

NOT all of us are privileged to go "overseas" to help, there is much to be done right here; and our women are undoubtedly doing their "bit" in a most spontaneous way, giving abundantly of their time and vitality as well as of their financial aid. Even so, there will be odd moments, possibly days at a time, as the hot weather approaches, when we shall realize that our efficiency will be increased by taking vigorous outdoor exercise, or by some recreation of one sort or another. We have therefore selected for you the best models for these purposes at, as you will appreciate, the most attractive prices. Should you be clever with your needle, you will see how readily most of the things can be copied.

To help further, there is a pattern for the unbuyable Eton suit in No. 4. Patternable, too, is the sport suit in No. 5, and the good-looking bathing suit in No. 14, the latter meeting the need of those who wish to protect their necks and arms. The bathing suit at the left of the lower center is just what will be welcomed gladly if you really need something new, yet refuse to pay more than is necessary for what is well made and becoming. The charm and simplicity of the sleeveless jackets and skirts at the center right speak for themselves. The wide belt of the jacket in No. 10 ties with sash ends, and the cunning little pockets can be buttoned for protection of their contents. The skirt with this jacket is of striped serge and has a back yoke which becomes a belt at the front.

The coat at the lower left may be had, also, made of crêpe de Chine or rubberized material, at a slight difference in price; and if one falls in love with the rain cap illustrated with No. 12, it can be ordered specially made. While we will gladly tell you where everything can be bought, that is not patternable—upon receipt of six cents in stamps, to cover the cost of postage and service, addressed to the Fashion Editors—we cannot do your shopping for you.

3. Since yarn is denied us, twine has been requisitioned to take its place, with such stunning results as this crocheted hat and bag, threaded with green ribbon. Set, $50.

1607-1608

4 and 5. The girl who chooses this sport suit above, with touches of plaid, will need just such a trig little beige straw hat with navy facing and perky bow. Hat, $10. Red quills, black streaked, smarten the red Milan hat which tops off the navy gaberdine Eton suit and maize blouse.

1622 1623

6

13

1621

14

10

11

12

6. A small but protective brim of leghorn, joined by a satin band to a soft crown of cerise chrysanthemum braid, makes motoring in comfort possible, especially when one's frock is protected by a coat of Palm Beach cloth like the one above. Price, $12.75; hat, $5.

13 and 14. Gay plaids are thoroughly at home against a background of sand dunes, so this taffeta bathing dress, with sleeves and collar to protect one from the caresses of a too ardent sun, will be correctly placed. If one prefers unrestricted arms and collarless neck, one will wisely choose a black poplin suit as shown on the left, piped in color. Price, $4.95. In vivid red rubber, with black tassel, is the cap; 45 cents. Bathing slippers in black satin, $1.75.

11 and 12. The sleeveless coat of navy taffeta above, with collar and pipings of beige satin, is worn with a skirt checked in yellow and white, with an overlaying plaid in black. Skirt, $6.75; coat, $6.90. A silken overhead raincoat, rubberized and plaid trimmed, $25.

NOTE—Patterns Nos. 1607 and 1622 come in sizes 16 and 18 years and 36 to 42 inches bust measure; Nos. 1608 and 1623 in sizes 16 and 18 years and 26 to 32 inches waist measure, and No. 1621 comes in sizes 36 to 42; price, 15 cents each, post-free. Send money, stating number and size, to the Pattern Department, The Ladies' Home Journal, Philadelphia, Pennsylvania.

Accessories from The Ladies' Home Journal, June 1918.

Fashion accessories from Pictorial Review, April 1923.

Within the illustration:

PARIS SAYS

4321
Paris—Regny

4314
Paris—Worth

4330

TINY hats of the new shiny cellophane straws, or composed entirely of lacquered flowerets, adopt the nose veil as a formal accessory. The sports mood is gayly expressed in the matched hat and scarf or 'kerchief, in painted or printed silks and linens. The scarf sketched at the left shows how jauntily a simple oblong scarf can be tied. Its plain border smartly sets off the brilliantly printed center.

Sports jewelry for Spring days is of three approved types: colorful strands of graduated beads; gold and silver chokers and chains, matched by brooches and bracelets; and curious onyx, shell, crystal and semi-precious sets copied from antiques. For formal dress, crystals, and crystals combined with pearls compose some of the smartest creations.

Belt buckles match hat brooches among the more expensive trifles of the ensemble. Gloves favor the pull-on as supremely modish. These are almost invariably of washable suède in the neutral tones of beige, grege and sometimes gray.

Coat 4307
Frock 4304
Paris—Premet

Jacket and
Blouse 4305
Skirt 3829

---

hat brooches" and "gloves favor the pull-on as supremely modish." Antelope and reptile purses are in vogue with matching shoes. This ad is full of information as regards accessories for the modern woman of the 1920s.

Comparing old photographs with the fashion magazine illustrations give us a realistic view of the people and what was actually being worn. On the top of page 20 is a class picture taken in 1924 of the Barnard Hall girls. Notice the style of dresses, the scarves and shoes, as well as short hairstyles that accommodate a cloche style hat. The illustrations in *Modes & Manners* of the same year show the stylized view of fashion accessories.

Accessories are described as "the hat is felt." Or "a flat envelope bag matches the low-cut lizard or alligator oxfords. Stockings of chiffon lisle or medium weight silk are the same neutral shade of the antelope gloves." This information helps to date items in your collection more accurately, as well as identify what accessories are appropriate to wear with various styles of garments, thus creating an authentic look for 1927.

1924 photo of Barnard Hall girls of Madison, Wisconsin.

It is these personal items that were worn or carried that bring us close to the life and times of the women in the past. As our lives become busier, we look back to what seems like a carefree life. As our clothing becomes more mass produced, we look back to the handwork and the love that was sewn into each individually produced accessory. At one time long ago, someone thought of a design and someone put that idea into form. Someone selected that piece to be in their shop and someone walked in and decided that it was the perfect accessory for their ensemble and budget. Whether decorative or useful, these cast-off fantasies have a living presence. And so it is with the accessories we treasure today, in each piece is the soul of the designer, the creator, and the wearer.

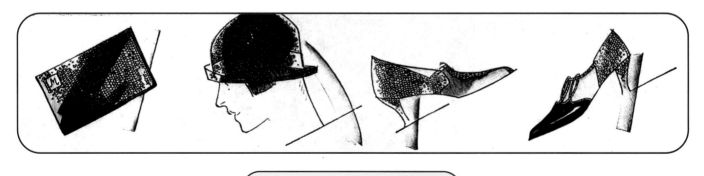

Modes & Manners, June/July 1924.

The Forecast Wardrobe and its Accessories

9-C   9-B

9-D   9-A

Delineator, November 1927.

SEASONING

Nylon spun to look and feel like wool, for these white stockings by Bonnie Doon, $1.95. Wanamaker

Wheatlmen in a neat underarm envelope, topped by a rolled cuff of soft grosgrain. Lord & Taylor

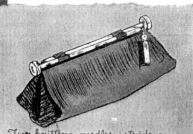

Ballast for your suits—wedge-heeled oxford with square eyelets and thong lacing, $9.95. Julius Grossman

Underarm pouch bag of capeskin, zipper-topped and roomy enough for knitting, $5. At Altman

Two knitting needles astride a huge pouch of faille, big enough for knitting and everything, $5. Saks 5th

Fringed square, blazing with Navy sayings, "Don't give up the ship", and the like, $2.95. Lord & Taylor

Tailored blouse of dark rayon crêpe, outlined with saddle stitching, by Joan Kenley, $3.50. Franklin Simon.

Wear Right's suited rayon, whip-stitched pullons, ten button length to crush down $1.50 Oppenheim Collins

More help for the WPB—domestic cotton, crocheted into a bow-topped cap, $3.95. Bonwit Teller

SKETCHES BY MARY HILL

83

Page of accessories from Mademoiselle, April 1942.

*"IT CAN'T BE WRONG"

Certainly, black is black. But black is right. So right it can't be wrong (except for picnics and breakfast). These are High-Noon-On dresses which can start out in the broad daylight without blinking and go on and on into the deep night. This is Big City Black. It's a paradox that black...opaque, covered-up... should be so cool on a summer's day.

• Left: Afternoon-of-a-Shirtwaist-Dress. Both twinkle with rhinestones, have pretty drapery, a nice simplicity. Enka rayon crêpe. Franklin Simon; Rich's; Bonwit Teller. Philadelphia.

• Below: First, long satin gloves, saddle bag. Above, black rose. All; Lilly Daché. Second: Befrogged belt, evening bag. Hattie Carnegie.

• Opposite: Little boat-neck, dolman-sleeve dresses of rayon crêpe. A cut-steel buckle fastens the beautiful satin bow on the foreground dress, secures the side drapery on the dress in the reflection. Saks-Fifth Avenue; Neiman-Marcus.

• All; Adele Simpson designs. Flato jewels

*SONG HIT: MUSIC BY MAX STEINER; LYRICS BY KIM GANNON

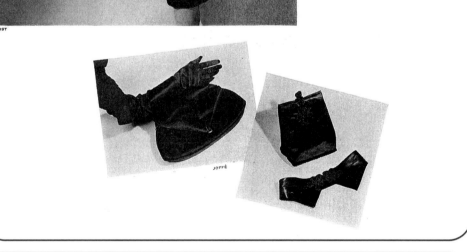

Gloves, hat, bag, and belt from Vogue, June 1943.

Photo Credit: © 2000 Chris Bryant

Apronstrings. A grouping of 1940s floral cotton aprons just hanging out, getting a breath of fresh air.

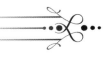

Aprons

The original term "apron" referred to a free-hanging panel attached at the front of the skirt, worn as early as the thirteenth century. "Apron" is from the Old French word "napperon," or the diminutive "nappe," simply meaning cloth. A napperon, or napkin, became an apron. In the middle ages an extra piece of cloth was tied over the skirt when sitting down at the table to protect the dress. Later this style was adopted by servants and a small bib top was added to protect clothing while working. Variations in color and style were then used to denote the artisan or trade of the workman.

From a functional protective cloth, it evolved to a decorative apron of lace or embroidered cloth seen as part of the seventeenth century fashion and into the eighteenth century. Many Scandinavian countries, as well as Russia, used the decorative apron as part of their traditional costume. The term "apron" is not often associated with what we think of as accessories but, in fact, it has become that something extra added to help in a secondary way.

A mere hundred years ago, aprons were an essential part of a lady's dress. Aprons were worn to clean the home, to cook meals, to garden, to care for children, to feed the chickens, to bake the bread, to make the soap, and the many other chores that defined a woman's role in society. And yet all the while women were wearing aprons they were also creating art. It was an art form practiced by American women in their homes — an art form that was frequently dismissed or overlooked. These women were a part of a culture whose system of values failed to appreciate the technical complexity and visual sophistication of their stitchery as art. It was expected

> "Beware of all enterprises that require new clothes."
> *Thoreau*

that each young woman would become proficient in needlework as part of her domestic role, but it was not considered an art form. Generally, it was relegated to the status of one more chore to be done. Their inspiration was not with the thought of fame, fortune, or even recognition, but only to create garments that would bring aesthetic and spiritual sustenance to themselves, their families, and friends.

The work of these women was familiar to almost every household and touched the lives of almost everyone. Sitting at her mother's knee, a young girl was trained in the fundamental technical skills of embroidery, quilting, lace-making, crocheting, knitting, and designing and sewing clothing. This artist had a scrapbag for a palette, and a needle for a brush. Although not recognized until recently as an art form, it was socially acceptable as a creative outlet because she was conforming to the domestic role of women.

Diagram of apron pattern, sold for 25 cents, Bazaar, 1872.

Pattern for apron and cap, The Delineator, October 1906.

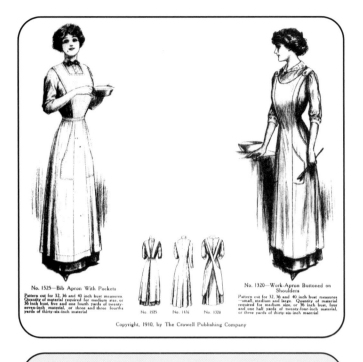

Patterns for two aprons, Woman's Home Companion, August 1910.

Those pieces that remain with us today serve as an important legacy for social and art historians. Much can be learned from those women who were able to synthesize their domestic role and their creative impulse. Preserving what might be termed "extraordinary art by ordinary women," who in many cases remain anonymous today, is the stewardship role we each take on as collectors.

Creating fashion and the making of a home were truly expressions of art, created primarily by women. Adding grace, warmth, and beauty to our lives, most of these women went about their work while wearing a variety of aprons. With little applause or financial rewards from community or family, acting out of love and an intense desire to improve their lives, they persevered in their creation of art, whether it was a hand-stitched quilt or hand-crocheted lace purse.

By preserving this art form we may revise women's work to reflect women's art, thus honoring those women who have gone before us. Aprons seem to carry a host of nostalgic memories of a simpler time when women's roles were clearly defined, albeit greatly restricted. Whether it is a red and white gingham apron with cross-stitched design or the cotton floral print Hoover apron

Six lawn aprons for one dollar, The Ladies' Home Journal, September 1915.

For YOU . . . or Your FRIENDS

DESIGN No. 1104. Here is a thought you might consider for developing into some charming and welcome Christmas gifts this year. It's a single design, containing three different aprons.

The first is your favorite easy-to-make dirndl type. And the other two are princesse-lined. To make the dirndl one is such an easy and such a gratifying task that you'll probably make up several—for yourself as well as for your friends.

Simply cut and edge the bodice, shir the waist, and then attach it to the sash ends and the bodice waistline. That's all there is to it. It's that easy to do.

Percale and other cotton fabrics are suggested. And rick-rack braid trimming is festive looking and easy to sew on.

Designed for sizes small, medium and large.

Apron for a Christmas gift, Woman's World, November 1938.

of the 1930s, aprons seem to conjure up the smell of home-baked cookies and warm bread, clean lemon-scented kitchens, a simpler, secure homelife.

From a time when aprons served as a functional part of dress to protect one's clothing from the work being done, to a decorative apron of lace or embroidered linen for special teas, to the fluffy cocktail aprons of the 1950s, we have come full circle. Aprons, if worn at all today, are usually worn only for food preparation. They are back to a functional status.

The following photos will only hint at the great variety of aprons one can find. They are all charming, from the frothy tea aprons

of silk ribboned, embroidered and lace, to the well-worn and stained aprons that we know were used to make many an apple pie. If these aprons could only tell us of the work they have seen.

Early pastel ads for "P and G" White Naptha Soap, The Delineator, June 1923.

Cotton aprons priced from $.59 – 2.98 from Wards catalog, 1947.

Variety of apron patterns available,
Modern Priscilla, November 1924.

PLENTY of aprons and house frocks have their place in the fall sewing schedule of every home woman. There are ginghams and chambrays, percales and prints, crêpes and cretonnes galore from which to choose, and a touch of hand embroidery will enhance the charm of many a simple model.

No. 2-1631. This apron is the sort one is glad to wear about the house, and is very pretty when made of a plain fabric, with trimming bands of another shade or color, and a few lazy-daisy and outline posies. It goes on over the head. Designed for sizes 34 to 44. Requires 3⅛ yards of material.

No. 2-1637. An apron for the kitchen, that is easy to slip into, has shoulder straps and ties at the back. When you make the apron of checked gingham, do the cross-stitching over the little checks; when you make it of plain material, the design must be stamped. Designed for sizes 36, 40, and 44. Requires 2⅝ yards of material.

No. 2-1655. A practical cover-all, fastening on the hips, just requires some bright blossoms in appliqué to dress it up. Designed in one size only. Requires 2¾ yards of material.

No. 2-1920. A frilly apron to wear when you get the Sunday night supper, is lovely when made of lawn or dotted muslin or organdy. It has a collar bib, and ties in back. Designed for one size only. Requires 1⅝ yards of material.

No. 2-2051. Another practical kitchen apron which goes on over your head and closes at the sides has gathers over the hips. Bright bindings and an appliquéd flower on the pocket are sufficient decoration. Designed for small, medium and large sizes. Requires 2 yards of material.

No. 2-2133. A slip-on morning dress which depends on its single stitch and lazy-daisy embroidery in pretty colors for charm. Designed for sizes 16 years and 36 to 44. Requires 3¾ yards of material.

No. 2-2176. A one-piece apron with back crossed and snapped to slashed edges at front, forming sleeves. Designed in one size only. Requires 1¼ yards of material.

No. 2-2178. This one-piece kitchen apron is designed in one size only. Requires 1⅝ yards of material.

Estimates are for medium sizes and 36-inch materials.

Cutting Patterns and Embroidery Transfer Patterns may be purchased by mail at 15 cents each, postage prepaid, if you address The Priscilla Company, 85 Broad Street, Boston, Mass.

48

*Summer parties call for
pretty dresses. The pink-
and-white gingham "cover"
dress has a princess line,
button front and puff sleeves.
Vogue Design No. 8356, 12 to 20.
The "conversation piece"
apron of organdy is appliquéd
with tiny felt flowers and
sequins. The blue-and-white-
tissue gingham has a sweeping
skirt, a simple bodice.
No. 8351, 12 to 20.
The apron, white organdy
embroidered with red cherries.*

Ladies' Home Journal, June 1954.

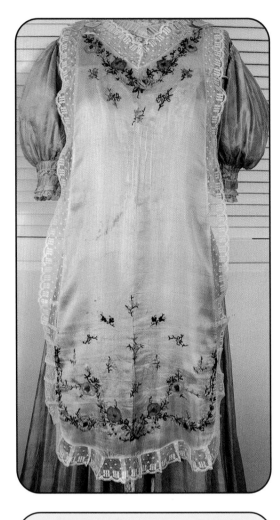

Close-up of the tea apron and detail of the silk ribbon work at neckline of tea apron.

Palest pink silk tea apron, trimmed in 1½" machine-made lace, silk ribbon folded roses, green variegated silk ribbon, and embroidery floss. This style apron is pinned at the shoulders, concealed by the pale pink silk ribbon bows. This feminine apron would have been worn for festive occasions, serving tea or receiving guests, dating to mid-teens. $35.00 – 50.00.

Half apron in soft aqua sateen cotton, trimmed with aqua crochet work on bottom hem and waistband with a cord woven through and tied in back, dating to early 1900s. $25.00 – 45.00.

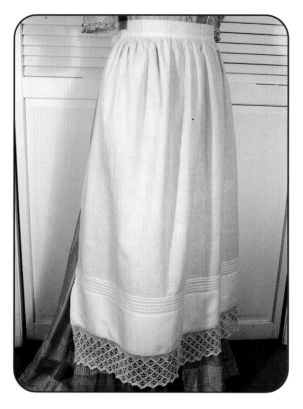

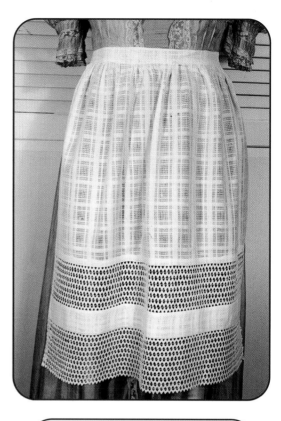

Half apron in white cotton with rows of tucks and white crocheted lace on hem, long ties in back, dating to early 1900s. $30.00 – 40.00.

Half apron in a window-pane weave cotton, with two rows of rick-rack lace trim, ties in back, dating to early 1900s. $25.00 – 35.00.

Close-up of the apron above showing the delicate weave of cotton fabric and the rick-rack lace trim. This early form of lace was actually made in the Victorian era; I have a cotton night-gown that is dated to 1870 from my family, which is trimmed with this form of lace.

Half apron of sturdy cotton, scalloped edge in a buttonhole stitch with lovely white on white flower embroidery pattern, small center pocket, dating from teens through 20s. $25.00 – 34.00.

Half apron in fine lawn with delicate machine-made lace insets, typical of the Edwardian period, 1900 – 1910. $24.00 – 33.00.

Fancy Tea Apron kit, complete with stamped fabric, embroidery floss, and directions by Bucilla, #5498. Many women made their own aprons from kits of this kind during the teens and 20s similar to the photo on the right.

Half apron of fine cotton, embroidered in blue Art Nouveau design, trimmed in machine-made lace, dating to mid-teens. This might have been a kit apron, such as the photo on the left. $19.00 – 29.00.

The Ladies' HOME JOURNAL

Lovely new designs in
BUCILLA
Reg. U. S. Pat. Off.
Embroidery Packages

The "BEBE DANIELS Apron *(Drawn from Photo)*

THE clever woman, when she runs away for a vacation, tucks in a variety of Bucilla Package Outfits to occupy those restful hours on porch and beach.

Looking toward the holiday season, she realizes that distinctive gifts, exquisite apparel for women and children and novel decorative pieces for the home, all can be made in a short time at a fraction of what their cost would be if bought hand-embroidered.

Naturally she chooses Bucilla Embroidery Packages, for she knows there are no tedious details of selecting materials, no complicated cutting or sewing. Each package contains, besides the stamped article of superior fabric, the correct Bucilla Guaranteed Washfast Flosses to complete the work, a lesson chart and a needle of the proper size.

In the department stores or needle art shops you will find a complete variety of Fall designs—or write for free descriptive circular showing articles to match those illustrated here, and many others. Use coupon below.

BERNHARD ULMANN CO., INC.
"Everything for Art Needlework"

Bucilla Package Outfit
5199—"Bebe Daniels" Apron of crisp maize organdie. Patches for Colonial girl figure and straps are of orchid dotted voile. Ready-made with pastel embroidery cottons to complete, $1.50.

Bucilla ad to make an embroidered apron, The Ladies' Home Journal, July 1924.

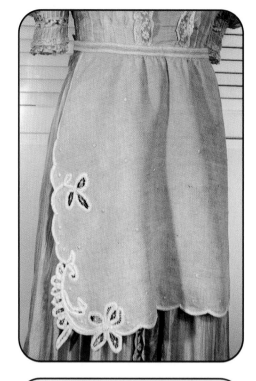

Half apron of ecru linen, trimmed with ivory Battenburg lace design and small embroidered dots overall, dating to mid-teens. $28.00 – 38.00.

Close-up of reverse side of apron, showing the detail of the embroidery and stitching on the back to give a shadow effect on right side.

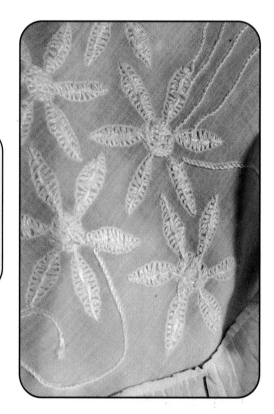

Half apron of fine white cotton lawn, white-on-white shadow embroidery design, with ruffled edge; dating to early 1900s through teens. $25.00 – 38.00.

Fancy black tulle tea apron, trimmed with metallic thread and silk ribbon embroidery at waistband and bordering hemline, early 1900s. $75.00 – 85.00.

Detail of ribbon roses, leaves, and metallic thread embroidery.

Long white cotton apron, tucking detail and hand-knitted lace with ecru silk ribbon on bottom, apron ties also trimmed. This must have been a very special apron made for a gift, however small stains in front indicate that it was well loved and used; dating to early 1900s. $40.00 – 50.00.

Close-up of the exquisite hand-knitted lace in a lovely diamond pattern, double rows of ecru silk ribbon woven through for a finishing touch. It is amazing to think of the time that it must have taken to make this lace!

Full pinafore style navy ging-ham apron, V-front and full pigeon breast bodice, nicely trimmed in smaller scale navy checked fabric, buttoned back; dating to early 1900s. $40.00 – 55.00.

Back view showing almost full coverage, two button closure.

Long half apron of navy ging-ham with small cross-stitch design on hem and pocket; very typical of early 1900s. $28.00 – 36.00.

Full cotton calico apron in small black pattern, rick-rack trim on bodice and pocket, ties in back; dating from teens through twenties. $19.00 – 29.00.

Half apron of black silk, very plain, perhaps for mourning, has a silk ribbon fancy bow at waist; dating to Victorian era. $25.00 – 35.00.

Half apron in small black print cotton, self-fabric ruffled edge, ties in back; dating from the teens to the twenties. $15.00 – 24.00.

Half apron in small calico print, entire apron is hand stitched with small ½" ruffle along the edge; dating to early 1900s. $22.00 – 36.00.

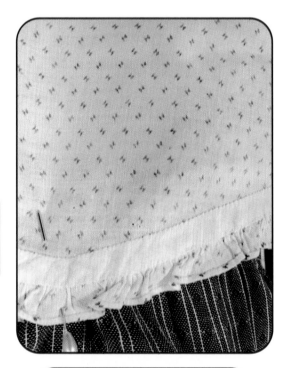

Close-up of the hand-stitched tiny hem of the ½" ruffle. Amazing handwork!

Close-up of crochet lace edging in photo at top right, which is intricate and attractive.

Half apron of black sateen cotton with attractive black and ecru 5" crochet lace edging on hem, pinned at waist; dating to Victorian era. $34.00 – 45.00.

Full black print cotton apron, trimmed with wide red bias tape, two side pockets, and ties in back; dating from 20s to 30s. $19.00 – 28.00.

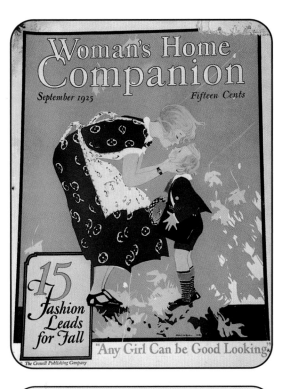

Woman's Home Companion, September 1925 issue. Charming cover with lady in apron and child. Originally fifteen cents.

Full white cotton apron, with embroidery detail around pockets and neckline. The apron is hand stitched, including a narrow hem with purple embroidery floss, 20s – 30s; $30.00 – 40.00.

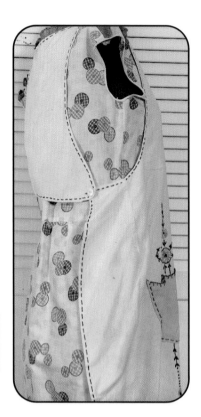

Back view of the photo at left also known as a "Hoover" apron, a common style that became popular during the Depression of the 1930s.

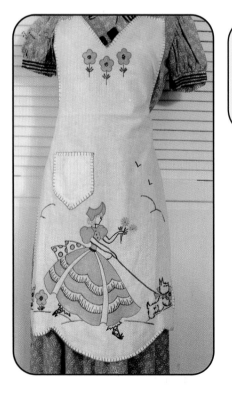

Full white cotton apron with a lady in elaborate dress walking her dog, pattern has been stenciled on, then outlined with embroidery; blanket stitch used to finish edges and pocket; dating from the 1930s. $45.00 – $55.00.

Full cotton apron in charming blue and orange print, trimmed in orange piping with two side pockets; 1930 – 1940s. $25.00 – 35.00.

Full white cotton apron with stenciled floral pattern, outlined with embroidery stitches, trimmed in red & white checked piping; 1930 – 1940s. $35.00 – 45.00.

Back view of simple tie back and very roomy for comfort.

Bib-front organdy apron in red and white pattern, with embroidery and lace trim, small triangle pocket and tie back; dating to 1940s. $30.00 – 40.00.

Bib-front organdy apron in green and white pattern with tie back and small triangle pockets, ruffled hemline; dating to 1940s. $28.00 – 35.00.

REG. U.S.   PAT.OFF.

ROYAL ♛ SOCIETY

Embroidery

Package Outfits

Your dealer now has on sale the new Fall line of these quality packages. There are Boudoir Caps, Blouses, Dressing Sacques, Tea Aprons, Combination Suits, Corset Covers, Nightgowns, Baby Dresses, Dolls' Outfits, Household and other decorative articles.

Each package contains the stamped material, either made up or ready for making, sufficient Royal Society Floss to complete the embroidery, full instructions and chart of stitches. Prices from 25c to $1.00 (except in Canada and foreign countries).

Royal Society Products Are Sold by Dealers Everywhere

Your dealer can supply or will procure the exact Royal Society item you want, either in Package Outfits, Embroidery Flosses; Crochet Cottons, Cordichet, Ball Floss, Strand Floss, or Celesta Twist, the new artificial Silk, fast color and washable.

Ask Your Dealer to Show You the New

ROYAL ♛ SOCIETY

Blue Bird Packages

Every embroideress will welcome these new and beautiful pieces. Besides the Scarf illustrated there are six other articles—Collar Bag, Laundry Bag, Necktie Rack, Whiskbroom Holder, Shaving Pad and Pillow. The designs are stamped and tinted in natural colors on tan "Needleweave," a new and durable material especially woven for embroidery purposes. These packages retail at 25c to 75c each, complete.

Send for the beautifully printed circular showing the Blue Bird Set in exact color

The "Blue Bird" For Happiness

H.E. VERRAN COMPANY
INCORPORATED
UNION SQUARE   NEW YORK

Ad for Royal Society embroidery package, which included the floss, stenciled garment, and directions to complete, priced at 25¢ – 1.00.

Contents of Royal Society apron kit with basic bib-front apron stenciled pattern ready to be embroidered, included Glossilla floss and direction sheet. Apron made of sheer organdy and already ruffled in contrasting green.

Full organdy apron in pale lavender with stenciled pattern of flowers, outlined in embroidery stitches, may have been a kit similar to the one above; dating to 1920 – 1930s. $40.00 – 55.00.

Full cotton apron in pink and white check with white organdy trim embroidered in black with flower to one side, tie back; dating to 1930 – 1940s. $30.00 – 40.00.

Full cotton apron with Scotties at home embroidered on front, said to be a child's apron, made by Joy's mom in the early 1950s. $37.00 – 49.00.
Courtesy of Joy Sigler.

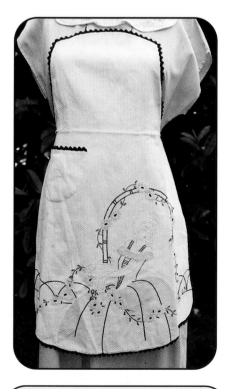

Back view.

Bib-front cotton apron with lovely lady appliqué and embroidered arbor of flowers, black rickrack finishing edges; dating to 1940s. $35.00 – 45.00.

Sweetheart bib-front of dimity with dainty floral design, edged with sheer ruffle, dating to 1940s. $25.00 – 35.00.

New-old gold and white checked cotton bib-front with Dutch motif border in black, red, and gold, eyelet lace edged pocket and top. Label still attached, "Fruit of the Loom," dating to the 1950s. $28.00 – 38.00.

Bib-front gray and red patterned cotton apron with contrasting striped cotton ruffle, red rickrack trim, dating to 1930s. $18.00 – 24.00.

Very sweet sheer white cotton half apron with long straps that tie in back, perhaps a household maid's apron dating to the 1920s. $15.00 – 22.00.

Half apron of natural duck with double sided clothespin pocket, quaint embroidery of blue-eyed dog hanging the laundry out to dry, dating to 1940s. $15.00 – 20.00.

Close-up detail of embroidery in photo on bottom right, page 42.

Sturdy cotton floral half apron, reminiscent of a 1940s tablecloth. $12.00 –18.00.

Dainty hankie apron in green and purple rose pattern, dating to the 1940s. $12.00 – 18.00. *Courtesy of Anne Phillips.*

Yellow organdy half apron with floral hankie trim, hankie used for small pocket, dating to 1940s. $12.00 – 28.00.

White organdy half apron with daisy hankie quartered, dating to 1940s. $12.00 – 18.00.

Cotton half apron with red, white, and blue patriotic hankies of WWII, military motif, dating to 1940s. $20.00 – 25.00.

Black organdy half apron with red floral hankie applied as large pocket, dating to 1940s. $12.00 –18.00.

Diamond shaped cotton half apron made of patchwork fabric from the 1940s, trimmed with rickrack. $14.00 – 19.00.

Cotton dishcloth made into a half apron, trimmed with crocheted variegated pansy pattern, dating to the 1940s. $18.00 – 25.00.

Crocheted cotton half apron in pink and white, dating to the 1940s. $14.00 – 19.00.

Crocheted cotton half apron in ecru with green waist ribbon, dating to 1940s. $12.00 – 18.00.

Souvenir half apron in cotton from Vancouver, lace and gray floral cotton trim, dated 1949. The date and place makes the apron especially collectible. $25.00 – 35.00.

Souvenir half apron in gold rayon from New York, with all the sights pictured, dating to 1950s. $25.00 – 35.00.

Aqua and white gingham half apron with rickrack incorporated into design on hem, pocket, and waist band, dating to the 1950s. $12.00 – 19.00.

Close-up detail of rickrack and stitching in photo above right.

Yellow and white gingham half apron with smocking along the top, which fits to the waist, dating to the 1950s. $12.00 – 19.00.

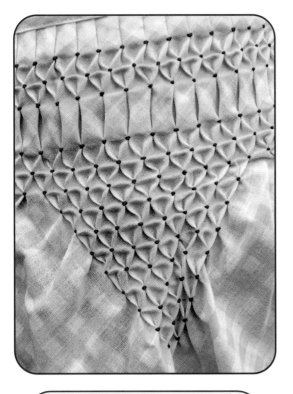

Close-up detail of smocking in photo on page 46 bottom right.

Waitress half apron in navy and white cotton, one pocket, dating to 1950s. $8.00 – 13.00.

Black and white organdy half apron, trimmed in rickrack, dating to 1950s. $9.00 – 14.00.

Charming red dotted cotton half apron, with white organdy ruffle trimmed in red rickrack, dating to the 1950s. $10.00 –15.00.

Half apron in sheer white organdy, faced with red apple print cotton under organdy for waistband, hem, and pocket, dating to 1950s. $9.00 – 18.00.

McCall's apron pattern #1279, dating to 1950s. Original price 25¢.

Pale lavender with rose pattern polished cotton in striking diagonal pattern, dating to 1950s. $9.00 – 18.00.

White cotton half apron, trimmed with pink and black pattern cotton on waistband, pocket, and hem, dating to 1950s. $10.00 – 15.00.

Pale blue hostess half apron with message "Your hostess requests the pleasure of your help in the kitchen after dinner," dating to 1960s. $12.00 – 18.00.

Yellow cotton half apron with white quilted cotton waistband and row of pockets at hemline, dating to 1960s. $8.00 – 12.00.

Blue denim and red bandana motif on half apron with button trim, dating to the 1960s. $8.00 – 12.00.

Sheer pink nylon half apron with lace trim and original tag still attached, dating to 1960s. $10.00 – 15.00.

Sheer white nylon half apron with Christmas stocking on pocket, dating to 1960s. $8.00 – 12.00.

White linen half apron with Christmas theme and "Greetings," dating to 1960s. $8.00 – 12.00.

"Buttons and Bows" apron pattern from Advance, compliments of Penney's. A promotion from the 1950s in conjunction with the movie "The Paleface" starring Bob Hope and Jane Russell.

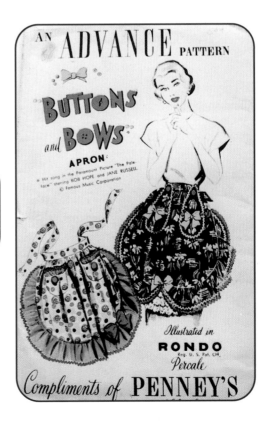

Fashion Wrapped Up. Gay 90s cape of cream wool with fuchsia silk shawl.

Photo credit: © 2000 Chris Bryant

Capes, cloaks, mantles, pelerines, shawls, and chokers. . . all were worn over the dress for fashion and for practical purposes. Usually considered outer-wear, certainly most ladies would want them to be a complementary accessory. Both cloaks and capes, gener-ally referred to as "mantles" in the 1800s, were outer garments without sleeves to constrict the costume. Falling full from the shoulders, cloaks could be all-enveloping from floor length to three-quarter length. Capes were similar, only shorter versions that were from fingertip length to as small as a mere flutter around the shoulders. Capes tended to be more orna-mented with lace, beaded passementerie, or ruffles.

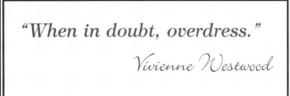

"When in doubt, overdress."

Vivienne Westwood

Beginning with the late 1830s and early 1840s many dresses were made with matching capes, often out of a silk fabric. These capes were generally unlined, often with fringe along the edge. These capes generally were fitted with darts at the neckline or a sloping shoulder seam which gave the characteristic fashionable look of the 1840s.

By the 1850s, fringe and ruching increased in pop-ularity. Because of the full pagoda sleeve line of the crinoline period, capes were often loose and full to accommodate the voluminous gown. The three-quar-ter length and short cape, worn for both day and evening, were usually in a circular cut, sometimes with a seam down the back. The longer light woolen cloaks often had a tasseled hood for warmth or other trimming falling from the top of the cloak. The burnous, or bernous, of the early 1860s was a shawl-like evening mantle of an exotic Arabian origin. Arabesque patterns were applied in borders of braid and stitching, particularly in striking contrast, such as black on light colors or white on black.

The full cloak began to lose favor in fashionable circles with the passing of the hoop dress of the 1860s. The shorter cape with a more fitted style became fash-ionable, which undoubtedly showed the bustle dress to its fullest advantage during the 1870s through the early 1880s. The material changed from the popular woolen fabric to the ever classic cashmere, poplin, and corded silk. Pleated frills were especially stylish on the closely fitting cape ending in a deep basque. The basque in back was often open at the center to accommodate the bustle. As the bustle began to wane in the late 1870s, the capes also streamlined in style with a more fitted look, but with sleeves cut as capes or square openings ending at the elbow. Some continued to have the long scarf ends hanging in the front, trimmed with the ever popular fringe of tied silk or chenille. Beaded passementerie was seen on most garments by the 1880s; as stated in the *Ladies' Treasury*, 1880, "every article for outdoor wear is beaded."

During the 1880s the long capes reached to just above the hemline, with fullness added by back pleats or larger gored sides. There was a great variety in the

THE SARAGOSSA.

Voluminous long cape covered the hoop dress of the 1850s – 1860s, ornamented with braid and tassels as shown in this fashion illustration, Godey's Lady's Book, September 1860.

53

shorter capes of this period, with the short sleeve shaping revealing the lower half of the dress sleeve. From the mid 1880s the sling sleeve was a distinctive style, formed by turning the front part of the mantle up inside, attaching to the back. The driving cape appeared about this time, as a plainer cloth cape for warmth. Also seen were the purely decorative short capes, heavily ornamented with beading, braid, frills, fur, feathers, and ribbons. The dominant color was black. Echoing the dress neckline, the capes had stand up collars or high mandarin band collars.

The large puffy leg-of-mutton sleeves of the 1890s gave rise to the full circular capes. These short full capes were the only reasonable solution for outer wear that would accommodate this extreme mode of fashion. These popular capes were made in a range of fabrics from tweed for sporting wear or traveling to plush and velvet for evening wear, trimmed with braid or appliqué, with a high flared collar. Full-length cloaks were seen again, often with a small yoke and a raised sleeve line with additional fullness for the large sleeves of the period. The inverted pleat, or Watteau pleat, also gave fullness to the capes. So dominant was the cape form, that a cape-like trimming of ruching or pleated frills was often seen on coats and jackets of the period, as shown in the Parasols and Umbrella chapter, page 207, right.

Capes continued their popularity into the twentieth century as an easy comfortable evening wrap. The materials varied from wool to velvet to mohair. After the Edwardian period the short cape was rarely seen unless it was a small fur cape for the shoulders, only worn for evening functions. In more modern times long rain capes became useful.

Full circular capes popular in the 1890s, with beading and fur trim as shown in The American Illustrated, October 1895.

Ad for circular plush cape of the 1890s, only $4.95 from Sears, Roebuck & Co.

Shawls

O uter wear could not be complete without some mention of shawls, which have been made in almost every material one can imagine. The technique for construction was often their ornament, such as the beautiful and delicate Chantilly lace. Many countries around the world influenced the popularity of the shawl. In the early Victorian period the shawl was the most popular summer wrap. Shawls came in many shapes, from squares to triangles to oblong. They were always simple and flat, but often of exquisite silks or paisleys.

Prior to 1840 the shawls tended to be smaller in comparison with later shawls. The size in this early period tended to be about one and a half yards square. With time the size increased, partly to cover the increasing skirt size of the 1850s. By the 1850s and 1860s shawls were two yards square, or as much as the double square of 64 inches by a 128 inches. The trend in size increased with the larger crinoline skirts.

The most valuable shawls are the paisley shawls of the Victorian era. However, there has been some confusion with regard to the term "paisley." This term refers to the Indian shawl woven of fine goat's wool in the characteristic Indian cone design, not the common paisley pattern we think of when using this term. These shawls were imported from India, while similar shawls were being made in Britain at Norwich and Paisley.

According to the *Lady's Newspaper* of 1847, "Shawls were never more in favour than the present winter. To say nothing of the products of the Indian looms or the highly and deservedly prized French cashmere, some of the newest specimens of our own British manufacture will find favour … To say which is the favorite colour for a shawl would be impossible, for the ground is completely covered by a rich mass of intricate and varied arabesques presenting an effect perfectly oriental."

Shawls were usually finished with fringed ends or borders. The knotting of the warp threads was the simplest of finishes. More elaborate knotting would create a lattice mesh effect around the edge of the shawl, often 15 to 20 inches in depth. Fringed braid could be sewn on, alternatively. Colors and patterns can date shawls, such as the tartan plaids of the 1860s. If the length was more than double the width, the shawls were referred to as "scarfs."

In the late 1850s – 1860s it was fashionable to wear

Chantilly lace shawl as shown in a fashion illustration in Godey's Lady's Magazine, July 1860.

light-colored silk dresses with contrasting black lace such as Chantilly. These light shawls of lace were popular for summer, either bobbin lace or machine net which was embroidered in black silk. The delicate and graceful patterns of Chantilly lace over the wide skirts were perfection in feminine attire. The size ranged from triangles of three yard lengths to two yard squares.

In the early 1900s the cape continued in popularity. Pelerines were ruffled bits of confection thrown about the shoulders to accent the costume, an accessory any lady could make from a length of chiffon and gathered silk ribbon.

Another example of the pelerine is the fur-edged velvet stole shown in pattern #7955. Also in fur, with stand-up collar, a pelerine can be more tailored in

A CHIFFON PELERINE AND MUFF

LOOSE jackets, capes and pelerines are much in evidence, being thrown about the shoulders on dress occasions when only a light wrap is required. The materials are varied, ranging from chiffon, of which the pelerine and muff illustrated are made, to velvet and fur. All are elaborately constructed.

No pattern is required for the pelerine shown at illustration I, as it is made entirely from straight lengths of chiffon and ribbon. A piece of seven-inch-wide ribbon is shaped around the neck and across the shoulders by laying dart-like tucks in at the neck edge and letting them run to nothing at the other; the ends reach just below the waist in front. No attempt at an absolute fit is made, only the general outline of the neck and shoulders being followed. Two thin layers of wadding are shaped like the silk but somewhat narrower, sachet powder is sprinkled between, and the edges of the silk are turned over the cotton. Another piece of ribbon, shaped in the same way, is placed under the sachet toward the padded side and the two are lightly tacked together.

Ribbon the same width is then sewed on full at about the middle of the sachet, so that it will extend well beyond it in a wide ruffle. A straight piece of chiffon, twice the width of the ribbon, is drawn up in inch-deep shirred tucks to half its width

at five-inch spaces. The chiffon is edged with a narrow ruche and falls over the ribbon, which is also edged with a ruche and extends three inches beyond the chiffon flounce.

Fancy ribbon, in the same general color as that used in making the pelerine, is tied in a succession of soft knots and tacked around the neck, the ends falling from the ends of the sachet piece in several loops. A longer end falls to the knee and a hemstitched chiffon flounce, one-half yard long and ten inches deep, is sewed at half the length of the ribbon, whence it falls like a deep, full tassel. The inside view in detail is given at illustration III.

The muff shown at illustration II is made of wadding covered with soft silk, the flat muff contained in pattern 7981 being used as a model. Chiffon to match the pelerine is shirred as represented at illustration IV, the tucks being one inch deep and the space

I.—PELERINE AND MUFF OF LAVENDER CHIFFON.

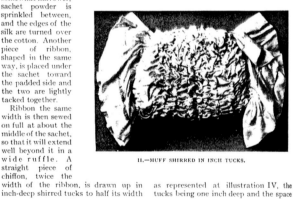
II.—MUFF SHIRRED IN INCH TUCKS.

790

The Delineator

Chiffon pelerine and matching muff, shirred and ruffled, The Delineator, November 1904.

The newest of winter accessories for outdoor wear, stole pelerine of velvet or fur with long ends in front, The Delineator, November 1904.

The old pattern may vary but slightly from the new, but sufficiently to rob it of its smartness.

Pelerine or neck boa as shown in The Delineator, October 1906

appearance. Both can be worn over a coat or long cape for a fashionable look.

The large embroidered silk shawl, an important accessory in the mid-Victorian era, had a resurgence of popularity from the early 1900s through the 1920s. They

were often used to drape over pianos in the parlor and referred to as piano shawls. The long silk fringe, often beautifully executed with hand knotting, added movement and intrigue as a woman loosely wrapped the shawl about her shoulders.

The Smartest Evening Wrap is a Shawl

This One of Cashmere and Yarn Can be Made at Home

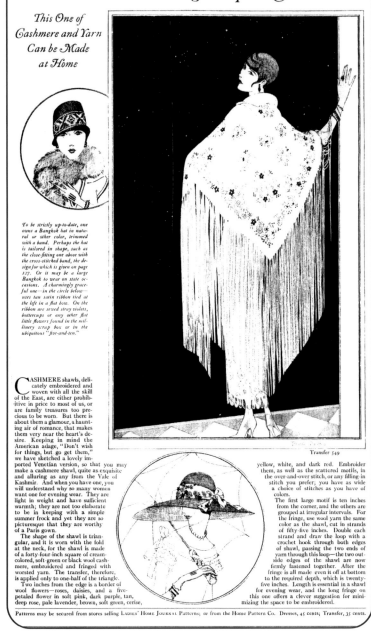

To be strictly up-to-date, one owns a Bangkok hat in natural or other color, trimmed with a band. Perhaps the hat is tailored in shape, such as the close-fitting one about with the cross-stitched band, the design for which is given on page 127. Or it may be a large Bangkok to wear on state occasions. A charmingly graceful one—in the circle below—uses tan satin ribbon tied at the left in a flat bow. On the ribbon are sewed stray violets, buttercups or any other flat little flowers found in the millinery scrap box or in the ubiquitous "five-and-ten."

CASHMERE shawls, delicately embroidered and woven with all the skill of the East, are either prohibitive in price to most of us, or are family treasures too precious to be worn. But there is about them a glamour, a haunting air of romance, that makes them very near the heart's desire. Keeping in mind the American adage, "Don't wish for things, but go get them," we have sketched a lovely imported Venetian version, so that you may make a cashmere shawl, quite as exquisite and alluring as any from the Vale of Kashmir. And when you have one, you will understand why so many women want one for evening wear. They are light in weight and have sufficient warmth; they are not too elaborate to be in keeping with a simple summer frock and yet they are so picturesque that they are worthy of a Paris gown.

The shape of the shawl is triangular, and it is worn with the fold at the neck, for the shawl is made of a forty-four-inch square of cream-colored, soft-green or black wool cashmere, embroidered and fringed with worsted yarn. The transfer, therefore, is applied only to one-half of the triangle.

Two inches from the edge is a border of wool flowers—roses, daisies, and a five-petaled flower in soft pink, dark purple, tan, deep rose, pale lavender, brown, soft green, cerise,

Transfer 549

yellow, white, and dark red. Embroider them, as well as the scattered motifs, in the over-and-over stitch, or any filling-in stitch you prefer; you have as wide a choice of stitches as you have of colors.

The first large motif is ten inches from the corner, and the others are grouped at irregular intervals. For the fringe, use wool yarn the same color as the shawl, cut in strands of fifty-five inches. Double each strand and draw the loop with a crochet hook through both edges of shawl, passing the two ends of yarn through this loop—the two outside edges of the shawl are now firmly fastened together. After the fringe is all made even it off at bottom to the required depth, which is twenty-five inches. Length is essential in a shawl for evening wear, and the long fringe on this one offers a clever suggestion for minimizing the space to be embroidered.

Patterns may be secured from stores selling LADIES' HOME JOURNAL Patterns; or from the Home Pattern Co. Dresses, 45 cents; Transfer, 35 cents.

The smartest evening wrap in cashmere, to be embroidered at home as shown in The Ladies' Home Journal, July 1924.

Irene Delroy all wrapped up in an embroidered silk shawl with silk fringe, The Theatre, June 1928.

Ad for choker of fox or marten by Hudson Bay Fur Co. in Seattle Post, social page of September 1925.

Springtime's Vogue!

The Season Wherein

CHOKERS

of Foxes and Martens
Hold Pre-eminent Sway

GLANCE at the devotees of Fashion as they swing jauntily along styledom's own avenues. Note the smart tailleurs . . . always in combination with flattering foxes . . . natural or dyed in the newest shades . . . also chokers, single and two-skin effects in baum, stone marten . . . and Hudson Bay Sable . . .

A selection not to be excelled anywhere awaits you.

Hudson Bay Fur Co.
INCORPORATED
819 First Ave.   1206 Fourth Ave.

Black faille shoulder cape, trimmed with delicate sheer silk ruffle, heavy black lace over chartreuse silk and black beading along the stand up collar; hook and eye front closure; lined with gathered chartreuse silk edging along hem, Victorian era. $150.00 – 200.00.

Black silk cape, unlined, came with black silk mourning gown from 1850s, 26" from neck to hem with 6" hand-knotted silk fringe. Black lace is hand stitched along the neckline and front; shaped over the shoulders and arms (gown not shown). $100.00 – 125.00.

Gold flannel wool fingertip cape with black soutache machine applied over all; hole punched design between soutache trim; gold ribbon ruffle around stand up collar; hook and eye closure at neckline with long ribbon ties, Victorian era. $165.00 – 195.00.

Burgundy velvet shoulder cape with black beaded passementerie trimming; front, collar, and bottom edge lined in black silk, large hook and eye closure at neck, Victorian era. $165.00 – 185.00.

Black plush fingertip cape with soutache design; lined with silk, fur-trimmed collar, hook and eye front closure, Victorian era. $110.00 – 125.00.

Black medium-length wool cape with applied soutache design, lined, fur-trimmed front and collar, hook and eye closure, Victorian era. $110.00 – 135.00.

Black wool fingertip cape with black lace ruffle along shoulder line, lined, trimmed with black silk ribbon; back view with inverted pleat, Victorian era. $95.00 – 115.00.

Camel colored light-weight wool knee-length cape with black soutache design in front, back, and collar, unlined, arm slits, hook and eye closure down front, Victorian era. $195.00 – 220.00.

Back view inverted pleat at hipline shown at bottom right page 59, as well as inside ribbon ties attached at back waist and tied inside front to give shape to the back as seen in this view. The shoulders are accentuated with the gathers and extra padding. Very flattering and feminine style of the period.

Ivory wool long cape, trimmed with pink silk panne velvet on cuffs, collar, and covered buttons, lined with pink silk, unusual mock sleeve design, Edwardian era. $225.00 – 250.00.

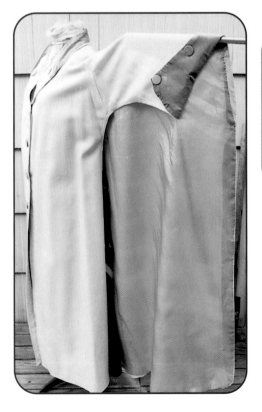

Side view of above right showing the simple but elegant mock sleeve design, which is open along the side seam and underarm to the velvet cuff which is just tacked down to simulate a sleeve opening when worn.

Black silk velvet short cape with three rows of deep tucks with wide hip band, gathered and rolled collar, lined with black silk, 1920s (back view). $75.00 – 100.00.

Pewter gray silk with two rows of Fortuny-like pleated georgette with stitched black cord design over all; large shawl collar and single large covered button closure in front. Cape is gathered in front to accommodate arms; late teens to early 1920s. $315.00 – 325.00.

Nile green cut velvet medium-length cape with arm openings in front, lined in ivory silk, dark maribou collar, frog with single covered button closure and tassle, late teens to early twenties. $275.00 – 300.00.

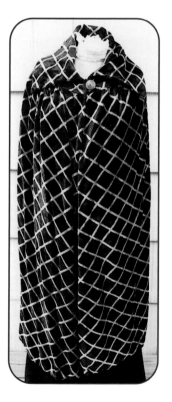

Black with white window pane pattern mohair mid-calf length cape, fully lined, single button neck closure, large collar, 1930s. $200.00 – 250.00.

Close-up view shows the nap of mohair fabric and window pane design.

Silver chinchilla shoulder cape, single hook for front closure, simple collar, lined in pewter brocade, 1940s – 50s; label reads "Teply, House of Fur, Portland, Oregon, est. 1898." Absolutely the softest, most luxurious fur ever! $250.00 – 350.00.

Black, long silk velvet cape, lined in ivory satin, no collar and no closure, simply designed, yet elegant over long gown of the 1930 – 1940s. $125.00 – 150.00.

Back view, showing the alignment of pelts and collar.

Classic white rabbit fur cape of the 1950s, lined with ivory satin, center front hook. $50.00 – 65.00.

Close-up view of back shoulder area.

Completely beaded capelet, rust colored seed beads and carnival glass blue bugle beads create medallion pattern, unlined, stand-up collar with front hook closure and small beaded balls trim entire edge of cape, Victorian era. $200.00 – 250.00 purchased at Persona Vintage Clothing.

Black beaded capelet, jet beads in an intricate pattern on faille fabric with stand-up collar, lined, with front hook closure, Victorian era. $200.00 – 250.00.

Back view of cape with beaded honeycomb open work over shoulders, usually made with heavy weight cotton thread which will last longer than bead work on silk, beaded fringe all around edge.

Close-up detail of lovely beaded design and beaded honeycomb on shoulder.

Close-up detail of pelerine ruffles and silk ribbon edging.

Black silk pelerine or boa made of pleated silk gathered in rows of ruffles, trimmed with gathered white edged silk ribbon, Victorian era. $110.00 – 135.00.

Black cut-velvet fitted cape, mandarin collar, floral motifs outlined in black beads, beaded fringe, with hook closure at neck, late-Victorian. $185.00 – 200.00.

Black silk ruffled boa, measures 78" long by 7" wide, Victorian era. $70.00 – 85.00.

Black silk ruffled neck piece, worn as an accent over a collarless cape or as an accessory for a plain bodice, hook closure and long ties, Victorian era. $40.00 – 55.00.

Black lace square shawl on net background, measures 50" by 48", machine-embroidered floral design, Victorian era. $95.00 – 125.00.

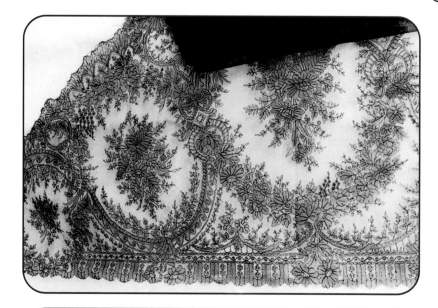

Close-up detail showing the outline thread on delicate floral and garland pattern of Chantilly lace.

Black Chantilly lace shawl, delicate floral and garland motif on triangular net background, scalloped edge, measures 106" along the diagonal, Victorian era. $150.00 – 165.00.

Long narrow black lace scarf or shawl, machine-made floral design on net, measures 108" x 17", Victorian era. $85.00 – 110.00.

Ivory silk shawl with colorful embroidered floral design, measures 56" x 37" with 18" silk knotted fringe, early 1900s. $150.00 – 175.00.

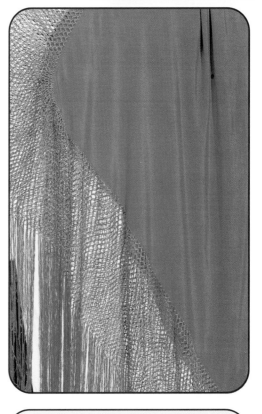

Ivory silk shawl with gold floral embroidered design in one quadrant, measures 56" x 52" with 20" fringe, early 1900s. $135.00 – 155.00.

Plain red silk shawl, measures 39" x 36" with an unusually deep fringe of 33" (11" hand-knotted), early 1900s. $125.00 – 145.00.

Plain black silk shawl, measures
60" x 62" with silk knotted fringe of
9", early 1900s. $115.00 – 135.00.

Ivory silk shawl with very fine overall floral and bird
embroidery from pale shades of yellow to deeper tones of rust,
measures 56" x 52" with 18" of intricate knotted fringe, early
1900s, $650.00. *Persona Vintage Clothing, Astoria, OR.*

Ivory silk shawl with delicate embroidery in
pastel shades of pink, lavender, and gray, measures
61" x 56" with 5" hand-knotted fringe, early
1900s, $350.00 – 450.00. Featured on cover and a
gift from Anne Splane-Phillips.

Black silk shawl with gold floral embroidery over all, measures 50" x 48" with 18" silk knotted fringe, early 1900s. $150.00 – 175.00.

Gossamer sheer silk tulle, soft gray in color with a glittery material impregnated in the tulle to simulate beads creating a lovely floral design on each end with scattered small motifs throughout the middle, measures 108" x 27", 1910s. $150.00 – 175.00.

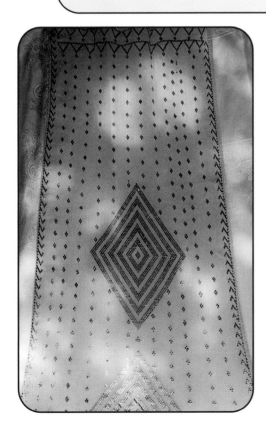

Egyptian Assuit cotton net shawl, 24" wide x 82" long, with thousands of tiny hammered silver pieces creating a high style deco design of three diamonds in the center, popular in the 1920s with the discovery of King Tut's tomb. So named for the city where they were made, Assuit, sometimes referred to as a wedding shawl. $185.00 – 200.00.

Close-up detail of silver design.

Exquisite handmade cream-colored lace collar, applied silk covered cord for design, black embroidered vines with tiny black beads for accent, Victorian era, front view. $110.00 – 120.00.

Petite shoulder cape for the boudoir made of black tulle with dot pattern, lace edged with tiny magenta bows along neckline and bottom. This boudoir cape came with the magenta silk corselet shown in photo, back view with small flared peplum and two covered buttons (the front laces under bust line), boned, lined with cream cambric, hand stitched, Victorian era. Very tiny and in mint condition. $200.00 – 225.00 for the set.

Back view of above, shows intricate design elements and beautiful handwork.

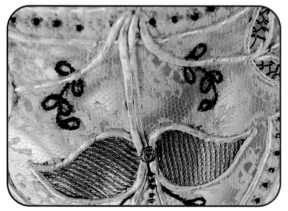

Close-up detail, includes tiny black bead accent and small gold bead used at the join of each leaf motif.

Ivory lace bertha collar, machine-made motifs on net background, front view. $55.00 – 75.00.

Photo of elderly lady with a cape of shiny fabric, perhaps a silk brocade. She appears to be holding a Bible in very weathered hands, still wearing her apron, after many years apparently as a homemaker. On the back of the photo, in pencil, "Mary Zeiter, borned 1800, age 93 when this was taken," which would place the cape, bonnet, and apron in 1893. For 93 years of age, she looks like a healthy, if not somewhat stern grandma. This is a fine example of the importance of questioning older relatives about family photos, making notes as to the names, dates, and other information that may be helpful to future generations.

Photo credit: © 2000 Chris Bryant

FANcy and FANtastic. An array of flirtatious fans with opera glasses.

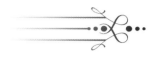
Fan, from the Latin vannus, means an apparatus for blowing the chaff from grain. Early people most assuredly used a simple palm leaf fan to separate the chaff from the grain or to help with starting a fire. Since the origin of man was near the equator, one can speculate that this accessory was also used as a practical solution to hot weather, by agitating the air with palm leaves or two bird wings joined together. The exact origin is obscure, but the fan as a feminine fashion accessory goes back thousands of years and can be seen in early bas-relief, sculpture, and paintings.

> *"The fan of a fair lady is the world's sceptre."*
>
> *Sylvain Marechal*

The early tombs of Tutankhamen of 1350 B.C. contained a fan chased in gold with a painted scene of the young king. The oldest Chinese fans are believed to be woven bamboo from the second century B.C., excavated near Changsha in the Hunan Province from the Mawangdui tomb. But the history of fans in China predates these, such as the feather fans used in ceremonies, even though they might not have survived time. The early examples were most likely fixed fans, not only to cool, but to shield the face in the presence of dignitaries. It is now thought that the brisé fan, made of carved or decorated sticks secured by a ribbon, was brought from Japan to China. The folding fan, as we know it, was modified from that brisé fan brought in by travelers.

The oldest Western fan dates to the sixth century and belonged to Queen Theodolinda, queen of the Lombards. This earliest of fans was a ceremonial fan, a flabellum, and is preserved in the basilica of St. John the Batiste at Monza, not far from Milan. Queen Theodolinda's fan has a silver-mounted handle with a purple vellum leaf decorated with gold and silver, its original box still intact. It was not until 1857 that the existence of this fan was widely publicized by a Victorian architect, William Burges.

Over time the fan evolved from a practical accessory to winnow grain or to move hot air for a lady, to that of a status symbol of the aristocratic and the saintly. Originally only natural materials such as palm leaves and feathers were used to make fans, but as time passed a great variety of materials were used including ornately decorated vellum, parchment, silk, feathers, gilding, painting, sparkling gems, and spangles. In the mid-sixteenth century these attractive novelties appeared in Europe with the fixed fan gradually being eclipsed by the folding fan, due to the convenience of carrying it when not in use. One could fold it and store it in a slim case, and tuck it into a boot or sleeve until needed. The folding fan became more popular and offered exciting possibilities for art in miniature. The whole leaf was used for decoration, the motif usually taken from tapestries, manuscripts, classical mythology, or biblical stories.

Fans, frequently assailed as unnecessary extravagances for the rich, were very expensive feminine accessories in the earlier periods. There was much criticism of fans as women's vanity since it had become a symbol of one's social status. A Fan Makers Company was established in London in 1709, as the industry already had stickmaker and fan painter specialists. This art form flourished and popularity increased. As trading activities expanded with the East India Company, the market for fans changed dramatically. Because fans were more available through travel and trade agreements, they were considered less of an occasional luxury and more of a necessity. Any woman with fashionable pretensions could afford this necessary accessory, even though it was a cheaper paper version.

Mass-production techniques satisfied an ever-increasing demand for this accessory as the popularity of fans heightened in the middle class. Despite the delicate appearance, fans were made to withstand much usage. Many fans of the aristocracy and royalty survive and can be seen in museums such as the Victoria and Albert Museum in London or Metropolitan museum of Art in New York.

Fan with ivory framework, silk leaf in butterfly design, Godey's Lady's Book, January 1871.

Lady with fan in fashion illustration from Godey's Lady's Book, January 1871.

From an 1894 dry goods source book, Japanese paper fans ranged in price from 50¢ per hundred to 75¢ each wholesale. The Japanese fan trade, including all the different grades imported, amounted to over $3,000,000.00 per annum. The most costly fans for general use were made of ostrich plumes and pearl sticks. These fans brought $60.00 apiece in the retail market, due to the increase in demand for ostrich which was also used extensively in this period for decorating hats and garments.

Storage, Maintenance, and Care of Fans

t is tempting to try to repair a damaged fan oneself, but it is advisable to leave restoration work to the professionals. It is best to retain any remnants of paper, silk, or ribbon rather than try to make it look better by replacing them with newer materials. Museums may be of help in recommending an appropriate glue to reattach a paper leaf that has become loose. If the rivet has been removed or lost, replacements can be found through The Fan Circle International, which is listed in the back under Resources. Fans should be kept out of the light to retain their color. Light, temperature, and air are factors in the life of a fan. Obviously, fans as well as other textiles should be in a smoke-free environment. Fans are best stored in the folded position, in acid-free tissue. If they are on display, they should be properly supported and allowed to rest after 2 – 3 months. The value of a fan is based on condition, age, and rarity. As with any collectible, the more authentic it is, i.e. not tampered with, the more valuable it is, not only monetarily but from a historical perspective. Because of their limited usefulness today, one should buy only those fans that are in good condition or appeal to one personally because of sentimental, artistic, or historic significance.

Parts of the Fan

The sticks, which can be made of ivory, bone, wood, mother of pearl, bamboo, or other suitable material, are the main frame of the fan. The outer sticks are usually more ornate or heavier in appearance and are referred to as the guards. The sticks are held in place by a pivot; the rivet is a screw that holds the pivot together. The mount or leaf is the cover for the fan which can often be various materials such as silk, a variety of patterned or painted papers, or other materials like feathers. The mount is where artistry and creativity show with spangles, embroidery, or painted motifs. Often there is a cord with a tassel attached for the lady to carry the fan over her arm when it is not in use.

Language of the Fan

A Victorian coquette would be able to communicate to her beau or would-be beau in a discreet and silent way by the movement of her fan. The significance of this silent language of the fan is as follows:

> *Shut the fan very slowly would mean: I will marry you*
> *Press the half-open fan to your lips would mean: Kiss me*
> *Threaten with a closed fan means: Don't be impudent*
> *Draw the fan across the cheek means: I love you*
> *Cover the left ear with open fan means: Don't tell our secrets*

This fan sign language was actually registered in the Patent Office of Washington D.C. Fans have been used over time to communicate one's status, offer salutations, signal an execution, cool one from the heat of the day, and to pass on secret messages. Their history has been long and colorful. Fortunately for us, many of these fans remain with us today and we can but wonder what their individual history has been.

Red ostrich feather, sticks painted to match, Victorian era, 13" in closed position. $120.00 – 145.00.

Black ostrich feather, tortoise sticks, Victorian era, 9" in closed position. $100.00 – 125.00.

Clipped pale pink ostrich feathers, with pierced celluloid sticks hand painted with delicate floral design, 1920s, 8" in closed position. $85.00 – 110.00.

Pale aqua ostrich, carved ivory sticks accented with gold, 1920s, 10½" in closed position. $85.00 – 95.00.

Pink ostrich feathers, four Bakelite sticks, 1910 – 1920s, 22" in length. $65.00 – 85.00.

Cream satin mount with detailed, hand-painted bird and fruit, white feathers trim the edge, ivory sticks, Victorian era, total length of 14" with feathers. $105.00 – 125.00.
Courtesy of Persona Vintage Clothing.

Cream marabou on ivory satin mount, plain ivory sticks, Edwardian era, 13" in closed position. $85.00 – 95.00.

Fixed peacock feather fan with wood handle, Victorian era, 12" in diameter. $85.00 – 95.00.

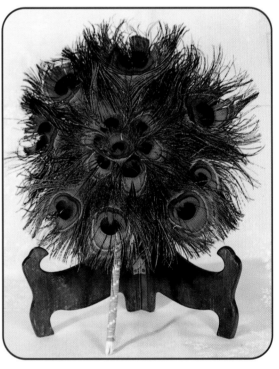

Rich purple satin mount on ivory sticks, Victorian era; 11½" in closed position. $75.00 – 95.00.

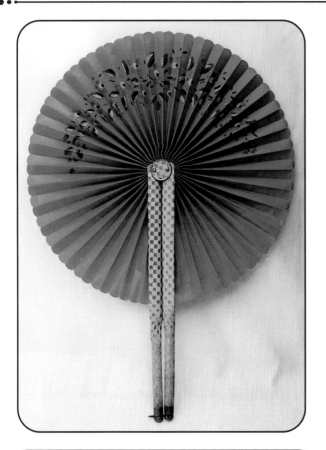

Vibrant red parasol, or cockade, fan with hand-painted design, interesting checkered handles that are clipped into open position, Victorian era, 10½" diameter. $95.00 – 115.00. *Courtesy of Jessie Allred Collection.*

Black paper parasol, or cockade, fan with intricate white outer design, the teal velvet covered handles are clipped into open position, Victorian era, 8" diameter. $90.00 – 110.00. *Courtesy of Jessie Allred Collection.*

Black paper parasol fan, partially closed, handles are clipped together to keep fan closed, Victorian era, 10" diameter. $75.00 – 85.00.

Telescope fan in closed position with wood handle, inlaid bird in flight (see page 80 top for open position), fan tassel on one end to pull and extend fan, 9". $150.00 – 175.00.

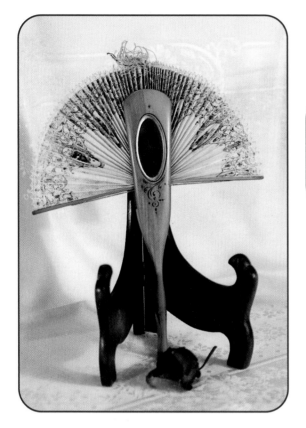

Telescope paper fan, extended half way from wood handle with oval beveled mirror on one side and inlaid bird design on back (see page 79 bottom right for closed position). Pale aqua paper mount has delicate printed pattern with lace edging, Victorian era, 9" across. $150.00 – 175.00.

Face screen or fixed fan of black wool, exquisite crewel embroidery in shades of green, rose, pale gold, and blue, edged in velvet with 6" wood handle, mid-Victorian, 10½" x 8". $100.00 – 110.00. *Courtesy of Jessie Allred Collection.*

Hand-painted sheer ecru silk gauze mount on carved wood sticks with silver painted design, original cord and tassel, Victorian era, 13½" in closed position. $75.00 – 85.00.

Sheer rust-colored silk gauze, hand-painted floral design, gilded wood sticks, Victorian era, 13" in closed position. $70.00 – 80.00.
Courtesy of Persona Vintage Clothing.

Ecru silk mount with hand-painted flowers, outer edge ecru lace, wood sticks with silver design, Edwardian era, 13½" in closed position. $75.00 – 85.00.

Ivory silk gauze embroidered with pale aqua flowers, pierced ivory sticks, 1910 – 1920s, 13" in closed position. $45.00 – 55.00.

Ivory silk mount with embroidered bird in foliage, delicate pierced ivory sticks, 1920s – 1930s, 9½" in closed position. $65.00 – 75.00.

Ivory satin mount with hand-painted design, beautiful grained wood sticks, Victorian era, 11½" in closed position. $65.00 – 75.00.

Coral marbleized celluloid brisé fan with gilded design on outer edges and hand-painted flowers, 1920s – 1930s, 4½" in closed position. $40.00 – 50.00. *Courtesy of Persona Vintage Clothing.*

Brisé celluloid fan with lovely hand-painted floral design in pink and green, original silk ribbon laced through sticks to hold in place, 1920s – 1930, 6" in closed position. $45.00 – 55.00.

Sweet printed cardboard fixed advertising fan, on back reads, "Frank H. Cooley Meats, Buena Park, Calif.," 1920s, size 8" x 11". $30.00 – 40.00.

Paper advertising fan in silver, red, and black floral design, on front reads "Toute La Provence, Mollinard Jeune, Grasse, Paris" and the back reads, "Perfume information and address to visit, the most interesting perfume factory in Grasse," 1920s, 9½" closed position. $35.00 – 45.00.

Paper advertising fan with lovely Gibson girl and her dog, wood sticks, back side reads "The Hollenden Restaurant, Cleveland," mid-teens, 10" in closed position. $40.00 – 55.00.

Brisé wood fan with Oriental scene painted below the pierced outer edges, held together with original silk ribbon, 1930s – 1940s, 6" in closed position. $35.00 – 45.00. Courtesy of Persona Vintage Clothing.

Lace-like pierced wood brisé fan, held together with original ribbon, 1930s – 1940s, 8" in closed position. $35.00 – 45.00.

Oriental fabric fan with cherry blossoms, Mt. Fuji, pagoda and peacock painted on fabric mount and sticks, souvenir fan from the 1950s, 13" in closed position, original box. $25.00 – 35.00.

Gray silk mount with Oriental scene hand painted on one side, pierced wood sticks, ivory guards with original tassel, 1940s – 1950s, 7" closed position. $35.00 – 45.00.

Round fixed paper fan with printed Oriental lady, pierced faux ivory handle, 1940 – 1950s, "Made in People's Republic of China" on back, 9" diameter. $20.00 – 30.00.

Round fixed paper fan with lovely printed Oriental lady, black lacquered handle and tassel, souvenir fan from 1950s, 9" diameter. $15.00 – 25.00.

Cream fabric on lacquered wood sticks with painted flamenco dancers and bull fight on mount and sticks, Spanish origin, 1940 – 1950s, 9½" in closed position. $20.00 – 25.00.

Black lace edged mount with hand-painted floral pattern, gold accent on black lacquered sticks, Spanish, 1950s, 12" in closed position. $25.00 – 35.00.

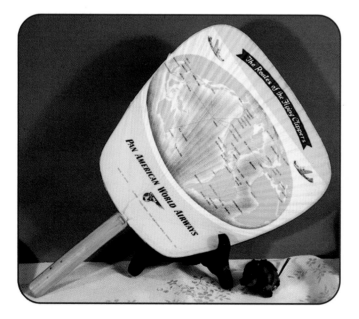

Fixed paper fan from Pan American World Airways showing the routes to the Orient and beyond, wood handle, 9" diameter. $15.00 – 25.00.

Fixed fan of hand-woven palm with tortoise, trimmed in feathers, a gift to my Dad from the Polynesian people in the 1950s when he was flying in the Marshall Islands, 14" in length. $45.00 – 55.00.

Oriental paper parasol fan with black metal handles, clip to hold open, souvenir from 1950s, 9$\frac{1}{2}$" diameter. $10.00 – 20.00.

Oriental paper souvenir fan with map illustration on mount, wood sticks, 1950s, 10" in closed position. $15.00 – 20.00.

Dramatic heavy paper mount with iris design on navy, five red lacquered sticks, original box labeled "Professional Kabuki Fan," from 1960s, 14" in closed position. $20.00 – 30.00.

Modern fixed advertising fan of cardboard depicting a Gibson girl and her beau, plastic handle, back reads "I'm a fan of Palmer-Wirfs," given at the entrance to the Portland Antique Show in 1999. $5.00.

Square paper fan with hand-painted floral design on mount, wood sticks, 16½" in width, early 1900s. $45.00 – 55.00. *Margaret Johntz Johnson Collection.*

Cockade fan with paper mount hand painted with flowers and birds, wood sticks, measuring 11½" diameter. $40.00 – 55.00. *Margaret Johntz Johnson Collection.*

Individual ecru crepe paper ovals attached to painted wood sticks, 8½" in length. $45.00 – 55.00. *Margaret Johntz Johnson Collection.*

Alternating red and green printed paper parrots on lacquered wood sticks, 8" in length. $60.00 – 80.00. *Margaret Johntz Johnson Collection.*

Multicolored paper geishas individually attached to silver decorated wood sticks, 10½" in length. $55.00 – 75.00. *Margaret Johntz Johnson Collection.*

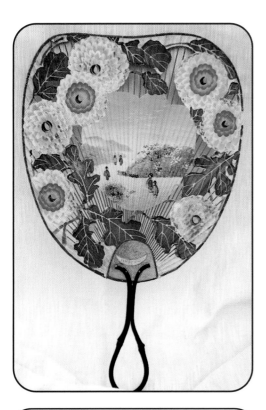

Fixed pierced paper with geisha design in muted tones, 10" wide with 5" handle, inscribed on reverse "Cambridge, August 1902." $45.00 – 65.00. *Margaret Johntz Johnson Collection.*

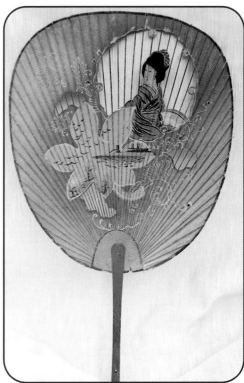

Fixed pierced paper fan with Oriental scene and chrysanthemums, 10" wide with 5" handle, inscribed on reverse "Miss Burt from Flo Tottenham." $45.00 – 65.00. *Margaret Johntz Johnson Collection.*

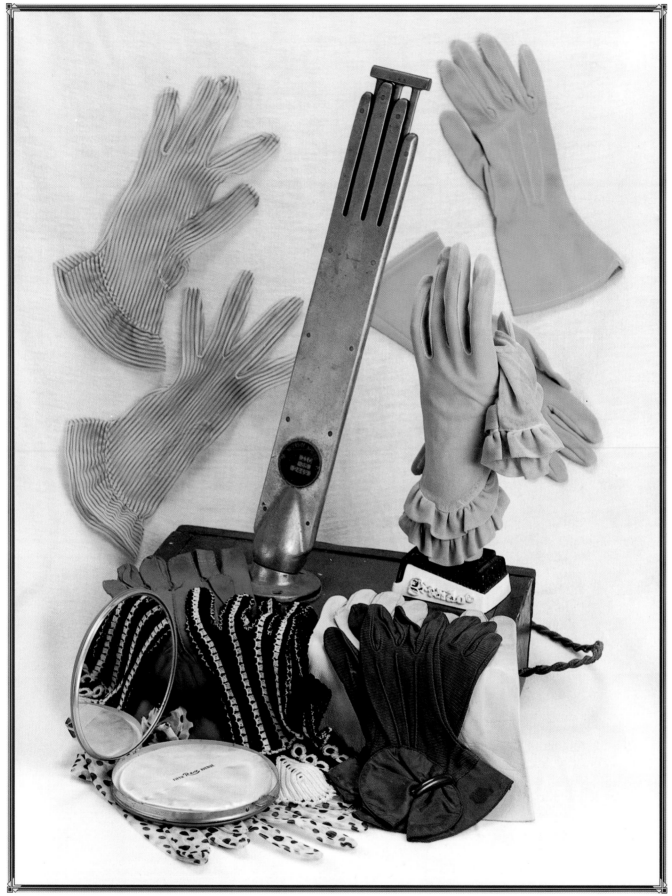

Taking Fashion in Hand. Variety of gloves with an electric glove press.

Photo credit: © 2000 Chris Bryant

Gloves

t is commonly held that the word "glove" evolved from the common Anglo-Saxon word "glof" meaning palm. The measurement term for the length of a glove is button. This measurement starts at the base of the thumb and is equal to one French inch which is only slightly longer than an American inch. Therefore a one-button glove is wrist length, a four to six button glove is about half way to the elbow, and formal length is a sixteen button glove (this term does not refer to how many buttons are on the glove).

As we enter the twenty-first century, gloves are used mainly for the purpose of keeping one's hands warm, useful accessories in cold climates. Gloves, however, have had a long and diverse history starting with the ancient Egyptians, Greeks, and Romans. It was not until the Middle Ages that gloves became an important accessory, used as a substitute for a signature. Gloves were so intimately associated with kingly power that monarchs were vested with authority by the delivery of a glove.

In the late Victorian period, at the coronation of English sovereigns, the ceremony of challenging by a glove was still observed. This custom started when Henry IV was crowned, and a knight armed for battle threw down his glove to any man who should dare to maintain that King Henry was not a lawful sovereign.

> *"If that from GLOVE, you take the letter G, then glove is love and that I send to thee."*
>
> *An old valentine verse*

This custom, the king's champion throwing down a glove at the coronation, was observed even for Queen Victoria's coronation.

As an accessory to dress for royalty, gloves were ornamented with pearls and precious stones sufficiently valuable to be left as legacies. These ornamental and jeweled gloves can be seen in museums today, reminiscent of the days when wealth was displayed by the accessories and clothing one would wear.

Mitts, sometimes referred to as mittens, are the characteristically Victorian accessory. These fingerless gloves were fashionable during the 1830s – 1840s for both day and evening. They were often hand-netted with an open work pattern in black or white silk. Generally the short length was worn for day, and the longer length for evening. During the next few decades these mitts were in and out of favor in the fashionable circles through the first decade of the twentieth century. Their popularity was resurrected in the late 1870s – 1880s. As stated in the 1879 issue *Queen*, "Long mittens are worn with demi-toilettes for dinner, but not for dancing parties. They are made in black and in colours to match the dress." Their use declined until 1900 when lace mitts and silk open mitts were again worn, often as accessories to a wedding ensemble.

KNITTED MITTEN AND BRACELET.

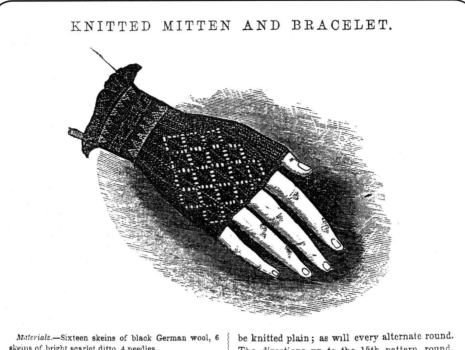

Materials.—Sixteen skeins of black German wool, 6 skeins of bright scarlet ditto, 4 needles.

BEGIN with the finest of the two sizes, and cast on 20 stitches on each of three needles, 60 altogether. Join into a round, and knit two rounds in black wool.

3d.—All scarlet.

4th.—* 3 scarlet, 1 black, *; repeat.

5th.—* 1 black, 1 scarlet, 2 black, *; repeat.

6th, 7th, and 8th.—Black.

9th.—* 5 s, 1 b, *; repeat.

10th.—* 1 s, 3 b, 1 s, 1 b, *; repeat.

11th.—* 1 s, 1 b, 5 s, 1 b, 4 s, *; repeat.

12th.—* 2 b, 1 s, 1 b, 1 s, 3 b, 1 s, 1 b, 1 s, 1 b, *; repeat.

13th.—* 3 s, 1 b, 5 s, 1 b, 2 s, *; repeat.

14th, 15th, and 16th.—Black.

17th.—Like 5th. *18th.*—Like 4th.

19th.—All scarlet.

Knit two rounds of black, and then take the coarser needles to form the hand, which is done in the following manner :—

Take half the stitches on one needle, and work *the pattern* on this needle only; the other half of the stitches will occupy two needles, being equally divided until you begin to form the thumb, when you will put 4 stitches only on one needle, and 26 on the other.

For the right hand the thumb needle will follow the long needle, for the left hand it will precede it. The needle with 26 on will always

be knitted plain; as will every alternate round. The directions up to the 15th pattern round, refer entirely to the long needle.

1st Pattern round, 1 n, (long needle).—K 15, m 1, k 15.

3d.—K 13, k 2 t, m 1, k 1, m 1, k 2 t, k 13.

5th.—K 12, k 2 t, m 1, k 3, m 1, k 2 t, k 12.

7th.—K 11, k 2 t, m 1, k 5, m 1, k 2 t, k 11.

9th.—K 9, k 2 t, m 1, k 1, m 1, k 2 t, k 3, k 2 t, m 1, k 1, m 1, k 2 t, k 9.

11th.—K 8, k 2 t, m 1, k 3, m 1, k 2 t, k 1, k 2 t, m 1, k 3, m 1, k 2 t, k 8.

13th.—K 7, k 2 t, m 1, k 5, m 1, k 3 t, m 1, k 5, m 1, k 2 t, k 7.

15th.—K 5, k 2 t, * m 1, k 1, m 1, k 2 t, k 3, k 2 t, * twice, m 1, k 1, m 1, k 2 t, k 5.

Begin now to form the thumb, thus, 4 stitches only being on the needle, k 2, m 1, k 2. The next round is, of course, plain. The third, fifth, and every other alternate round, k 2, m 1, knit all but the last 2; m 1, k 2. In the 3d row there is 1 to knit between the 2 made stitches; in the 5th there are 3, and so on, until there are altogether 25 on the needle (that is, an increase of 21), which forms the thumb. Then, k 2, m 1, k 2 t, k 17, k 2 t, m 1, k 2; which do in every alternate round until the length for the hand is done; the directions sufficing for the thumb, until separated from the fingers; the following directions refer wholly to the long needle.

Directions for "knitted mitten and bracelet," or knitted mitt with wrist. Quite a popular style in the mid-Victorian era for ladies to make at home, Godey's Lady's Book, August, 1856.

LONG BLACK SILK MITTEN.—NETTING.

Materials.—Fine black crochet silk, and three meshes—two steel round and one flat bone mesh. The steel meshes this size—O— and this—o—; the flat mesh this width ——

These mittens are for a full-sized hand; if required smaller, they can be reduced three or four stitches every way.

Net on the large steel pin 42 stitches; work 14 rows; net 8 stitches, make a stitch on the eighth stitch to begin to form the thumb; finish the row. Net 3 rows, and on the eighth stitch of 4th row make 1 stitch, net 1, make 1; finish row. Net 3 rows, on eighth stitch again make 1 net 3, make 1; finish row. Net 3 rows, on eighth stitch make 1, net 5, make 1; finish row. Net 3 rows, on eighth stitch make 1, net 7, make 1; finish row. Net 3 rows, on eighth stitch make 1, net 9, make 1; finish row. Net 3 rows, on eighth stitch make 1, net 11, make 1; finish row. Net 3 rows, on eighth stitch make 1, net 13, make 1; finish row. Net 3 rows, net 23 stitches, turn back, and net 15; net these fifteen stitches, thirteen rows, and one row, with the small mesh. The thumb must now be joined in netting stitch down as far as the thirty-four stitches, which remained when it was begun. Net along these thirty-four stitches, then two more rows, and in the 3d row, when you come to the eighth stitch, where the thumb is, take 2 stitches together; finish the row. Net 1 plain row, and on the eighth stitch of the next again net 2 together. Net plain rows until the mitten is sixty-six stitches from the commencement. Then 1 row with the flat mesh, netting 2 into every stitch; 3 rows with the smallest mesh; then with the largest steel mesh net into every other stitch. Net 1 more row, and this end of the mitten is finished. Net the two edges of the work together in the same manner as the thumb.

38*

Directions for "long black silk mitten," mitts were handmade by netting, Godey's Ladys Book, November 1860.

Both evening and day gloves tended to be short prior to 1850. The *Lady's Newspaper* of 1847 wrote, "Gloves continue to be worn as they have been for some time past, covering about one-third of the arm and edged with trimmings of lace or ribbon." Gloves during this period were usually white, occasionally pale shades of pink or yellow, and usually trimmed at the top with a ribbon ruching, flowers, or lace. Daytime gloves were at the wrist with a single button, in light colors of kid. Some gloves of the mid-1800s had a silk tasseled braid and clip for closure or a short lacing of silk cord at the back of the wrist. An article in the *Queen* magazine from 1862 welcomed spring with "the countless pairs of mauve, lemon, pink and my favourite pale — gray" gloves.

In the 1800s it was said that for a glove to be of superior quality it must pass through three kingdoms: Spain to dress the leather, France to cut the glove, and England to sew the gloves. France, however, took the lead in glove making in the late 1800s. Grenoble, France, became the largest manufacturing center of kid gloves. Grenoble was centrally located to countries raising goats and had the special qualities of water for the dyeing of leather, with over 300 different shades available. The annual production of kid leather gloves in Grenoble in the early 1890s was about 1,200,000 dozen pairs! To accomplish this, over 25,000 people were employed, mostly women and children. Over 9,600,000 kid goat skins were used in the production of gloves per year; the kids being so young, on average only three gloves were cut from one skin.

By 1865 short gloves for evening were going out of style, as they lengthened from four or five to six buttons. During the 1870s gloves reached half way to the elbow. Many gloves after 1880 reached beyond the elbow, ornamented with lace or embroidery and fastening with four buttons at the wrist. At this time, the type of dress worn often determined the length of glove. As stated in the *Ladies' Treasury* from 1882 "When the sleeves are short the gloves must cover the elbow."

Gloves of the four button length were the most common during the 1890s.

Madame Rowley's Toilet Mask

(OR FACE GLOVE).

THE FOLLOWING ARE THE CLAIMS MADE FOR MADAME ROWLEY'S TOILET MASK, AND THE GROUNDS ON WHICH IT IS RECOMMENDED TO LADIES FOR BEAUTIFYING, BLEACHING, AND PRESERVING THE COMPLEXION :

1st. The **Mask** is **Soft** and **Pliable** and can be **Easily Applied and Worn** without **Discomfort** or **Inconvenience**.

2d. It is durable, and does not dissolve or come asunder, but holds its original shape.

3d. It has been **Analyzed** by **Eminent Scientists** and **Chemical Experts**, and pronounced **Perfectly Pure** and **Harmless**.

4th. With ordinary care the **Mask** will **Last for Years**, and its *valuable properties* **Never Become Impaired**.

5th. The **Mask** is protected by letters patent, has been introduced ten years, and is the only **Genuine** article of the kind.

6th. It is **Recommended** by **Eminent Physicians** and **Scientific Men** as a *substitute for injurious cosmetics.*

7th. The **Mask** is as **Unlike** the fraudulent appliances used for conveying cosmetics, etc., to the face *as day is to night*, and it bears no analogy to them.

8th. The **Mask** may be worn with **Perfect Privacy** if desired. The **Closest Scrutiny** cannot detect that it has been used.

TRADE MARK
Reg'd

The Toilet Mask (or Face Glove) in position to the face.
TO BE WORN THREE TIMES IN THE WEEK.

9th. It is a **Natural Beautifier** for **Bleaching** and **Preserving** the **Skin** and **Removing Complexional Imperfections**.

10th. The **Mask** is sold at a moderate price, *and one purchase ends the expense.*

11th. Hundreds of dollars uselessly expended for cosmetics, lotions, and like preparations may be saved by those who possess it.

12th. Ladies in every section of the country are using the **Mask** with gratifying results.

13th. It is safe, simple, cleanly and effective for beautifying purposes, and never injures the most delicate skin.

14th. While it is intended that the **Mask** should be **Worn During Sleep**, it may be applied, *with equally good results*, at **Any Time**, to suit the convenience of the wearer.

15th. The **Mask** has received the testimony of well-known society and professional ladies, who proclaim it to be the greatest discovery for beautifying purposes ever offered to womankind.

A FEW SPECIMEN EXTRACTS FROM TESTIMONIAL LETTERS :

"I am so rejoiced at having found at last an article that will indeed improve the complexion."

"Every lady who desires a faultless complexion should be provided with the Mask."

"My face is as soft and smooth as an infant's."

"I am perfectly delighted with it."

"As a medium for removing discolorations softening and beautifying the skin I consider it unequaled."

"It is, indeed, a perfect success—an inestimable treasure."

"I find that it removes freckles, tan, sunburn and gives the complexion a soft, smooth surface."

"I have worn the Mask but two weeks and am amazed at the change it has made in my appearance."

"The Mask certainly acts upon the skin with a mild and beneficial result, making it smoother and clearer, and seeming to remove pimples, irritations, etc., with each application."

"For softening and beautifying the skin there is nothing to compare with it."

"Your invention cannot fail to supersede everything that is used for beautifying purposes."

"Those of my sex who desire to secure a pure complexion should have one."

"For bleaching the skin and removing imperfections I know of nothing so good."

"I have worn the Mask but three nights, and the blackheads have all disappeared."

"The Mask should be kept in every lady's toilet case."

"I must tell you how delighted I am with your Toilet Mask, it gives unbounded satisfaction."

"A lady was cured of freckles by eight nights' use of the Mask."

"The improvement in my complexion is truly marvelous."

"After three weeks' use of the Mask the wrinkles have almost disappeared."

"My sister used one for spotted skin, and her complexion is all that can be desired."

"It does even more than is claimed for it."

"I have been relieved of a muddy, greasy complexion after trying all kinds of cosmetics without success."

COMPLEXION BLEMISHES

MAY BE HIDDEN IMPERFECTLY BY COSMETICS AND POWDERS, BUT CAN ONLY BE REMOVED PERMANENTLY BY THE TOILET MASK. BY ITS USE EVERY KIND OF SPOTS, IMPURITIES, ROUGHNESS, ETC., VANISH FROM THE SKIN, LEAVING IT SOFT, CLEAR, BRILLIANT AND BEAUTIFUL. IT IS HARMLESS, COSTS LITTLE AND SAVES ITS USER MONEY. IT PREVENTS AND REMOVES

✦ WRINKLES, ✦

AND IS BOTH A COMPLEXION PRESERVER AND BEAUTIFIER. FAMOUS SOCIETY LADIES, ACTRESSES, BELLES, ETC., USE IT. VALUABLE ILLUSTRATED PAMPHLET, WITH PROOFS AND FULL PARTICULARS, MAILED FREE BY

The Toilet Mask Company, 1164 Broadway, New York.

☞ Apply NOW, while you have our address before you, as this advertisement appears only occasionally. Please mention "THE QUEEN OF FASHION."

Ad for Madame Rowley's Toilet Mask or Face Glove, among other amazing complexion beautifiers, claimed to prevent and remove wrinkles, with testimonials from well-known society and professional ladies, The Delineator, November 1893.

Kid gloves were finished in either "glace" or suede. Glace means the smooth polished look that was so popular for most evening gloves. Suede gloves were made lusterless in appearance by removing the thin, almost transparent outer layer of the skin by simply peeling it or shaving it. Suede gloves were introduced in the 1860s and continued to be fashionable into the 1880s, until "Her Majesty, having forbidden the *gant de suede* gloves to be worn at the drawing rooms — no longer admissible in dress circles," according to the *Ladies' Treasury*, dated 1882.

Softness and freedom from blemish were the principal factors in the value of kid skins for glove making. Many imitations were put on the market, including colt, sheep, antelope, llama, kangaroo, and monkey, but kid skins can be recognized by their incomparable fine texture, thinness, and suppleness. Perhaps that is where phrases like "handle with kid gloves" or "fits like a glove" come from. Kid gloves have always been the most desirable, even into modern times.

Gloves are the bane of woman's existence—not because they wear out quickly, but because they soil so easily.

Take your own case. How often have you ruined a pair of white kid gloves, getting aboard a crowded street-car or out of a carriage?

Some day, some one will invent a glove that can be washed. Until then, the best way to improve the appearance of gloves that have become soiled (other than sending them to a cleaner) is to use Ivory Soap Paste. It will not remove dirt that has become ingrained in the leather; but anything short of that disappears before it as if by magic.

IVORY SOAP PASTE:—To one pint of boiling water add one and one-half ounces of Ivory Soap cut into shavings; boil ten minutes after the soap is thoroughly dissolved. Let it cool.
Put glove on hand. Dip a soft flannel cloth into the Ivory Paste and rub it over the soiled parts. Remove with another soft cloth. Let the glove dry on the hand.
Ivory Paste can also be used to clean white kid and satin slippers, straw hats, canvas shoes, etc. It will keep for months if placed in a glass jar with a screw top.

Ivory Soap - 99⁴³⁄₁₀₀ Per Cent. Pure.

Ad for Ivory soap showing a lady being fitted for kid gloves, with the suggestion of cleaning your kid gloves with Ivory Soap Paste when they are soiled from boarding a crowded street-car or getting out of a carriage. And of course soiled gloves are the bane of a woman's existence! The Delineator, October 1906.

Fabric gloves of silk, lisle, and cotton were also popular. Machinery was used in the manufacture of these gloves. In cutting, a number of folds of fabric were placed one upon another and a blade or punch would cut the shape and size required. There was a specially designed sewing machine which would stitch the gloves together, they were sent to the dyer, then sent to the finishers to be dressed, banded, and boxed. Often the fabric gloves were woven with double fingertips, making them more durable.

Glove making was a major industry in Germany; however, England held the reputation for the finest silk Milanese gloves. By the end of the 1880s silk gloves had lost favor in fashionable circles. It was written in *Woman's World*, 1888, "Silk gloves have long ceased to be fashionable though thousands of women wear them."

Silk gloves regained popularity again in the Edwardian era, as noted in the numerous ads for silk gloves in the magazines of the times.

"NIAGARA MAID" Silk Gloves—the 20th Century standard of perfection—embody the best features of the old silk glove, but eliminate its faults.

An innovation that adds strength to the silken threads is the "NIAGARA PROCESS"—which has brought "NIAGARA MAID" Silk Gloves to the high standard that has endeared them to thousands of pleased wearers.

Ask your dealer to show you "NIAGARA MAID" Silk Gloves, which come in every new and beautiful color, in long or short lengths, plain or embroidered, at a price to suit every purse.

Always better for your money than you ever bought before—unless they were "NIAGARA MAID."

Quarter sizes, in addition to the regular sizes, insure precise fit.

Look in the hem for the name—and if your dealer cannot supply you with "NIAGARA MAID" Silk Gloves— send your money order direct to us, stating size, color, style and price, and we will have them promptly delivered to you through your dealer.

Two-clasp Short Gloves, $.50, $.75, $1.00, $1.25
Long Silk Gloves, $.75, $1.00, $1.25, $1.50
Embroidered Silk Gloves, $2.00, $2.50, $3.00, $4.50
Men's Gloves, $1.00, $1.25
Misses' Gloves, $.50 to $1.00

Every pair of "NIAGARA MAID" Silk Gloves is fully guaranteed.

NIAGARA SILK MILLS,
Dept. A, N. Tonawanda, N. Y.

> *Ad for Niagara silk gloves, with double the wearing life, smart fit, and costing only half the price of kid gloves, The Ladies' Home Journal, June 1908.*

> *Ad for Niagara silk gloves, "the 20th century standard of perfection," priced from 50¢ to $4.50, The Ladies' Home Journal, June 1909.*

Look for name "Niagara" in the hem

They are creating no end of comment all over the country. Beyond comparison with other silk gloves. More satisfactory than kid gloves that cost nearly double.

A special process of treating the silk—the Niagara Process— gives to Niagara Silk Gloves double the wearing life the usual silk gloves possess.

It makes them retain their smart fit and style as long as they last.

Washing after washing cannot make them lose their beautiful coloring, nor the closely woven silk its rich luster.

Niagara Silk Gloves

can be procured in every fashionable style and color suitable for every occasion—morning, afternoon and evening.

Sold at fashionable shops everywhere.

If you have any difficulty in finding what you want, send us money order, stating size, enclose sample you desire to match or harmonize and we will have them delivered through your local dealer.

16 Button Length, $1.50 to $2.00 a pair. Prices governed by thickness of silk.

NIAGARA SILK MILLS,
North Tonawanda, N. Y.

"Making Good"

Whether applied to man or merchandise, both must "make good" or make way.

Dewey, for instance, "made good" at Manila, and the country paid him homage.

With merchandise, the "KAYSER" Patent Finger Tipped Silk Gloves have "made good" for over a quarter of a century. To-day they are the standard in the glove world, and the enormous demand for gloves bearing the name "KAYSER" attests the fact that the women of the world have set their stamp of approval upon them. Verily, they have "made good."

"KAYSER'S" gloves must "make good" or make way for a new pair free, the guarantee ticket insures this.

If any pair falls short of the "KAYSER" standard, or your expectations, we want the dealer to replace that pair at our expense. The guarantee ticket does this.

Any "KAYSER" glove that does not "make good" must make way.

"KAYSER" Gloves "cost no more" than the ordinary kind.

LOOK IN THE HEM

for the name "KAYSER," the hall mark by which the critic knows "the genuine."

Short Silk Gloves, 50c, 75c, $1.00, $1.25, $1.50
Long Silk Gloves, 75c, $1.00, $1.25, $1.50, $2.00

JULIUS KAYSER & CO., Makers
NEW YORK

Ad for Kayser, with the patented Finger Tipped Silk Gloves for over a quarter of a century, priced from 50¢ – $2.00, The Ladies' Home Journal, June 1910.

Real photo postcard of confident young lady wearing her coat with large-brimmed hat and her leather gloves, about 1910.

Although this book deals with ladies' accessories, there is an interesting fact relating to the production of men's working gloves in the late 1800s. In the city of Gloversville, New York, there were 140 separate glove factories which manufactured two-thirds of men's working gloves. The annual output in the early 1890s from this one town was over $20,000,000.00 annually.

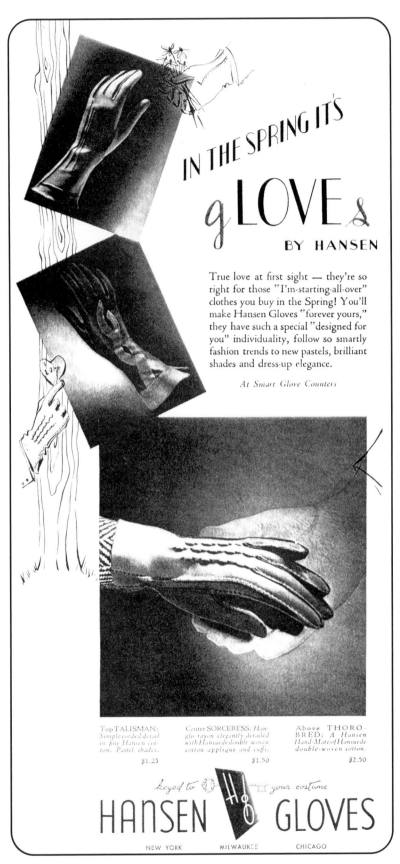

IN THE SPRING IT'S

g LOVEs

BY HANSEN

True love at first sight — they're so right for those "I'm-starting-all-over" clothes you buy in the Spring! You'll make Hansen Gloves "forever yours," they have such a special "designed for you" individuality, follow so smartly fashion trends to new pastels, brilliant shades and dress-up elegance.

At Smart Glove Counters

Top TALISMAN: Simple corded detail in fine Hansen cotton. Pastel shades. $1.25

Center SORCERESS: Hanglo rayon elegantly detailed with Hansuede double-woven cotton applique and cuffs. $1.50

Above THORO-BRED: A Hansen Hand-Mate of Hansuede double-woven cotton. $2.50

keyed to your costume

HANSEN GLOVES

NEW YORK   MILWAUKEE   CHICAGO

Ad for Hansen Gloves, with new pastels, brilliant shades, and dress-up elegance, Mademoiselle, April 1942.

STREAMLINER — unequalled for slenderizing the hand. Black, White, Navy and newest Latin-American colors. $1.

PETUNIA—dressmaker detail, with petal top. Black, White, Navy, Dusty Pink, Dusty Blue and Pebble Beige. $1.

FIESTA—a softly tailored semi-dress glove with fascinating side shirring. Liberty Red, Black, White, Navy, Dusty Pink, Dusty Blue and Pebble Beige. $1.

Hands

GRACEFUL AS SPRING...IN GLOVES BY SENDRA

You'll walk hand in hand with beauty in these
bewitching new gloves by Sendra. Vibrant with
the youthful lilt and lift we so need
today, they grant that final note of charm that
lovely hands deserve. In the liquid, slenderizing grace of
"Streamliner"—the suave Latin-American
simplicity of "Fiesta"—the exquisite petalled
detail of "Petunia"—you'll find
that intimate perfection only classic designing
can achieve. Ask for Sendra
Gloves at finer stores everywhere
...you'll thrill at their
moderate cost.

Sendra

EISENDRATH GLOVE CO., 2005 Elston Ave., Chicago
Official glovers to American Airlines

Ad for Sendra gloves that grant that "final note of charm that lovely hands deserve," priced at $1.00, Mademoiselle, April 1942.

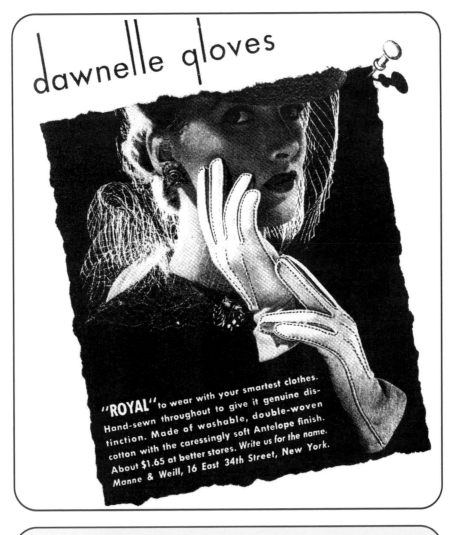

Ad for Dawnelle Gloves, made of washable cotton with the "caressingly soft Antelope finish," Mademoiselle, April 1942.

We've harvested
the "fall look"
with leather accents

Gloves bound to draw comment: hand-stitched
leather accents on soft double-woven cottons.
$4.00 to $6.00 the pair.
At fine stores everywhere.

Van Raalte
GLOVES · STOCKINGS · GIRDLES · LINGERIE
Because you love nice things

Ad for VanRaalte gloves, in all fine stores everywhere, priced at $4.00 – 6.00, Mademoiselle, 1942.

Throughout the Victorian and Edwardian periods gloves were the symbol of gentility. The social status of a lady or gentleman could practically be determined by the quality of their gloves. To be appropriately dressed, women of the 1940s and into the 1950s always wore matching or coordinating gloves as accessories to their ensemble. Short white gloves were expected for church on Sundays for young girls, even into the 1960s. By the 1970s, sales for gloves diminished as more and more women discarded the fashion accessory as superfluous.

The last thirty years of the twentieth century gloves have been primarily practical, and one cannot but wonder if some of the feminine mystique has been lost. A lady's gloved hand can be mysterious and desirable. Perhaps it is the "hidden" aspect of a gloved hand that is most alluring.

Muffs

uffs were a fashion accessory carried throughout the Victorian period into the early 1900s to keep the hands warm. In later decades the muff was more a fashion statement than a necessity of warmth. Prior to 1850 the muff was usually fur, which varied from ermine to chinchilla to sable, depending on the fashion finances. The average size for this era was nine inches long with a circumference of about 20 inches. Muffs were filled with down or cotton wadding, usually lined with silk, often quilted, and drawn up on the ends with a cord or ribbon. During this period, muffs often came with a matching set of fur cuffs as mentioned in the *World of Fashion* in 1845, "with their usual accompaniment, these useful manchettes."

As stated in the *Queen*, 1863, "we are accustomed in England to see small muffs, if they are barely large enough to admit the two hands their dimensions are considered quite sufficient." Smaller muffs were the fashion from the 1850s to the 1870s. Although sable was the first choice, velvet muffs with fur trim on the ends were also used. Skunk became a popular choice of fur for the 1870s, as well as astrakhan, which is a curly lamb.

Beginning in 1879 through the 1880s, new shapes and materials were seen. Muffs were made of plush, satin, and velvet, trimmed with lace, fur, or sometimes feathers. They went from the simple muff form to a looser, softer form containing a pocket or inner purse. A large bow or small stuffed bird might ornament the muff of this period. As the century came to a close, muffs went from a medium to a larger size. The larger, flatter cushion muff became the new fashion, often with the head and tail of the animal used for ornamentation.

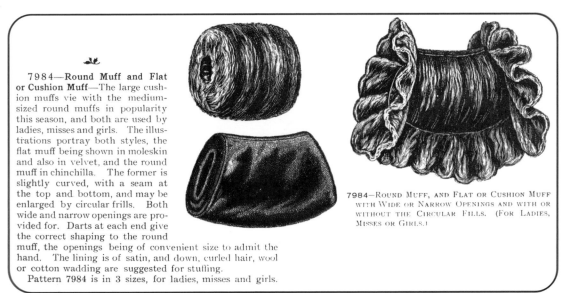

7984—**Round Muff and Flat or Cushion Muff**—The large cushion muffs vie with the medium-sized round muffs in popularity this season, and both are used by ladies, misses and girls. The illustrations portray both styles, the flat muff being shown in moleskin and also in velvet, and the round muff in chinchilla. The former is slightly curved, with a seam at the top and bottom, and may be enlarged by circular frills. Both wide and narrow openings are provided for. Darts at each end give the correct shaping to the round muff, the openings being of convenient size to admit the hand. The lining is of satin, and down, curled hair, wool or cotton wadding are suggested for stuffing.
Pattern 7984 is in 3 sizes, for ladies, misses and girls.

7984—ROUND MUFF, AND FLAT OR CUSHION MUFF WITH WIDE OR NARROW OPENINGS AND WITH OR WITHOUT THE CIRCULAR FILLS. (FOR LADIES, MISSES OR GIRLS.)

Pattern #7984 for three different muffs, the round muff shown in chinchilla and the slightly curved cushion muff in moleskin or velvet. Circular frills could be added as shown in the third view. The Delineator, 1904.

Real photo postcard (unused) of lady with fur neck choker and matching fur muff of medium size, ca. 1910.

Real photo postcard (unused) of lady with matching fur neck choker and smaller muff of contrasting color to her coat, ca. 1910.

Real photo postcard (unused) of lady with fur boa and muff, note her large hat and leather purse, ca. 1910.

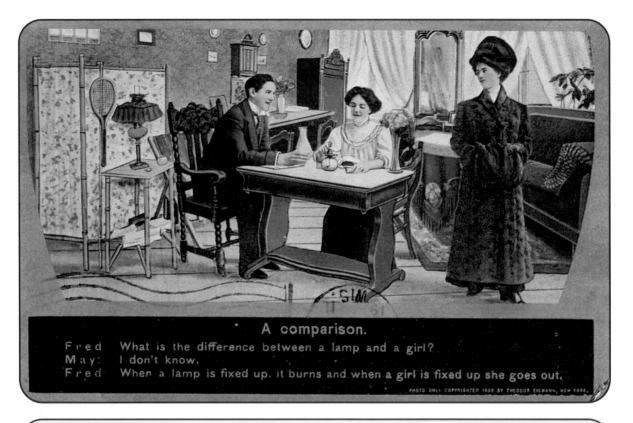

A comparison.

Fred   What is the difference between a lamp and a girl?
May: I don't know.
Fred   When a lamp is fixed up, it burns and when a girl is fixed up she goes out.

PHOTO ONLY COPYRIGHTED 1909 BY THEODOR EISMANN, NEW YORK.

Postcard of lady in long fur coat with matching hat and muff, showing postmark of "1911 WIS" just below desk. Dated postcards are excellent ways to date styles.

Real photo postcard of lovely lady with matching ermine fur stole and flat cushion style muff, adorned with the black tipped ermine tails. Ermine are of the weasel family of rodents, prized for their pure white fur in winter pelage, similar to rabbits that are brown in summer and white in winter for camouflage. Some call ermine "winter mink."

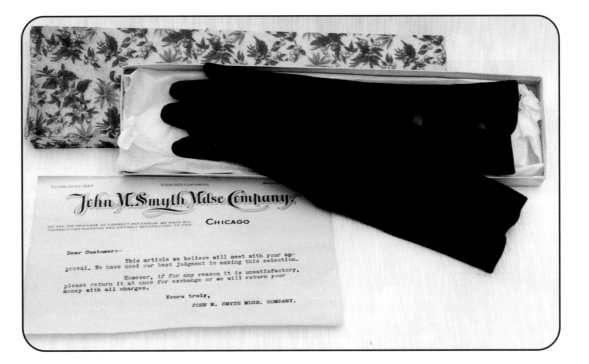

Black cloth gloves for cold weather, with burgundy lining and two wrist snaps, in mint condition; in original gift box with letter from the "John M. Smyth Mdse. Company" of Chicago, early 1900s. With gift box and documentation, $45.00 – 65.00.

"Valuable information about gloves" included in the box with black cloth gloves above. This insert shows the proper way to fit gloves, with instructions for washing and cleaning gloves.

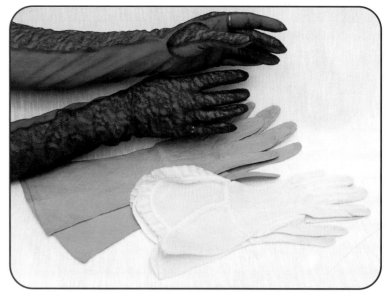

Three pairs of fabric gloves: long, brown sheer gloves with sheer lace on top; medium length gold linen; gauntlet style white cotton, dating from 1920s to 1930s. $15.00 – 30.00 per pair.

Three pairs of crocheted gloves: White hand-crocheted gloves with lovely pattern date to mid-teens, ecru with rust date to 30s – 40s, and ecru short are considered more modern. $25.00 – 35.00 per pair.

Four pairs of dark gloves: from the top, mid-length black net with solid fabric palm, button closure at the wrist; wrist length navy crocheted with white accent; very delicate navy netted gloves; and full length sheer evening gloves with three-button wrist closure and original "Van Raalte" tag. $15.00 – 35.00 per pair.

Five pairs of silk gloves: long ecru silk evening gloves with small ruffle; simple long magenta gloves; long rich brown gloves with open work provocatively baring the wrist and arm; long black silk with white braid accent; short ecru with fancy braid trim at wrist. $18.00 – 55.00 per pair.

Two pairs of 1940s gloves: great green gloves with wrist detailing and Bakelite accent; gauntlet style navy fabric with contrasting ivory lining. $18.00 – 28.00 per pair.

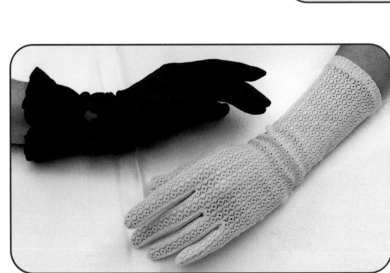

Two pairs of 1940s: Black fabric gloves with button wrist accent and butter yellow lacey summer gloves. $15.00 – 20.00 per pair.

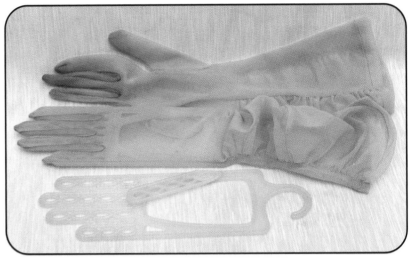

Pale pink nylon mid-length, gathered on the back, shown with plastic glove dryer. After washing, insert the glove form and hang to air dry. $10.00 – 20.00.

Two pairs of 1940s: magenta wrist length fabric and suede gloves and plum ruched at the wrist fabric gloves. $10.00 – 20.00 per pair.

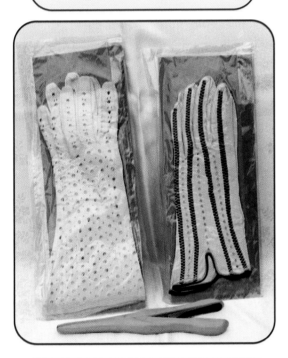

Four pairs of black leather gloves: mid-length black leather with black beaded design; mid-length black leather with a pair of soutach frogs on the back; mid-length black leather with small floral pierced design, lovely scalloped edge; short tailored black leather gloves with double row of rhinestone trim at wrist. 15.00 – 35.00 per pair.

Two pairs of leather gloves: white leather wrist length, navy stitched design with pierced open work; white leather with pierced open work all over; both in mint condition still in original sealed cellophane package, shown with wooden glove stretcher. $15.00 – 30.00 per pair.

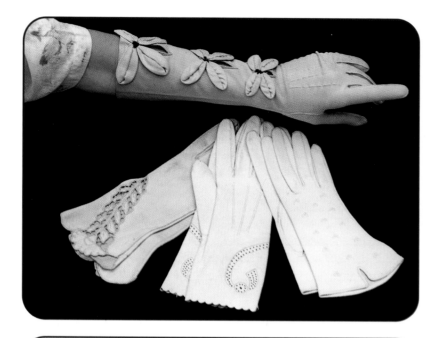

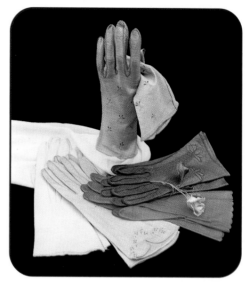

Four pairs of light leather gloves: Palest pinky-beige suede mid-length gloves with interesting trio of leather-stitched flowers on back; ecru wrist length gloves with very pretty cutwork effect; white wrist length with stitched swirl design, small scalloped edge; creamy white wrist length gloves with subtle raised design all over. $18.00 – 48.00 per pair.

Five pairs of leather gloves in shades of red: palest pink plain unadorned wrist length gloves; delicate pink with pierced floral design at wrist; red leather gloves with scalloped edge; maroon wrist length gloves with stitched design; light mauve wrist length gloves with stitched floral design all over. $15.00 – 25.00 per pair.

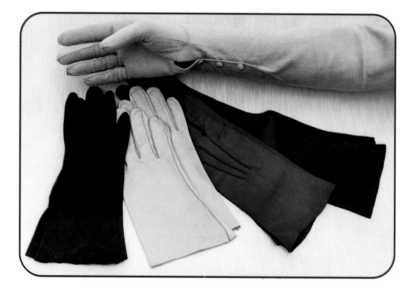

Five pairs of leather gloves: long ivory gloves reach to above the elbow with three small buttons at wrist for fit; navy medium length tailored gloves; great green wrist length gloves with back stitching detail; pale blue short gloves; classic black short gloves with back stitching detail. 8.00 – 32.00 per pair.

Five pairs of leather gloves: elegant long dark cocoa brown suede gloves; tawny gold pigskin wrist length gloves; black and cream deco design with small triangles at wrist; camel and gold wrist length gloves with pointed edging; cream wrist length with chocolate brown zigzag design. $20.00 – 45.00 per pair.

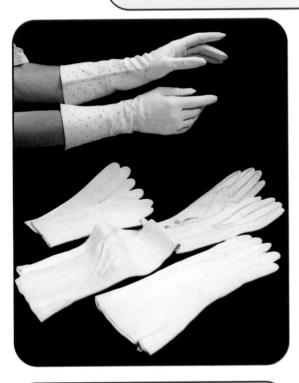

Various lengths in cream to white leather gloves: medium length rich cream glove with pierced design; classic white short gloves; elbow length ivory leather gloves with three-snap closure at wrist; medium length white leather with back stitching. $10.00 – 30.00 per pair.

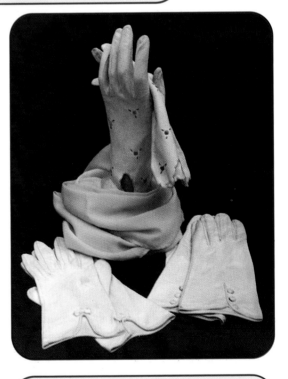

Three pairs of short white leather gloves: floral embroidered gloves with notch at wrist; creamy white leather gloves with miniature bow detail at notch; white gloves with three small leather covered buttons on back. $15.00 – 20.00 per pair.

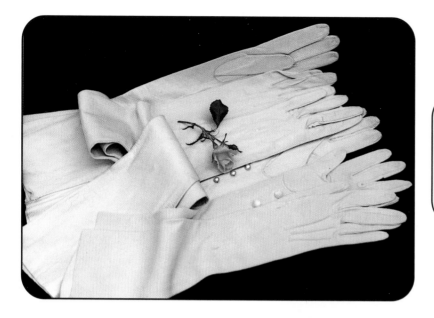

Three pairs of long evening leather gloves: ivory smooth leather with snap closure at wrist (not shown); creamy white smooth leather gloves with three small pearl buttons at wrist for closure; soft fawn suede gloves with mother-of-pearl button closure. Depending on size, $25.00 – 50.00 per pair.

Four pairs of various beaded gloves: long evening gloves from early 1900s with sequined and embroidered design on ivory kid; short gold seed beaded ivory cloth gloves; white cloth medium length gloves with white seed beads and small pearls at edge; winter white cloth gloves with seed beads radiating from wrist design. $20.00 – 65.00 per pair.

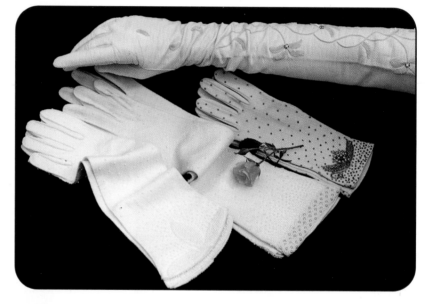

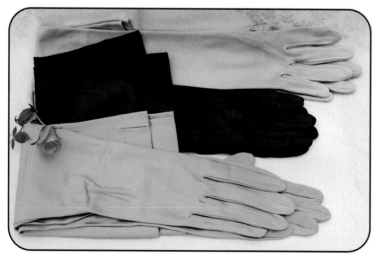

Three pairs of 1950s long evening gloves in pale mint green, dark green, and chartreuse shiny stretch fabric gloves. $15.00 – 20.00 per pair.

Five pairs of medium length 1950s cloth gloves in pale blue, beige, red with scalloped edge, very plain pale pink, and classic black. This gathered medium length glove was often worn with a ¾ sleeve coat covering the arm. $10.00 – 20.00 per pair.

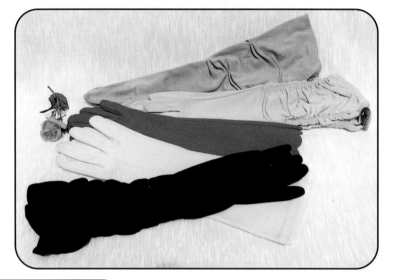

Three pairs of metallic 1960s evening gloves in shiny silver, sparkle silver stretch fabric, and gold metallic fabric. $10.00 – 20.00 per pair.

Five pairs of classic 1950s cloth gloves in various styles and shades of cream to white. $10.00 – 15.00 per pair.

Seven pairs of nylon gloves from 1940s to 1950s, from ruffled to ruched, in various pastel shades, ultra feminine. $10.00 – 20.00 per pair.

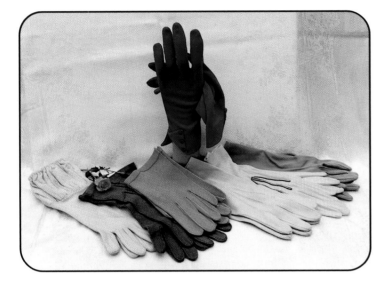

Seven pairs of cloth gloves in various styles and shades of pink, purple, coral, pale blue, butter cream, lime green, and red. $10.00 – 20.00 per pair.

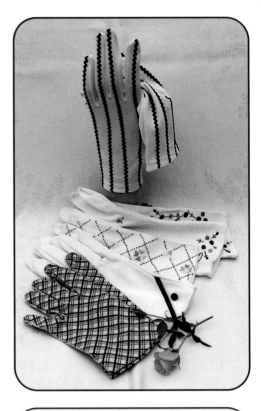

Five pairs of short cloth gloves variously trimmed in navy blue rickrack, embroidered flowers, and red and blue plaid, 1950s – 1960s. $15.00 – 20.00 per pair.

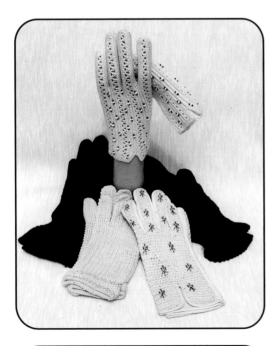

Five pairs of knitted 1950s – 1960s gloves in cream with bead and embroidery trim, black, navy, and pale pink. $8.00 – 15.00 per pair.

Four pairs of short leather: beige 1950s driving gloves; 1960s white leather with black hand stitching on the back; early 1900s, short ivory leather with snap closure; mint condition white leather 1950s gloves. $9.00 – 15.00 per pair.

Black sheared beaver muff, 12" in length with a wrist ring attached by a black silk ribbon. $35.00 – 55.00.

1940s Simplicity pattern #4777, for mitts, purse, and hat, originally 25¢.

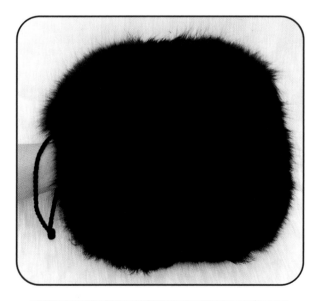

Black fox muff, zippered pocket inside for hankie and comb, 13" in length. $35.00 – 60.00.

Black bear or badger with much coarser fur, 12" in length with tortoise-like wrist ring. $40.00 – 65.00.

Leopard muff-purse, zippered for convenience of carrying necessities, 18" in length. $75.00 – 100.00.

Unusual sheared beaver purse-muff, frame is double hinged to open with two small barrels sliding over the single barrel for closure of purse, hands kept warm in the side openings of the muff with black ribbon handle. $45.00 – 75.00.

Simulated Persian lamb muff, 16" in length with zippered side opening for carrying the essentials, 1940s. $20.00 – 30.00. Courtesy of Kathleen Davin.

Matching white ermine zippered muff with black plastic ring, and small ermine hat with black felt on top of crown and back tab, 1930s. Set, $135.00 – 165.00.

andkerchiefs, or hankies, have an interesting history. In ancient times the handkerchief was a mere bit of silk used by the priests at the alter. Indeed, for many years priests were the only people in Europe allowed the privilege of using handkerchiefs. This use was restricted to the altar for propriety. It was called a "facial" and kept with the other vestments. Eventually the grand ladies of court began borrowing the idea of small squares of silk to wipe their eyes or noses. Over time these gentlewomen gave their pretty little handkerchiefs as tokens of love and friendship. Gentlemen began wearing these small (three to four inch squares) in their hatbands to show the favors of their mistresses.

In time ladies began to embroider the edges of these handkerchiefs with fancy stitches or special emblems. Empress Josephine, who was lovely, did not have perfect teeth. Because she was self-conscious of this fault, she carried a small lace-edged handkerchief with her and constantly raised it to her lips in an effort to conceal this dental problem. It was the ladies of the French court who followed suit from the Empress's example, and soon the fashion of handkerchiefs came into general use.

The ladies and gentlemen of the European aristocracy soon adopted the convenience of these handkerchiefs to absorb a sneeze or muffle a cough. The ordinary handkerchief, once used only by priests and royalty, spread to the common citizens. It became an indispensable accessory and an article of apparel for anyone wanting this personal convenience. Handkerchiefs were often carried and held to the nose while walking in an area that might have a disagreeable odor. Indoor plumbing was not a common utility in the 1800s. Ladies might walk about the streets with handkerchiefs to their noses.

The staple in any wardrobe would be the plain white hemstitched linen handkerchief. The grades of linen came from Belfast, Ireland. Even today an Irish linen hankie is known to be the best quality. However,

> *"In his holy flirtation with the world, God occasionally drops a handkerchief. These handkerchiefs are called saints."*
>
> *Frederick Buechner*

"finish" is the key to quality and the detail determines price. Ladies did not find favor with poorly finished handkerchiefs, they wanted to have the best hemstitching or lace available on this small fashion accessory they carried. It was the sign of a well-bred young woman.

There were large quantities of cotton handkerchiefs imported from Switzerland, hand-embroidered and worked on machines. Most of these imported hankies were produced in St. Gall, Switzerland. In point of quality, the hand-finished linen goods were far superior to the less expensive Swiss cotton. No matter how fine a cotton handkerchief may be, it cannot be compared to a linen one. Cotton loses its finish and color sooner than the linen hankie, after several washings. Because of the difference in expense, however, there was always a demand for the cotton hankies of Switzerland.

While the classic white hankies were favored in Europe, printed patterns on hankies became popular in the U.S. in the late 1800s. The original printing process was labor intensive and took more initial financial outlay. At one time some mills had as many as 60,000 engraved designs, some for a single-color design, and some for two or more designs. The cheaper designs were engraved on copper rollers, which could later be turned off in a lathe for later engravings. Often a first edition might print as many as 1,000 dozen handkerchiefs. If the pattern was a popular one, the roller would be preserved for future printings. The finest engravings were made on wooden blocks which were printed flat. These blocks would be preserved for future printings.

America's pockets were lined with colorful squares of fabric that depicted everything from a presidential campaign to a 400-year exposition. Commemorative handkerchiefs carried the message back home as souvenirs. These little snippets of history were emblazoned with symbols of patriotic and moralistic themes. There were "Protection" handkerchiefs used to promote candidates' campaigns in 1888.

Fashion Squared. Little lacey squares of fabric that proper ladies carried.

Photo Credit: © 2000 Chris Bryant

Silk hankies were primarily imported from China and Japan, which had the technique for making beautiful silk very cheaply. These hankies were either finished or imported in what was called "in the piece"; that is, not separated or hemmed. The finishing was done as piecework by women in America. It was easy work that could be done at home by women who needed to make a little extra money for the family. Often young girls were employed as cheap labor for this type of work which needed little training. Most young girls had been brought up with the basic sewing skills necessary to finish a hankie.

> *Large variety of pure linen handkerchiefs, starting at 3 for 49¢, The Ladies' Home Journal, December 1899.*

No. 383.—Ladies' Embroidered Silk Handkerchief. This beautiful ladies' handkerchief is of pure silk, warranted. It is a delicate pale pink in color, and has scalloped edges embroidered in blue silk, and is also embroidered around the entire outer edge in a design representing stars and grasses in pink and old gold. It is very delicate and pretty, and cannot fail to be appreciated by every lady who receives it. Understand that it is not a so-called silk-finished or imitation silk handkerchief, but one that is warranted of pure silk throughout. We will send this Embroidered Silk Handkerchief by mail, post-paid, also THE PEOPLE'S HOME JOURNAL for one year, upon receipt of only **Fifty Cents;** or we will give the handkerchief *free* to any one sending us a club of **Two** subscribers for one year at 35 cents each or **Four** subscribers at 25 cents each. Or we will send the handkerchief post-paid, without subscription to the paper, upon receipt of 25 cents.

> *Delicate pale pink silk handkerchief, with scalloped edges and embroidery, sent with the subscription to a magazine for fifty cents! The People's Home Journal, December 1894.*

December, 1899

Christmas Handkerchiefs

Nothing More Suitable for Gifts
...
Nothing So Easy to Purchase by Mail

Our Holiday Catalogue, the most artistic book of its kind ever issued, is filled with illustrations of beautiful *Pure Linen* Kerchiefs, from which we select a few to show here.

Unlaundered Handkerchiefs

We make a specialty of Pure Linen Hand Embroidered Unlaundered Handkerchiefs. These are just as they come from the homes of the peasants in Ireland, where they are embroidered by hand. They have not been washed, starched and boxed, but simply bundled up and sent to us, dirt and all: we get them at just about ⅔ the price that same goods laundered would be, so we are able to give unusual bargains in these. They wash beautifully.

...

If you should buy any of them and they should not wash clean to your satisfaction, send them back and get your money.

Unlaundered Initial Handkerchiefs

Top series (A, F, K),	. 3 for 49c.	
2d " (W, N, C),	. 25c. each	Ladies'
3d " (T, M, A),	. 50c.	"
4th " (N, W, S),	. 25c.	Men's

1st and 2d Rows (14, 17, 16, 21, 23, 22), . . 3 for 49c.
3d and 4th " (239, 73, 240, 63, 261, 253), . 25c. each
5th and 6th " (618, 610, 609, 623, 621, 620), . 50c. each

Ladies' Pure Linen Embroidered Handkerchiefs
LAUNDERED AND FINISHED

207, 25c.
209, 25c.
206, 25c.
338, 50c.
584, 50c.
539, 50c.
711, 75c.
702, 75c.
703, 75c.
704, 75c.
705, 75c.
707, 75c.

These are our direct importations, and you pay no middleman's profit.

...

Here are Some Choice Novelties:

806, $1.00
807, $1.00
804, $1.00
932, $1.50
933, $1.50
935, $1.50
944, $2.50
941, $2.50
943, $2.00

Duchess and Point Lace Handkerchiefs

Duchess and Point Lace
D 40 $4.00
D 50 $5.00
D 75 $7.50
D 85 $8.50
D 100 $10.00
D 125 $12.50
D 150 $15.00
D 250 $25.00

We bring from Belgium the most extensive lines of these high-art creations shown in America, and our prices are more moderate than in stores that pay New York rents.

...

MODERN LACE-MAKING

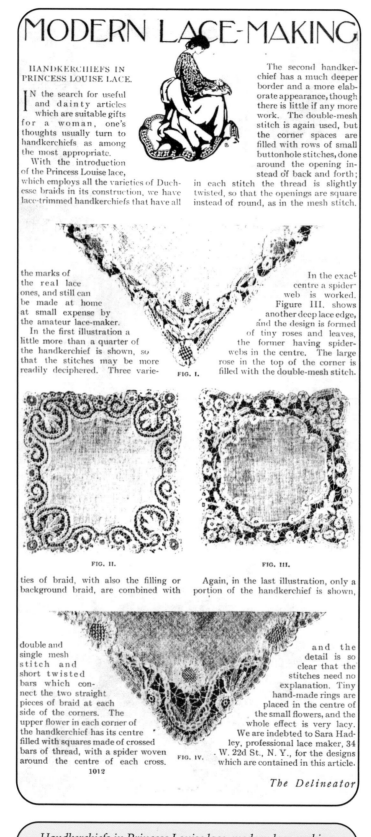

HANDKERCHIEFS IN PRINCESS LOUISE LACE.

IN the search for useful and dainty articles which are suitable gifts for a woman, one's thoughts usually turn to handkerchiefs as among the most appropriate.

With the introduction of the Princess Louise lace, which employs all the varieties of Duchesse braids in its construction, we have lace-trimmed handkerchiefs that have all the marks of the real lace ones, and still can be made at home at small expense by the amateur lace-maker.

In the first illustration a little more than a quarter of the handkerchief is shown, so that the stitches may be more readily deciphered. Three varie-

FIG. I.

ties of braid, with also the filling or background braid, are combined with

double and single mesh stitch and short twisted bars which connect the two straight pieces of braid at each side of the corners. The upper flower in each corner of the handkerchief has its centre filled with squares made of crossed bars of thread, with a spider woven around the centre of each cross.

1012

FIG. II.

FIG. III.

The second handkerchief has a much deeper border and a more elaborate appearance, though there is little if any more work. The double-mesh stitch is again used, but the corner spaces are filled with rows of small buttonhole stitches, done around the opening instead of back and forth; in each stitch the thread is slightly twisted, so that the openings are square instead of round, as in the mesh stitch.

In the exact centre a spider-web is worked. Figure III. shows another deep lace edge, and the design is formed of tiny roses and leaves, the former having spider-webs in the centre. The large rose in the top of the corner is filled with the double-mesh stitch.

Again, in the last illustration, only a portion of the handkerchief is shown, and the detail is so clear that the stitches need no explanation. Tiny hand-made rings are placed in the centre of the small flowers, and the whole effect is very lacy. We are indebted to Sara Hadley, professional lace maker, 34 W. 22d St., N. Y., for the designs which are contained in this article.

FIG. IV.

The Delineator

Handkerchiefs in Princess Louise lace, modern lace-making techniques of the early twentieth century, The Delineator, December 1904.

Directions for fancy handkerchiefs with insets of flowered organdy and blocks of pink lawn, linen, and lace joined with a rolled hem, and insets in shield and butterfly designs, The Delineator, 1904.

Real Irish Linen
Handkerchiefs

Just send us your name and address on a postal and we will mail you **FREE** our handsome **Christmas catalogue** which illustrates and tells all about Brayburn Irish Linen Handkerchiefs.

You can buy them direct from our Irish Mills through our American house

Special.—To introduce our Brayburn real Irish linen handkerchiefs we will send six assorted patterns beautifully embroidered in an artistic hand painted box postpaid for **$1.45.** This is a welcome Christmas present. We refund the money if you are not more than satisfied.

BELFAST LINEN MFG. CO., 80 Valpey Bldg., Detroit

Ad for real Irish linen handkerchiefs, six embroidered handkerchiefs in an artistic hand-painted box, postpaid for $1.45, The Delineator, 1904.

LISSUE
THE NEW FABRIC HANDKERCHIEF

At all good stores. If your dealer cannot supply you, send us his name and 25c. for sample to be mailed to you prepaid. *Handsome booklet and sample of fabric free on request.*

Address Dept. 12
THE TOOTAL BROADHURST LEE CO., Ltd.
92 Grand Street, New York

Soft as thistledown; fine as gossamer; and durable. Colors guaranteed indelible. Six free for one that loses color in the laundry. Also in *all white*. From England to you for 25c. The registered "LISSUE" label appears on each handkerchief. Insist on the genuine.

New "Lissue" fabric handkerchief from England, 25¢, The Delineator, March 1911.

FANCY HANDKERCHIEFS

FOR the insets the old-fashioned faggoting stitch, in which no threads are drawn, was employed. This stitch is illustrated in the November DELINEATOR, where several collars are shown.

Pieces cut from organdy lawn that is

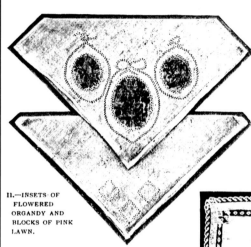

II.—INSETS OF FLOWERED ORGANDY AND BLOCKS OF PINK LAWN.

printed in little bouquets of roses on a white ground, are inset in the handkerchief shown at illustration I. The corner of the handkerchief was basted to a square of paper, bouquets cut from the organdy in oval shape and turned under one-eighth of an inch all around were laid on the handkerchief with care as to correct position, and the outline was marked on the handkerchief with a sharp pencil. The linen was then cut away an eighth of an inch from the pencilled outline and this one-eighth of an inch was turned under, making the pencilled outline the edge of the opening. The inset pieces were basted in the opening and the edges connected with the faggoting stitch, working across from the inset piece to the handkerchief.

Colored lawn folded into three-eighth-inch squares is inset in the handkerchief

shown at the second illustration. Three squares are inset in each corner.

The example pictured at illustration III. is made from a piece of fine handkerchief linen. The border design is drawn on paper and a square of pink lawn is basted over it. The white linen is then basted in the centre of the square, space being left between for the Valenciennes insertion. The edges of the lawn are rolled, and the lace is over-handed to them with a fine needle and cotton.

The shield-shaped inset in the handkerchief shown at illustration IV. is intended as a background on which an

III.—LINEN AND LACE JOINED WITH A ROLLED HEM.

initial or monogram may be worked.

A more intricate design is shown at illustration IV. After the butterfly inset is faggoted in place a few of the same stitches are taken in each of the large wings and a row of fine French knots is made between the open-work rows.

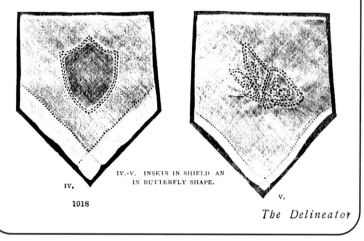

IV.-V. INSETS IN SHIELD AND IN BUTTERFLY SHAPE.

IV.

1018

V.

The Delineator

It was in 1924 that the paper tissue for removing cold cream was introduced by Kimberly-Clark. By the 1930s the convenience of disposable tissues almost entirely usurped the role of the purely practical hankie.

General use of the little hankie declined, just as the corset and parasol faded from fashion. Hankies, especially with fancy trimmings, became more of an accessory to carry than to actually use.

Ad for printed handkerchief of the month by Burmel, Vogue, June 1943.

One may wonder, "Where are all these hankies today which were printed in the 1800s?" Remember, these were considered personal items that were disposable, after all why would one keep something that had been used daily until it was worn out? Only the wedding hankies, or other special keepsake hankies would be carefully tucked away, to take out years later and hold for the sake of memory. We have the good fortune as collectors to appreciate these little square bits of history, and wonder just who did carry this small square of fashion?

Care & Storage

ost hankies that we find today are affordable. They are small and easy to store. It is important to remember that they are textiles and can suffer from the same problems of larger collectibles such as quilts or shawls. Keep them away from bugs and other creatures, lest they become dinner. Avoid situations that will bring about the dreaded mold and mildew. If possible store them flat as opposed to folded, or wrap them around a tube (empty paper towel roll, covered in aluminum foil works well). Use acid-free tissue or cotton sheeting to store them. If they are to be framed, carefully stitch them onto a fabric backing and don't allow the glass to rest on the hankie. Most professional framers know the proper materials that will preserve your treasured token. Handkerchiefs should be washed only under the most careful conditions, some are too fragile while others may become even more faded. It is known that some early nineteenth century handkerchiefs will fetch an amazing $3,500.00 price, while some twentieth century keepsakes can bring several hundred dollars. Shouldn't we cherish our keepsakes from the past?

> *"The maple leaf wears a gayer scarf*
> *The field a scarlet gown,*
> *Lest I should be old fashioned*
> *I'll put a trinket on."*
>
> *Emily Dickinson*

Lady wrapped in scarves.

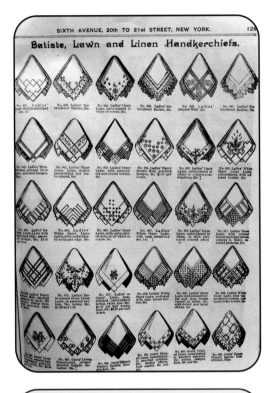

Fine white linen bordered with a fine Battenburg type lace, butterfly design on the corners, early 1900s. $65.00 – 85.00.

Page advertising "Batiste, Lawn and Linen Handkerchiefs" for ladies in H. O'Neill & Co. Fall and Winter Catalogue, 1890 – 91, priced from 13¢ – $1.00 each.

Three hankies: pink linen with filet lace butterfly in one corner, stitched edging in darker pink; white lawn hemstitched with fine hairpin lace edging; ecru Princess lace on net background. These three hankies are examples of distinctively different lace styles. $25.00 – 55.00.

Four hankies: white Irish linen with original tag, edged in green crochet trim; cream linen with lacey pink crochet trim; white linen with scalloped white crochet trim; blue Irish linen with original tag, edged in two-tone ecru crocheted lace. $5.00 – 15.00.

Four hankies: small square peach cotton with hand-embroidered, appliquéd lace design in one corner, dating to 1920s; white cotton machine-embroidered heart design with original tag "Made in Switzerland," dating to 1950s; white cotton appliqué and embroidery with original tag "Made in China," dating to 1950s; fine white cotton with blue embroidered pansies in one corner. $5.00 – 12.00.

Seven hankies from one woman's estate in Astoria, Oregon. All hankies were monogrammed "A. L. H." and each one distinctly different, as fine examples of lace edging, Madeira work, hemstitching, and embroidery. With such exquisite taste, one can only speculate about the life of this woman and what she was like. $10.00 – 15.00.

Three examples of WWI silk hankies, each embroidered "Souvenir of France," machine-made lace and machine embroidered. These wonderfully feminine confections were easy to mail home to sweethearts, wives, and mothers, and served as subtle patriotic propaganda. $15.00 – 20.00.

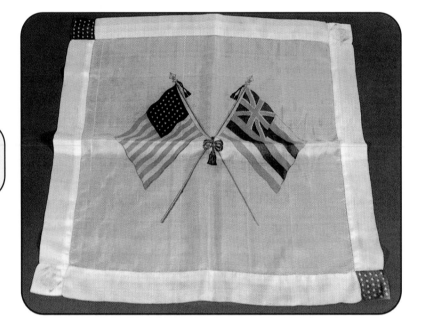

Large white silk commemorative hankie with American-British flags in center, printing in corner is too faded to read, measures 17" square. $22.00 – 42.00.

Three printed cotton hankies: "The Whimsey Report on the Birds and Bees" with original tag, "Carol Stanley" in corner; a 1961 calendar hankie with automobile motif on all four sides; a 1959 calendar hankie with scalloped edges. $10.00 – 30.00.

Four cream silk hankies: delicate pink embroidered flowers with original tag "100% silk"; purple-edged smaller square with embroidered flowers and "Portland 1905" commemorative hankie; pink, yellow, blue embroidered flowers with blue scalloped edge; blue embroidered with pink edge. $10.00 – 20.00.

Five cotton hankies: showing a variety of styles, sizes, and trims from shadow appliqué, to cut-work on the peach, tiny tatted edge on white, Madeira work on the blue and white. $7.00 – 15.00.

Four hankies: three folded hankies are great examples of Madeira work on cotton lawn; unfolded hankie is appliqué and hemstitching on cotton, rolled hem. $10.00 – 18.00.

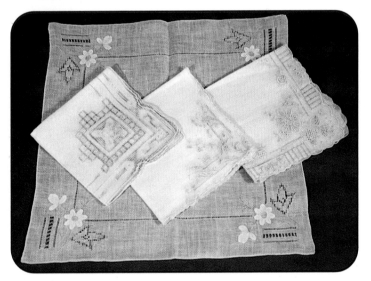

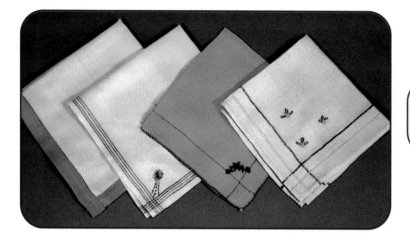

Four hankies in pongee silk, variously trimmed. Usually pongee is the natural ecru color, rarely do you see the vibrant color such as this rose shade. $5.00 – 15.00.

Seven white cotton monogrammed hankies with various trims, crocheted edgings, and embroidery. $7.00 – 15.00.

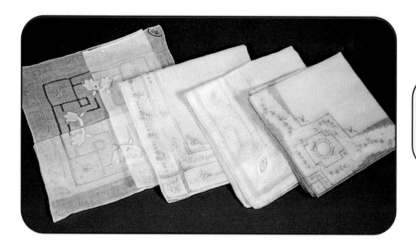

Four white cotton hankies: lawn that has original tag and fold is hemstitched and appliquéd white on white; the other three are finely embroidered and hemstitched. $10.00 – 18.00.

Four cotton hankies with various embroidered floral motifs, two with original tags. $9.00 – 15.00.

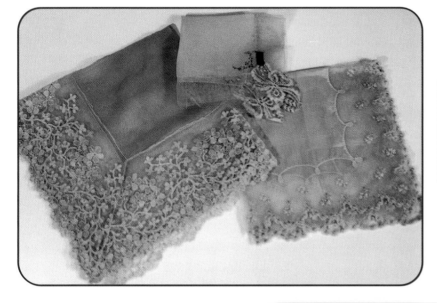

Three fancy silk hankies: the sheer pink silk georgette has a deep border of delicate ecru lace, measures 16" square; the small peach with hand-painted floral design in corner has original tag which reads "Marv-o, re. U.S. Pat.," measures 9½" square; the aqua silk has a deep embroidered sheer silk border and measures 14" square. $18.00 – 28.00.

Ivory wedding hankie made of a fine lawn center, with 4¼" deep machine lace, early 1900s, measures 17" square. $28.00 – 38.00.

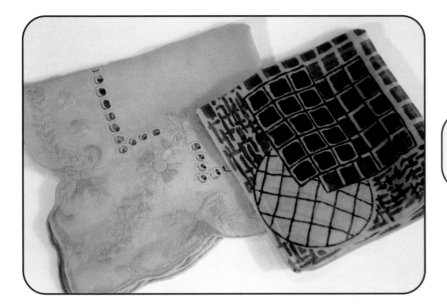

Rust silk hankie with embroidered floral design and eyelet work; cotton hankie in green and black deco design with plain rolled hem. $10.00 – 18.00.

Three white cotton hankies: the smaller one is a modern Battenburg lace; ivory machine lace hankie and an example of drawn work on white cotton. $5.00 – 12.00.

Six cotton hankies with variety of floral patterns and colors, popular in the 1940s and 1950s. $5.00 – 12.00.

Gift hankie book in semi open position, blue on ivory paper bound, ribbon on spine, dating to 1940s. Purchased from Persona Vintage Clothing, Astoria, OR. $15.00.

Gift hankie book in open position, showing three cotton floral hankies folded like a fan. Very creative and unusual presentation.

Gift package of three cotton hankies in blue, green, and gold with embroidered designs in corners, never used. $15.00 – 20.00.

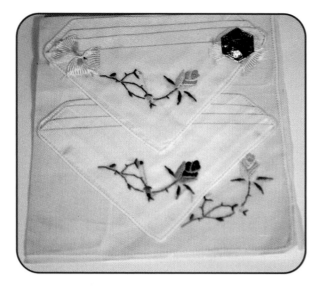

Three gift packaged white cotton hankies with embroidered rose in corners, original tag and ribbon still attached, never used. $12.00 – 18.00.

Lovely fawn colored silk hankie holder edged in delicate ivory lace, decorated with silk ribbon flowers and streamers, matching powder puff on wand trimmed with folded roses, dating to early 1900s, may have been a wedding gift. Set, $45.00 – 55.00.

Pink cotton commemorative large hankie or scarf, reads "Souvenir of Columbus Exhibition, 1892." On the left side of the central round depiction of Columbus's ship is "1492" and to the right is "1892," measures 27" square. $65.00 – 85.00.

Deep aqua silk scarf with dancing figures showing a variety of popular dances and the year they were in vogue, center reads *"The Big Apple, 1937."* $35.00 – 45.00.

Long peach silk scarf with beautiful machine embroidered flowers and hand-tied fringe, dates to 1930s, measures 50" x 18½", fringe measuring 9". $45.00 – 60.00.

Cream silk scarf with Oriental embroidered central motif and delicate floral border in pastel shades, measures 26" square. $50.00 – 65.00.

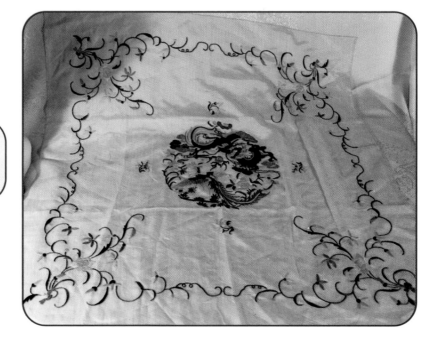

Photo Credit © 2000 Chris Bryant.

Ahead of Fashion. Five designer hats: feathered Lilly Dache, red poppies Leslie James, pink straw Hattie Carnegie, black fox Schiaparelli, beaded Dior.

140

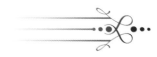

ats are transforming in their power! They will change a mood, relieve depression, inspire curiosity, express creativity, eliminate invisibility! Hats are a means of "topping it off," adding a touch of panache to an otherwise ordinary ensemble. They get us out of our routine, and make others wish they had the fashion nerve, or verve.

You could say hats are a woman's mystery. It is a mystery that unfolds, creating allure and feminine mystique that cannot be had instantly. It is almost as if a hat has a spirit all its own, and only becomes apparent when it is worn. A hat is not alive on a hat stand, it has no meaning on its own. A hat is part sculpture, part architecture, part trimming, and part craftsmanship. It is wearable art. It is a bouquet we wear on our heads. And always a hat expresses emotion, especially when the wearer feels an affinity to that particular style.

The history of hats is long and varied. For centuries they were symbolic of one's status, whether socially, religiously, or nationally. Hats were visible signs of one's wealth, political beliefs, occupation, or religion. Hats or head coverings have also been a shroud of submission historically, and continue to be so in many countries even today. Of course hats have also been a practical necessity in cold weather climates. Generally hats and headwear denoted the importance of the wearer.

Originally it was a man's accessory from classical times onward, as with many accessories. Rarely did women wear hats until the end of the sixteenth century. By the Victorian period, a proper lady was not seen in public without a hat or bonnet. In the mid nineteenth century the bonnet, which covered the hair and made a wide frame for the face, with an extended brim, was in fashion. Even indoor functions, like the opera, were attended with the appropriate headdress or ornamentation.

Bonnets were usually always lined with silk or muslin. "No one article in the whole range of female costume is more important in its effects than that comparatively small piece of satin, silk or other material that forms the lining of the bonnet" as stated by Mrs. M. J. Howell in the *Handbook of Millinery*, 1847. Trimming inside the brim was as important as the outside trimmings of lace, ribbon, and flowers.

*"Three things a woman can make out of anything…
a salad, a hat, and an argument."*

John Barrymore

OPENING IN BONNETS, HEADDRESSES, LINGERIE, ETC.

OPENINGS being the fashion of the day, and the principal occupation of the female portion of a city community during October and November, we commence our round of sight-seeing with an inspection of Brodie's elegant cloaks—for which we refer our readers to our more lengthy "Chitchat." Genin's juvenile fashions will come next in review, the Bazaar being brightened by Mr. Taylor's selections from over the water. Of this gentleman's taste and courteousness, no regular visitor of Genin's needs to be reminded. Meantime we open our own novelties, commencing with a simple but extremely tasteful headdress, suited to a young married lady, for opera, or an evening reception.

Fig. 1.—Front view, showing the division of the hair into two rouleaux which are marked by two small jewelled or ornamented hair-pins, placed over the ear; these are softly shaded by the outline of the plumes at the back of the head.

Fig. 2.—The back hair twisted into a smooth coil, on each side of which pure white ostrich plumes are arranged turning in towards it at the end. Plumes are sometimes worn by young ladies, but are more suitable for those who have

Fig. 1.

Fig. 2.

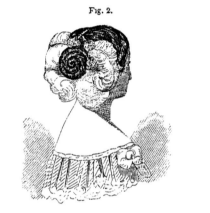

a right to be addressed as "Madam," though not sufficiently staid for chaperones.

in the same manner, over the cape; this bow is sometimes placed quite to the left, and has a

Fig. 3.

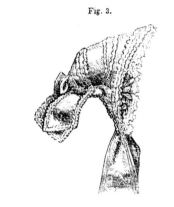

Fig. 4.

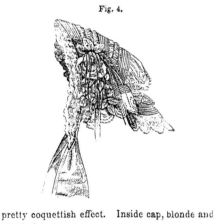

Fig. 3.—Simple bonnet of green French velvet, with fine satin quillings, a little darker shade, of the same color. Broad bow of velvet, edged

pretty coquettish effect. Inside cap, blonde and myrtle leaves.

Fig. 4.—Bonnet of drawn silk and blonde;

447

Front and back views of plumes worn by young ladies, or suitable for "those who have the right to be addressed by 'Madame.'" The side views of a small bonnet with lace, braid, and ribbon trims as shown in Godey's Lady's Book, November 1856.

HAT (Fig. 1).—The shape may be made of black stiff net and black wire; cut it out as Fig. 2 for the crown, and cut through the four straight lines up to the dotted one, and bend the latter down; then make into a round by creasing the sides where they are cut through, and tack them together with black thread. Procure a piece

of black silk velvet, and cut it the size of the round of Fig. 2, and it will form Fig. 3. For the brim, cut out of the same net the shape of Fig. 4, and cut out the round hole for the crown, and through the black lines at the top and bottom, turn up the dotted lines, and tack round inside of them a thin piece of wire, then fold over the top and bottom, where it is cut through, and sew the sides together. Cut a piece of black silk velvet on the cross, and shape it from the dotted lines to the circle in the middle of Fig. 4, and tack it under the brim of the hat; cut another strip of the same velvet on the cross, and bind the whole of the edge of the brim very neatly. Put in the crown, and fix it to the brim by sewing it all round, and the rough edge with a small piece of sarsnet ribbon, lining the inside of the crown with Persian silk, and it will form Fig. 5. Get a small white ostrich feather, rather long, and tack it inside of the brim on the top of the hat, carry it to the back, fasten it there, and allow

Fig. 1.   Fig. 2.

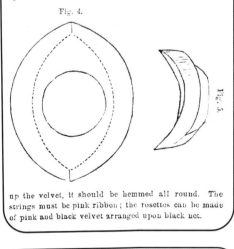

Fig. 3.

it to hang over a little. Cut some more strips of black silk velvet on the cross, and make up a nice large bow upon black net, and ends of the same; but before making

Fig. 4.

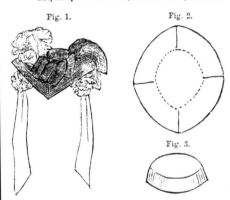

up the velvet, it should be hemmed all round. The strings must be pink ribbon; the rosettes can be made of pink and black velvet arranged upon black net.

Directions for making the base of a hat from stiff net and wire, Godey's Lady's Book, July 1860.

THE RESILLA.
(Front view.)

A NEW style of covering for the head, which, on account of its lightness, will advantageously supersede the wadded hoods worn in the carriage in going to and returning from the opera and evening parties. It will also be found very useful of a warm evening when it is pleasant to sit in a balcony or veranda, and when it is especially necessary to protect the head by some light covering against the chilly dews which fall after sunset. It forms a light and graceful covering for the head, whilst, at the same time, it shades the neck.

We give the instructions for working the Resilla in the Work Department, accompanied with an engraving showing a back view of the same.

Beautiful illustration of the new style evening head covering, "worn in the carriage in going to and returning from the opera and evening parties," Godey's Lady's Book, August 1860.

143

Fig. 23. Fig. 24.

Fig. 25. Fig. 26.

Four illustrations of stylish bonnets with detailed
ornamentation, Godey's Lady's Book, January 1871.

Group of bonnets showing the trailing ribbons and fabric sashes in the back, note the widow's veiled bonnet in the lower left of illustration, Godey's Lady's Book, January 1871.

RIDING HABITS.
(*See Description, Fashion Department.*)

Riding habits with the appropriate veiled hat resembling a man's top hat in shape, Godey's Lady's Book, March 1871.

The bonnet from 1840 to 1850 kept the same shape, with the downward curve of the lower edge from the back of the crown, as seen on page 175. After 1850 the general shape was one of more open form, opening more widely around the face, with crown growing lower and smaller. As written in *World of Fashion* in 1853, "it is the peculiar form of crown which gives this appearance, by being made low and sloping towards the back." Worn well back on the head, this bonnet looked as if it were slipping off. The 1860s ushered in the spoon bonnet, so named because the front brim rose high, narrow, and more pointed with receding sides. The curtain in back was longer in the late 1850s and early 1860s than it had been.

Up until the 1850s the bonnet was the only acceptable fashion. However, by 1850 the wide-brimmed straw hat was being worn for summer at the seaside or in the country as casual wear. By the late 1850s, hats were becoming fashionable for informal occasions, at first for the younger ladies because "of course they are not suited to elderly ladies," stated in the *World of Fashion,* 1857. The hats for summer were usually made of straw or horsehair plait; the winter hats were of velvet or felt. Although not a new material, felt had not been used for fashionable bonnets for over three decades. Trimmings were restrained, with the favored velvet ribbon, feathers, and if flowers were used they were placed at the front.

The 1870s found the bonnet, as such, completely out of favor in exchange for a mere puff or lace fluff with small flowers and ribbons. As stated in the *Englishwoman's Domestic Magazine* from 1870, "no such thing as a bonnet is now in existence, and what is so called is a mere ornament for the head — a puff, a diadem, a lace fluting, a bonnet of flowers, a band of ribbon." As with any period of time, the hairstyles had an influence on what kind of hat could be worn, as well as what was fashionable. In general hats of the 1870s were more elaborately trimmed than what was seen in the previous decade.

A favorite fabric for hats that was seen in the 1880s was plush; beaver also appeared after 1887. Straw hats were seen all year as mentioned in *Woman's World* in 1888, "Throughout the year, straw is the one material that never goes out and vast numbers of straw bonnets are made with rows of velvet alternating with the straw." The Gainsborough, a large hat with one side turned up, was popular most of the decade. Another fashionable style was the postilion or post-boy hat with a high crown also called the flowerpot.

The stiffened straw hat with a ribbon band and flat brim, in a sailor style, was popular for sports in the late 1880s into the 1890s. Sometimes the brim was curved upward with a wired ribbon bow of velvet, but most of the hats of this style were plain and tailored. To retain a vestige of the high toque, the ornamentation of feathers or stiff bows was designed with a vertical effect. Wings and whole birds were often used on hats of this period. The 1890s ushered in a variety of shapes and sizes in hats with the principal materials being felt, velvet, chip, and straw, with flower and feather trimmings continuing their popularity.

Young lady in old photograph with a definite vertical design on her hat of roses and ribbons. She is wearing a jacket or coat with the cape detail mentioned in the chapter on cape styles for the 1890s. Back is marked "Eudora Gillette Weed, age 18."

149

Lovely lady in wicker chair with enormous leg-of-mutton sleeves and elaborate lace collar; her hat is probably straw with the 1890s vertical sweep of flowers. Mrs. Greenfield of Portland, Oregon. All photos of Mrs. Greenfield courtesy of Elaine Greenfield.

Dramatic example of bird wings decorating a most fashionable hat of the 1890s. Lady is Mrs. Greenfield of Portland, Oregon.

Same lady as in photographs on page 150 without the hat, note the hairstyle. Wonderful example of how a hat can add that bit of panache!

The largest center for the manufacture of hats in the 1890s was Danbury, Connecticut. Danbury had nearly as many hatters as all other cities in the U.S. combined, producing over 6,000,000 hats a year. In 1894 New York City turned out $5,000,000.00 worth of caps with at least 500 styles. Each step of manufacture was handled by a different person from cutting the material, blocking the crown, sewing the sides, with the finishing work usually being given to young girls. The earnings for this piecework was 50¢ – $2.00 per dozen caps.

Catalog sales were robust. In the 1894 – 95 Montgomery Wards catalog the millinery department offered to furnish any style of trimmed or untrimmed hat in any desired quality or cost. A reasonable charge was made for trimming a hat from 15¢ to 75¢. Prices for straw were 35¢; fur felt $1.50, and plumes ranged in price from 15¢ for cocque feathers to ostrich at 43¢. In the Sears, Roebuck Catalogue of fall 1900 a "Ladies chambray sun bonnet made of good, fast color, laundered, bow strings in back and full cape" was available in black, navy, light blue, and pink for 25¢. Sears offered a velvet covered turban (untrimmed) for 75¢, an English felt untrimmed hat for $1.10, sweeping bird of paradise spray (6 stems) for 50¢, and padded bird wings for 35¢.

In the early 1900s as dresses became slimmer, hairstyles became fuller and hats became larger to accommodate this Gibson girl look. Charles Dana Gibson, a prolific artist, was influential in the ultra-feminine style of the Edwardian era. Lingerie hats were soft, sweet confections of lace, silk, or tulle and flowers on a wire frame.

THE FASHION DEPARTMENT
FOR JUNE 1908

From the fashion department of The Ladies' Home Journal, June 1908.

Scene in a millinery shop: ladies with sweeping dresses trying on large lovely hats, illustrated in The Ladies' Home Journal, June 1908.

The Altar of Her Beauty

Illustration of plumed Edwardian hat, The Ladies' Home Journal, June 1908.

A Dress of Gingham for the Morning and One of Dotted Swiss for the Evening

Fashion illustrations of spring and summer dresses with the fashionably large hats of the season, The Ladies' Home Journal, June 1908.

According to *Vogue,* "In 1910 etiquette demands hats be worn out of doors, regardless of weather." As the silhouette became less bolstered and skirts narrower, the visual importance of hats increased. Fashion magazines of the day had extensive articles on new hat styles, construction tips from milliners, and all the latest trims.

Real photo postcard of two sailors and lady with very large hat with contrasting plumage, ca. 1910.

Will you be my Valentine?

Hand-colored Valentine of lady with large garden party hat. On the back is a place for one-cent stamp, addressed to "Esther Swanson, Merriam Park, Minn."

Real photo postcard of serious woman wearing a fur neck choker and matching muff (with heads), and huge hat ornamented with several bird wings and button or jet disk, ca. 1910.

Beautiful ad for Castle Hats of distinguished quality and design, *The Theatre*, March 1910.

AMERICAN FASHIONS FOR AMERICAN WOMEN

Good-Style Street Hat in Blue Straw.
Designed by N. F. Morrill

Tailored Hat for Morning Wear.
Designed by N. F. Morrill

Black Mohair Braid Toque for Traveling.
Designed by Willard J. Valentine

New Walking Hat With Feather Quills.
Designed by L. H. Bakom

The Out-of-Town Hat

Drawings by Jessie Barrick

Girlish Hat in Shaded Red Silk Poppies.
Designed by Rowena Rice

Tan Straw Toque With a Band of Bluets.
Designed by Charles Kurzman

Violet Toque With Shaded Roses.
Designed by N. F. Morrill

All-Flower Toque of Pansies for Silk Dress.
Designed by Charles Kurzman

THIS wide variety in styles of out-of-town hats is given for the woman who desires a correct and becoming hat to wear with more informal clothes, and for traveling. The first one is in very good style for street wear, and well carried out in dark blue straw faced with an inch-wide blue velvet band, finished with black satin cord. Crown and brim are draped with a Persian silk square of harmonious colors.

A TAILORED hat for morning wear is necessary for the well-dressed girl. The second hat on the top row with the square buckle is in light blue straw, though any becoming color may be chosen. The top of the brim is covered with blue pongee; band, buckle and tie are of shadow cretonne in old rose, blue and écru design, edged with the straw. The hat is made on a wire frame: crown measures about seven inches across and four high, brim five inches wide.

THE girlish poppy hat, which would be suitable to wear in the afternoon with a foulard or pongee dress, is bright and youthful in all red. The crown is four inches high, rounded, and the brim rather narrow, about two inches and a half on the straight side and four on the rolled. This is faced with red China silk, shirred. Silk poppies of medium size in different reddish tints are sewed close to the hat all over the crown and part way on the brim.

A FLOWER-TRIMMED toque, like the tan-colored straw with bluets and a large blue velvet bow in the back affords an opportunity for a charming combination of colors, but the choice of flowers should be determined by the complexion of the wearer. Use a turban wire frame to fit the head rather closely. Cover it with a fancy pattern of tan-colored straw, arranging the crown in folds. A wreath of bluets and a large wired bow of wide blue velvet ribbon complete the trimming.

VERY new and smart is the trimmed sailor hat for a linen suit. Black and white striped ribbon five inches wide is made into the large flat bow directly in the front of the hat, which is white mohair braid with a black edge. The style is simplicity itself, fresh and cool looking to wear in either the morning or afternoon. Crown of hat seven inches across and four high, brim six inches wide. About five yards of ribbon would be needed for such a large bow.

Trimmed Sailor Hat for Linen Suit. Designed by N. F. Morrill

White Straw With Persian Band. Designed by Charles Kurzman

FOR a good, serviceable traveling hat the mohair braid toque may be depended upon to last an entire season. While it is in all black the quality of the straw renders it light and summery, and the wings are soft and graceful. A toque of this style will require clever handling to insure becoming lines. It is made on a wire frame, bent to fit the head, and covered with rows of braid.

SHOWN in the upper right-hand corner of this page is a very new style of walking hat trimmed with feather quills. The straw is cream color, crown four inches high and five across, rounded; the brim flares high on the left side and lower on the right, while at the center back it is flat, as shown in this small illustration. A deep facing and a fine cord of black satin make a striking combination of trimming with the white feather quills.

A SEMI-DRESS hat like the all-flower toque in pansies is most useful to wear with the afternoon silk or pongee gown. It is a happy medium between the tailored and the picture hat. It is made on a wire frame, fitting the head closely, with a slightly extended rim covered with pansy-colored straw. Cover frame with violet maline on which sew purple-tinted pansies. A crushed band of velvet to tone in with them is wound around the flowers, ending in a full bow.

ONE of the most conservative styles in this season's toques is the one of violet straw draped in folds and trimmed with shaded roses. It is more suitable, perhaps, for the woman of forty than for a young girl, and it may be made in any color to suit a costume. An ordinary toque frame may be used as a foundation, but the draping must be carefully done in order to keep the correct lines and proportions. The trimming is simply a flat bouquet of shaded roses.

PERSIAN band trimmings on this white hat (faced with black) are distinctive both in color and form. For the band and the side piece the Persian strip (gathered) is veiled with black chiffon and piped with cherry-colored silk. This is sewed to a straight band of black satin a quarter of an inch wider on each edge. The buckle has a black satin edge half an inch wide, and measures six inches long and four wide, with Persian center.

NOTE—The American Fashion Editors will take pleasure in answering by mail any inquiries about the designs in this department and about clothes in general. A stamped, self-addressed envelope should be inclosed.

American Fashions for American Women, toques and sailor styles stylishly trimmed in flowers, feather quills, wide ribbons, The Ladies' Home Journal, June 1910.

The Lingerie Hat

Drawings by Anna May Cooper

White Silk Lace Over Blue Silk. Designed by N. F. Morrill

Cream-Colored Point d'Esprit and Tea Roses.
Designed by Willard J. Valentine

Very New and Youthful Rolled-Brim Lingerie Hat.
Designed by Rowena Rice

MANY changes and new becoming lines are introduced in this season's lingerie hats. The one above in cream-colored point d'esprit shows one variation in having a shirred crown and brim. The drapery, which is drawn in soft folds from crown to brim, is held by a wreath of tea roses with a bow of brown ribbon velvet at the side. Made on a white wire frame, flat brim four inches wide, round crown eight inches across.

FOR the silk lace design over blue silk use a large-sized white wire frame with drooping brim six inches wide, and large bowl-shaped crown. Cover first with pale blue China silk, and over this arrange the lace, corded about every two inches, and drooping almost plain over the brim and a little below the edge. Six or eight chiffon and satin roses in pale pink with foliage form the trimming.

ESPECIALLY attractive is the girlish and fluffy lingerie hat made of lace and plaited ruffles on a white wire frame with drooping brim about four inches wide. Full crown of lace. Three ruffles of lace-edged net fall from the crown to the brim, the latter covered and faced with narrow lace. There is a pink ribbon band at the top of the crown ending in a bow at the back; spray of pink buds and forget-me-nots.

THIS new lingerie effect in straw and lace is one of the most becoming of lingerie hats for a young girl. Of Mexican straw, round crown seven inches across and four high; straight, drooping brim four inches wide; three ruffles of lace-edged net around crown, single pink rose nestling on the side. In the shops are many similar shapes in the lovely new straw braids which lend themselves well to this simple trimming.

IN THE picturesque lingerie hat or bonnet effect the lines are very becoming to a small oval face. It should be made on a high-crown wire frame especially fitted to the head, with an extended brim of about two inches covered with écru tulle; crown of Leghorn plaited on to the frame. A loose band of Dresden ribbon goes around back of the lace ruffles; large pale pink rose at side of front.

A VERY youthful effect is obtained in the new rolled-brim hat of cream-colored silk-dotted net trimmed with a crushed band of wide satin ribbon in apple green (requiring two yards) and a large pink rose with foliage at each side. It is made on a white wire frame with the net gathered quite full and corded on each wire. The rounding crown measures about seven inches across and four high, and the brim is five inches wide.

DEPARTING even more from last season's all-ruffle or embroidered lingerie hat is this new turban with the net crown—a touch of lingerie combined with the conventional. Made on a large turban frame, brim four inches wide, covered and faced with white straw; large crown covered flat with white silk and white net put on full, caught here and there to the crown. One large silk rose is placed directly on left side.

ON THE right just below an excellent example of the milliner's art is shown in this becoming hat for the mature woman. It is made on a wire frame of conventional shape, and medium size brim, about three inches wide, covered with two rows of lace of ivory white. Flat crown eight inches across and three high, covered with white net; wreath of roses alternating in deep and pale pink tones ending in a cluster at the right of the front.

THE lingerie hat of Mexican straw (center in bottom row) shows simplicity and good style in every way. Crown six inches across and four high; brim five inches wide covered with three rows of lace (requires six yards two inches wide); for band around crown, and large bow of pale blue satin ribbon eight inches wide, five yards are needed. One delicate pink rose at right of front.

ONE of the most unusual of the season's lingerie hats is that of lace braid shown in the lower right-hand corner. Made on a white wire sailor-shaped frame, large round crown nine inches across and four high; brim four inches wide. About one piece of braid would be needed to cover the frame, sewing it on in rows. Crushed (bias) band of black chiffon velvet six inches wide, and clusters of pink roses.

Girlish and Fluffy in Lace and Ruffles.
Designed by Rowena Rice

Young Girl's White Lingerie Turban.
Designed by Rowena Rice

A Lingerie Effect in Straw and Lace.
Designed by Rowena Rice

Becoming Hat to a Mature Face.
Designed by Helen Taylor

A Picturesque Lingerie Bonnet Effect.
Designed by Charles Kurzman

Lingerie Hat of Mexican Straw. Designed by Rowena Rice

A Sailor Shape Made of Lace Braid.
Designed by Willard J. Valentine

The Lingerie Hat with trimmings of shirred silk, gathered ruffles, fabric roses, very large bows, and lace, The Ladies' Home Journal, June 1910.

The Mature Woman's Hats

Selected by Ida Cleve Van Auken: With Drawings by M. E. Musselman

NO LONGER does fashion relegate the woman past the youthful years to circumscribed styles in diminutive bonnets, as worn but a short time ago. Nowadays one wisely chooses a hat, toque or bonnet in the size and shape most becoming, the color, materials and manner of wearing the hat giving the dignified tone of maturer age more than the method of applying the trimmings or the design of the hat as a whole.

Black tulle softly veils the roses which form such a pretty trimming on this hat of blue straw braid with the shaped brim.

Fascinating bonnet made of horsehair braid with loops of satin ribbon framing the face, trimmed with violet plumes.

Graceful large hat of purple Milan straw, faced with satin, and with shaded ostrich plumes encircling the crown.

A charming small hat, rolled high at the left side, draped with mouse-gray faille silk, drawn in a bow across the back.

High-crown hat, made of split straw braid in dull blue, with a satin ornament trimmed with rows of silk soutache braid.

The soft standing brim of this hat is faced with smoke-gray satin, with crown and bow of filmy white tulle veiled with gray.

ONE of the most charming and simple forms of trimming for a small hat or toque is with a draped crown of silk or tulle, using the same material for a bow, at the side or back, depending upon the shape of the hat, as in the toque directly above and the one in the center on the left. Flowers are worn on hats and bonnets for the mature woman, in small clusters, or when more profusely used, as on the hat in the upper left-hand corner, their too pronounced coloring is subdued under a veiling of tulle, or gold and silver lace may be substituted with pleasing effect. For either a bonnet or a large hat ostrich plumes are lovely as a trimming, giving a grace of line and softening beauty not found in the stiffer forms of adornment. Another pretty ornament is the butterfly poised on the bonnet shown on the right. This may be used on a large or a small hat.

Toque of pliable hemp braid in a soft amethyst tone, trimmed with Cluny lace caught at each side with a cluster of roses.

A lace butterfly, trimmed with jet beads and iridescent spangles, is used on this bonnet, draped around the outer edge with beaded net.

The Mature Woman's Hats, notice the return of the bonnet in the two styles on the right, The Ladies' Home Journal, March 1911.

Lovely photo of lady in large sheared beaver hat with flat brim and mound of ostrich plumes, circa 1910.

How to repair your own Willow Plumes described in our circular, free with every order.

If We Have No Store In Your Town
ORDER BY MAIL

Our catalogue (free on request) explains why we can produce the finest Plumes in the world and sell them direct to the consumer at one-half what other Plumes sell for. Instead of adding the customary middleman's profits of 60% we only add 10% above our manufacturing cost, which saves you 50%.

If you order by mail, one of our shoppers will select for you the choicest Plume obtainable at your price.

Our motto: you must be satisfied.

FRENCH PLUMES (Guaranteed)

18 inch Plumes, extra quality . . . . **$ 6.75**

18 to 19 inch Plumes, specially full and rich **$10.75**

DROOPING WILLOW PLUMES

22-24 inches, double hand knotted, 16 to 17 inches wide **$12.75**

Broadway Willow, 28 inches long, 22 to 24 inches wide, covering the largest hat **$20.00**

We do not pay express charges. Upon receipt of 50c to cover express charges we will send you any of the Plumes advertised here C. O. D. for examination. If not satisfactory you may return same.

Booklet illustrating 50 Paris hats trimmed with London Plumes, including instructions how to trim your own hat, sent free.

London FEATHER CO.
London, New York
Newark, Chicago
21 West 34th St.
NEW YORK

SEND ALL MAIL ORDERS TO
21 West 34th St., New York, N. Y., Department — 30

Ad from the London Feather Co. in New York, note the "drooping willow plumes for $12.75," 22" – 24", double hand knotted, 16" – 17" wide. The barbs on these plumes are extra long because as many as two additional barbs were hand tied onto the original barb. This work was usually done by children because their tiny fingers could more easily accomplish this tedious task. This is apparently before child labor laws.

BUY DIRECT FROM THE FARM

We sell at Producers' Prices and Deliver Free

California's matchless climate and Cawston's twenty-five years' experience and superior methods of manufacturing insure perfection.

We raise our own ostriches. We pluck the plumes, dye, curl and manufacture them in our own factory on our Farm.

Cawston Ostrich Feathers

RECEIVED 7 PRIZE MEDALS
AT LEADING WORLD'S EXPOSITIONS

Cawston male ostrich feathers have life, lustre, strength and beauty not found in other feather goods. They retain their curl and wear for years.

YOUR OLD FEATHERS VALUABLE

Send them to us and we will dye, recurl and make over into willow plumes.

HOW TO ORDER

You can first secure our catalogue and order from it, or you can send any amount you wish to pay for a plume or a boa and leave the selection to us. Or send $5.00 for a Cawston "Selected" Plume, or $10 for a Cawston "Special" Willow. Both come in black, white or any solid color, and are leaders with us. MONEY RETURNED IF NOT PLEASED.

CATALOGUE SENT FREE

Cawston Ostrich Farm

P. O. Box 4   South Pasadena, CALIFORNIA

Ad for Cawston Ostrich Feathers, established in 1886, primarily using the male ostrich plumes. The birds were not killed to produce feathers for hats.

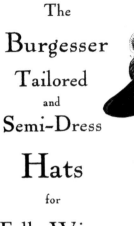

The
Burgesser
Tailored
and
Semi-Dress
Hats
for
Fall *and* Winter

combine the quality and style that characterize all models bearing this trade mark.

On sale at all leading dealers throughout the United States and Canada

Designed and Introduced

by

A. D. Burgesser & Co.

149-151 Fifth Avenue
New York

Ad for A.D. Burgesser & Co. of New York for tailored and semi-dress hats for fall and winter, The Theatre, November 1911.

New Veils and Midseason Hats

By Edith M. Weidenfeld

Drawings by Gertrude L. Pew

The fashionable helmet shape softened in effect by marabout and feather trimmings

The latest picture hats are made with double brims in rolling effect

together with small dots. This veil looks well with the tailored hat, as does the one shown just below it, which has a diamond-shaped cobweb pattern, with the diamonds outlined with small chenille dots.

All face-veils, whether arranged on a tailored hat or a dressy shape, should be carefully pinned around the edge of the brim of the hat, allowing the lower edge of the veil to come just below the chin. The veil should be inconspicuously fastened with hairpins just below the barrette in the back of the hair, thus drawing it closely at the lower edge. Twisting the veil under the chin, to take out the fulness, spoils the shape of the veil, and surely detracts rather than adds to its pretty effect. The ends of the veil are tied, and tucked out of sight.

THERE is no particular season nowadays, so it seems, when women are not specially interested in new hats and new veils. Just now it is the midseason hats, and the new Paris veils to go with them, which are occupying the attention of the woman of fashion.

Of course, the veils are necessary because the winds are high and cold right now, and because the hats bought in the early fall need a freshening touch or two. Then there is another because—the latest edict from Paris, which says: It is the fashionable woman who is the veiled woman right now; so, even the prettiest of our American women will let the glow of their cheeks and the luster of their eyes be only half revealed through the meshes of a veil.

The fashion in veils is varied; that is, varied in style and design, rather than in mesh. The cobweb veil is without doubt the favorite, and it is seen both plain and combined with dots—small, medium, and large. The plain cobweb veils come in simple designs, hexagon, octagon, and conventional flower patterns; but no matter what their design, they are used for face-veils only. Other face-veils have the foundation mesh in cobweb, and are ornamented with chenille dots. To describe the many patterns would be impossible, so great is their number. Illustrated at the bottom of this page, however, are some of the best of the designs.

The foundation of the veil at the extreme left is cobweb. The large, hexagon figure is made of small chenille dots, and the center of the conventional flower in the middle of each hexagon is also chenille. This veil may be worn appropriately with a dress or semi-dress hat of velvet, beaver, or fur. The hat, however, must be moderate in size, for the face-veil, which, to be correct, should cling close to the face and hair, is not in good taste when flowing loosely from a picture shape.

In the same class with the veil just described is the plain cobweb-mesh veil. This pattern, because of its simplicity, is much worn by the conservative woman. Next to it in favor is the one shown just below it. Though more elaborate in style, it is so fine in weave that when properly arranged over the face the effect is very soft and dainty. The other three veils are appropriate for the more tailored hats. The foundation of the one at the extreme right is sheer, but the small chenille squares in black and white, forming a checked pattern, are quite heavy. The veil shown next to the one with the hexagon pattern has a plain square design, the squares seemingly held

Novelty veil with design omitted where veil fits over face; arranged in new way

Lately the face-veil has had a decided rival in the lace veil, and it seems likely that this latter veil will enjoy its decided popularity for several months to come. From time to time there are new patterns and weavings, but there never has been quite so unique an idea as the one shown in the veil on the hat illus-

Veil in lace flower-design

Fringe-trimmed veils are the vogue

Fashion favors the veil of filet lace

trated in the center of this page. Although the lace veil is very picturesque and exceedingly becoming, it has had a decidedly bad feature, which was this: when drawn over the face, it was almost impossible to see through it, and it was quite as impossible for the passer-by to see the face behind it. Now this has all been done away with, by having the center of the veil of plain mesh just big enough around to fit over the face. Of quite as much importance as the simple mesh feature in this cobweb veil is the very new and very correct arrangement of the veil itself. The top of the veil is shirred in the center front, and fastened to the brim of the hat with a silver butterfly. At the side the veil is not fastened to the hat, but arranged in soft folds as shown in the illustration. At the back it is again shirred, but not quite so much; and at this point it is fastened, and the ends hang in graceful loose folds.

Other attractive lace veils are also shown on this page. One has a plain mesh ground with dots and large leaves, done in the running stitch, scattered over its surface. The lower edge is finished with a border of the leaves and tiny flowers in lily-of-the-valley effect.

The special feature of one of the newest fashionable veils here pictured has its border of fringe. Filet net veils are also much favored this winter.

A word or two must now be said about the midseason hats. The most fashionable, without doubt, is the velvet hat in small, medium, and moderately large models. It is simply but effectively trimmed with bands of feathers or marabout. A very good style is the helmet shape shown at the left of this page at the top. This type, which is apt to be severe, is considerably softened by its trimming, a band of marabout and three soft plumes. With this hat the lace or face veils for dress wear are appropriate.

No veil, however, would be correct worn with the picture hat illustrated in the right-hand corner. It is too large a shape on which to arrange a veil satisfactorily, and nothing is more unattractive than a poorly arranged veil. The hat in itself is unusually charming, and, aside from that fact, shows two of the latest hat fashions in Paris: one, the double-brim effect, with the lower brim of velvet and the upper of cloth-of-silver; and the other, the use of the Prince of Wales tips, which are really very small ostrich-plumes.

To wear with a tailored suit, the hat illustrated in the center of this page is smart in style. It is black felt, trimmed with green velvet and a green velvet wing edged with marabout. Either the face-veil or the draped lace veil may be worn with this hat.

Fine cobweb veils, both plain and combined with chenille dots, are the favored face-veils this season. Illustrated above are five cobweb veils with chenille dots, one showing a checked design in black and white, and a plain cobweb veil

New Veils and Midseason Hats, "fine cobweb veils, both plain and combined with chenille dots, are the favored face-veils this season," from Woman's Home Companion, February 1912.

Real photo postcard of couple, lady with tailored hat with very wide band and narrow brim, also handbag, ca. 1912. *Courtesy of Beth Bown.*

VAN RAALTE
Veils

Made in U. S. A.   At All Good Shops

THE TRELLIS continues to be the vogue in veilings. It is a distinctive Van Raalte creation and comes in a variety of beautifying designs.

Remember Van Raalte Veils—wash without wearing—stretch without tearing—outlast three ordinary veils.

Write for Miladi's Veil—a treatise on the wear and care of veils. Address Dept. X.

E. & Z. Van Raalte, Fifth Ave. at 15th St., N. Y. C.

For your protection this little white ticket is on every yard. Look for it.

Nice ad for Van Raalte veils, with the distinctive "trellis" which continues to be the vogue in veilings, *The Ladies' Home Journal, September 1915.*

Undulating of Brim Is the New Fall Sailor

By MAUDE ANDERSON

INDICATIONS point to simplicity of shape and trimming in the new hats. The dominant ideas are expressed in two styles—small close-fitting toques, and the sailor, the newest type of which has been selected for this month's millinery lesson. Sailor shapes display drooping and undulating brims rather than the straight brim worn in past seasons, and many novel slashed-brim effects are being shown among the more extreme models.

Trimmings are as simple as the shapes, and the colors are dark. Blue and black lead, but Bordeaux red, dark seal brown, bottle and laurel green and rich deep shades of purple will also be favored. Grays and tans are being shown, too, and sometimes two shades of one color, or two colors in one material are employed.

Fancy ostrich trims many smart hats, and there are all sorts of beaded motifs appliquéd on the brim or the side of the crown. Crewel embroidery forms a novel but very effective decoration on a black velvet hat. Cut jet, and nickel buckles are among the novelty trimmings. Velvet is the favored material for covering hats, but satin, and novelty plushes, as well as pressed felt will be worn.

The wide, roll-brim sailor illustrated is a stunning model which promises to be very popular during the coming months. It is made of black velvet, with a shirred facing of silk on the upper brim and is a very simple hat for the beginner to start with. The trimming consists of a fancy feather arranged diagonally across the front and caught in the center with a jet buckle.

The materials required for making this model are: one yard of black velvet, one-half yard of black silk for the top brim, one fancy feather divided in half, one jet buckle, one piece of black frame wire, one yard and a half of heavy satin wire for the edge wire, one spool of black tie-wire, one pair of wire cutters and nippers combined, to make the frame, and one yard of crinoline to line the frame, for a foundation upon which to arrange the outer material.

To make the frame, always begin with the head wire. For this cut a piece of wire thirty inches long, form it into a circle by lapping the ends until it measures twenty-four inches around, and fasten the overlapping ends with tie-wire. Cut four pieces of wire each twenty-six inches long, for A, B, C and D as shown in Illustration No. 2.

Wire (A) is the front wire. On this wire measure three and one-quarter inches for the brim wire. Then bend wire up and measure two and one-half inches for the height of the crown band, then bend wire again at right angles, and measure eight and one-half inches across the crown; bend wire down and measure for the back of wire (A) two and one-half inches for the crown band and five inches for the brim. This frame is made in one piece.

Wire (B) is the left side-front wire. On this wire measure four inches for the brim wire. Then bend wire up and measure two and one-half inches for the height of the crown band, then bend wire at right angles, and measure eight and one-quarter inches across the crown, bend wire down and measure for the back of wire (B) two and one-half inches for the crown band, and three and one-half inches for the brim.

Wire (C) is the right side-front wire. On this wire measure two and three-quarter inches for the brim wire. Then bend wire up and measure two and one-half inches for the height of the crown band, bend wire again at right angles, and measure eight and one-quarter inches across the crown. Bend wire down and measure for the back of wire (C) two and one-half inches for the crown band, and four and one-half inches for the base of the crown band.

Wire (D) is the side wire. Measure on the right side three inches for the brim wire. Then bend wire up and measure two and one-half inches for the height of the crown band, bend wire again at right angles and measure seven and one-half inches across the crown. Next bend wire down and measure on the left side of wire (D) two and one-half inches for the crown band, and four and one-quarter inches for the brim.

Now tie these four main wires, A, B, C and D to the head wire by bending each wire around the head wire with nippers and arranging them at equal distances apart, and in their right places. It is better sometimes to attach each wire to the head wire after you have measured it off, and allow on each wire for turning over the edge wire. Tie the center of the cross wire of the crown with tie-wire to keep in place until this part of the frame is entirely finished and braced. Now cut a piece of frame wire

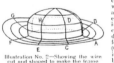

Illustration No. 1—Shirring the facing for the top of the brim

Illustration No. 2—Showing the wire cut and shaped to make the frame

Illustration No. 3—Fitting the facing to the under part of the brim

thirty inches long, join it into a circle and lap the ends until it measures twenty-five inches around, tying the overlapping ends with tie-wire. Then place this at the top of the crown band, and tie to each wire, attaching a brace wire between this wire and the center of the cross wires, and a brace wire in the center of the crown band. The more brace wires used, the stronger the frame will be, and the better it will keep its shape.

The next step is to attach the edge wire to the brim. For this take a piece of the heavy satin wire measuring fifty-two inches, and form into a circle by lapping the ends until it measures forty-seven inches around, fastening the overlapping ends with tie-wire. With the lapped ends of the edge wire at the back, using the nippers, bend the free end of each of the brim wires over the edge wire once, at the point marked off. Clip off the superfluous wire at the ends, and pinch the ends down flat to make a neat finish, so the wires will not stick through when the facing is applied. It is necessary to put two brace wires on the brim. As the frame is already shaped, it is easy to attach these intermediate wires, by laying them on top of the brim wires at equal distances apart, and tie to each brim wire with the tie-wire keeping the lapped ends at the back where they do not show.

Having completed the frame, it must next be covered. Take the crinoline and fit it to the underside of the brim, smoothing it and pinning it to position. Cut out the head size and make little slits in the crinoline up to the head wire; cut around the edge wire, but allow enough to turn over. Transfer this facing to the upper brim and sew around the head wire. Turn the outer edge over the edge wire and sew to position. Repeat the first part of these directions for facing the underbrim. Cover the crown as smoothly as possible with the crinoline, laying it in plaits around the base of the crown.

The foundation of the hat is now completed. To trim, start with the velvet, and on the underbrim pin to the front wire (A); stretch it across the underbrim, and pin it all around the edge wire, then cut off the crowns, but allow one-quarter inch to turn over the edge wire. Sew this to position, then cut out the head size, and cut little slits up to the head wire, then sew to position. Illustration No. 3 shows how this is done.

To make the top brim for the hat, take the silk and cut three strips, each five inches wide. Join them together making one long strip. Cut a piece of the frame wire forty-five inches long. Now take this wire and sew it on the edge of the strip of silk. As you go along, pull the thread, to shirr it on the wire. After this is done start at the back and pin the wired edge of the silk strip to the velvet that you turned over the edge wire, having the shirring evenly distributed on the wire. Sew to position to cover up the raw edge of the velvet on the top brim. The remaining edge draw to the base of the crown land in small plaits, and sew all around the head wire.

With the velvet that is left make a small tam to fit the top of the crown, running a shirring thread on the edge of the circle. Slip this over the crinoline-covered crown, draw up the thread, and sew to position around the wire above the base wire of the crown. Cut the remaining velvet on the bias, and cut from this bias piece two strips three inches wide. Join the strips together, and hem both raw edges so the strip will be two and one-half inches wide. Then sew one end, draw the other around the side of the crown band, and sew to the first end, slip-stitching the top of the velvet strip to the top of the crown band. Slip-stitch the other edge to the base of the crown band. If desired, both edges may be piped with silk.

To trim, divide the feather in half as illustrated in the large picture and sew on the front, finishing off the ends where they are joined at the center, with the jet buckle.

This hat could be trimmed very simply with wide ribbon. Make a full bow with wired loops slanting the same way as the feather, but have the bow to the left or right side close to the crown band. Small ribbon rosettes may encircle the crown, placed so that they just touch, or small motifs of wool or crewel embroidery could be appliquéd around the crown.

For the lining of this hat take a piece of soft silk twenty-six inches long, and four inches wide, and on one edge put a hem one-quarter inch deep. Sew the other edge around the head wire and tack a small piece of silk up against the inside of the crown. Run a piece of baby ribbon through the hem, draw up to fit the head comfortably, and tie in a small bow.

Illustration No. 4—The finished frame covered with crinoline to form a foundation

Though simply trimmed, this black velvet sailor is decidedly fetching

Two gay and gorgeous black and white feathery butterflies lightly poised themselves on a huge black velvet hat and Knox fastened them down securely, added a few finishing touches in the way of patent leather pipings, and created a masterpiece

The Question of Hats

A flowery path blazed by some of our well dressed Ladies of the Stage leads to the new bonnet of Spring

A ring-around-a-rosy of shaded pink, garlands a Rawak hat and lends excitement to the plaited brown grosgrain ribbon running up into a peak in the back.

When the best horsewomen in the country ride the best horses in the country they wear the best riding hats to be found in the country. A Knox model of Hatter's Plush.

When Miss Anna Pavlowa posed for the introduction of the Universal's "The Dumb Girl of Portici," she wore this hat (lower left) created by Rawak and christened the "Pavlowa-Portici" in honor of the occasion. It is made of shiny black Milan Porcupine straw, ornamented by a green braid and dangling tassel, and is specially good for Southern wear.

It looks good enough to eat, this Smolin wheat-straw hat, for the rough prickly finish of the material is strangely reminiscent of a certain kind of breakfast food! Four velvet apples in dull contrasting shades that apples are not, and a blue crêpe facing form its interesting trimming.

Undulating of Brim Is the New Fall Sailor, with all indications pointing to simplicity in shape and trimming for the new hats in Pictorial Review, October 1915.

New styles for well-dressed ladies of the stage, The Theatre, January 1916.

With beauty, naturalness and wide dramatic experience as assets, Marjorie Rambeau has forged her way quickly to the front of the stage. The fine authority with which she plays the leading role in "Cheating Cheaters" quite justifies her previous good work in "Sadie Love" and "So Much For So Much." Miss Rambeau is wearing one of the New Knox Fall Models.

KNOX
MILLINERY
FIFTH AVENUE   AT FORTIETH ST.

Ad for Knox Millinery with Miss Rambeau wearing one of the New Knox Fall Models in plush or fur, The Theatre, October 1916.

The invention of the automobile was also a strong influence on the hat styles in the second decade of the twentieth century. By necessity the size began to diminish, narrowing and becoming smaller. The use of feathers declined due to groups protesting the killing of birds for decoration. A wide range of fabrics and artificial trims became fashionable during the second decade. There were still ladies of fashion who chose feathered hats into the late teens.

Lady of fashion photographed in an extreme feather hat and fur trimmed coat, ca. 1918.

Real photo postcard of a lady by a lake, with hat similar in style to one on page 166, appears to be velvet with artificial flowers.
Courtesy of Beth Bown.

THE LADIES'
HOME JOURNAL

In This Issue: Charley Ross—The Unforgotten Lost Boy

JULY, 1924
Volume XLI, Number 7

THE CURTIS PUBLISHING COMPANY, PHILADELPHIA

10 CENTS By subscription $1.00
In the United States and in Canada

Fabulous cover with flowered crown and wide-brimmed straw hat, a perennial favorite for summer, The Ladies' Home Journal, July 1924.

The cloche, introduced in 1917 with a small brim, was acclaimed as the hat for the 1920s. "Cloche" came to mean any close fitting hat with or without a brim, usually a rounded crown. Women's right to vote, their increased interest in sports, and the necessity of being more practical were all instrumental factors in the hat styles of the 1920s. The newer bobbed hairstyle allowed for the change from large crowns to the close-fitting new fashion.

Patterns for Midseason Hats

No. 5034

No. 5031

NO. 5034. *Tete de negre* georgette crêpe forms the entire top of the large poke featured in this model. The upward sweep of the wide brim reveals the hair at the back. The lines as graceful as a picture hat are modernized to suit present-day needs. A spray of flaming cactus flowers is fastened flat on the brim at the right side. These flowers are different from any you have seen, and directions for making them come with the pattern. A smooth straw plateau in a dark shade forms the brim facing.

NO. 5031. Lace is draped over a wire form to make a bow for this jaunty small hat. The transparency of the lace gives softness to an otherwise tailored model. Taffeta makes the plain cap crown and top brim. Smooth straw is used for the facing. Sand taffeta with brown lace and straw; copen blue taffeta with navy blue lace and straw; or black taffeta and lace with white straw facing make attractive color combinations. The model is suitable for church, formal afternoon, and informal evening wear.
All Priscilla hat patterns are 35 cents each. Order by number.

No. 5036

OLD blue lace ruffles the edge of the quaint straw brim of model No. 5036. Old blue silk *gros de laundre* in the same shade forms crown and facing. Hand-made flowers and fruits in pastel shades hold the lace to the side crown at the front. Every thrifty household has an old milan or leghorn straw hat which may be remodeled to make this charming design.
Hat patterns are as easy to use as dress patterns, complete instructions are given, covering every step in the making, from frame to trim.

No. 5035

NO. 5035. The textile design of a beautiful old English shawl gave the idea for the hand-made flowers which trim this model. Dull orange, sand, beige, leather, and moss-green shades of georgette are used for the making of the flowers. Beige georgette crêpe makes the crown and top facing. Leaf-brown milan straw is used for the facing of the tricorn brim.

NO. 5037 has singular grace of line, as well as the *chic* effect naturally attributed to a smart sailor. The side of the square crown is covered with blue bias folds, which soften the otherwise severe effect.
Starlike hand-made flowers encircle the base of the crown. Flowers and hat are made of two different colors; the flowers matching the facing shade. Black and white leather and beige, rust and navy, sand and green, are good combinations.

No. 5037

A variety of hat styles for midseason from those with the elegant shaped brims to no brims, Modern Priscilla, July 1924.

THERESA MAE HAT SHOP

offers the distinction of Paris in hats designed for every type of feminism.

No. 223 on State Street

Ad for the Theresa Mae Hat Shop, University of Wisconsin Barnard Magazine, 1925.

A WARNING to WOMEN who wear Tight Hats

BOBBED hair has created a vogue of close fitting hats—and physicians say that tight hats are probably responsible for much of the baldness among men.

HERE are two simple rules for keeping your hair vigorously healthy in spite of the injurious effect of tight hats.

—◦(1)◦—

Keep the scalp clean! Shampoo regularly with Wildroot Taroleum Shampoo. Made from pure crude and pine tar oils, it cleanses deep down to the hair roots yet does not leave the hair harsh or dry.

—◦(2)◦—

Massage and brush the hair vigorously every day. Once or twice a week saturate the scalp with Wildroot Hair Tonic. This reliable tonic stops dandruff, invigorates the hair roots and leaves the scalp antiseptically clean. The most widely used hair tonic in the world.

YOU can't start these treatments too soon. Invest in these two bottles today. Wildroot hair preparations may be obtained at drug stores, barber shops and hair dressers' everywhere. Accept no substitutes.

WILDROOT

HAIR TONIC   TAROLEUM SHAMPOO

Ad for Wildroot and a "warning to women who wear tight hats," McCall's, August 1928.

1475-149

Exquisite Paramount press photo of Marlene Dietrich in "The Scarlet Empress," an example of pure elegance in the way she wears this fur hat and muff, 1934.

Escaping the Depression of the 1930s through glamorous movies launched one of the most innovative and exciting periods in hat fashion. It was the economics and politics of this period that were reflected in the fantasy hats of the 1930s. Milliners are swift and accurate barometers of mood, and to relieve the depressing state of mind with very little in the way of materials, they became more creative. Schiaparelli's "toy toppers" actually look as if they might have been little party favors worn on the head! It was in the last half of the decade that the crown shriveled away and the brim won out, and like a sloping plate, was worn down over the forehead at a very jaunty angle.

7400—Coat. The British influence has its say in this new tweed reefer with its jaunty fitted lines. Designed for 12 to 44. For 16—3½ yards 54-inch material, 2⅜ yards 39-inch lining.

7382—Little Women's Frock. Heavy linen on homespun woolen for the shorter woman. Designed for 12½ to 46½. For 20½—2⅜ yards 54-inch material, 1 yd. 36-in. contrast. Width 1⅜ yd.

7271—Frock. Gay wings of white at the neckline point the way to flattery. Designed for 14 to 52. For 16—3⅝ yards 39-inch material, ¼ yard 39-inch contrasting. Width about 1¾ yard.

7314—Coat. Designed for 12 to 40.
7276—Frock. Designed for 12 to 46. For 16—3⅛ yards 50-inch fur cloth, 2½ yards 39-inch lining for coat, 2⅜ yds. 54-in., ⅝ yd. contrast for frock.

7400 7382

LITTLE WOMEN 7382

7400

TWEEDS not only dominate the sporting picture, but have entered the metropolitan scene with savoir faire. Homespun and loosely-woven, hand-loomed woolens have a new softness of texture and are developed in the season's smartest colors—the tobacco browns, dark woodsy greens, clay rust, wine and a cheery raspberry. Plaids in subdued, smoky colors and small checks are combined with plain woolens. Wool crêpe and jersey in black make those important "little" dresses that form the background of a smart winter wardrobe.

For more formal daytime wear, wools are smooth and sleek and have a feeling of luxury. Cellophane threads shine through deep rich shades, gold and silver strands gleam in the depths of black and brown, or highlight clear vivid shades. Cords and diagonal weaves are good and duvetyn and velvety-surfaced woolens fashion coats and frocks of distinction. Broadcloth, long eclipsed, again steps to the fore and some smart innovations are wool net, wool lace and embroidered jersey.

Even during the evening wool weaves new enchantment, as smooth-surfaced sheer woolens with delicate threadings of gold or silver are used for some of the most stunning evening gowns ever! In fact, it's a safe bet that if a woman mentions a "perfect lamb of a frock," she means exactly that, this year!

7314

7271 7276

7271 FOR BEGINNERS   Coat 7314 Frock 7276

Examples of the sloping hats of the late 1930s, Pictorial Review, October 1934.

·· COAT SILHOUETTES

DON'T be flustered by the bewildering variety in the new coat fashions. Just remember that the Big Three are the slim, semi-fitted coat in formal woolens, the tweed reefer and the boxy three-quarter coat. As evidence of the importance of semi-fitted lines we offer Nos. 7380 and 7396. Things to note are the smooth shoulders, modified sleeve interest and exciting collars. Collars, by the way, are making news—breaking out in rippling fulness or framing the face in luxurious "pouch" effect.

The British influence is having its say in tweed fashions. You'll see what we mean if you turn to No. 7400 on page 61. It's the new reefer with superbly fitted double-breasted lines, wider revers and big patch pockets. Another last-minute success is the swagger coat in fur cloth—it's the perfect answer to what to wear over your suit. And don't hesitate to make it. With the new loose, easy lines, raglan sleeves and simple collars, you'll find it simple to put together.

THE coatings to watch are, first, the tree-bark types with a smoother, modified surface, the suède-finished woolens and woolens with just a hint of a bouclé or diagonal weave. In tweeds the classic homespun and hairy weaves are best in fog checks and Glen plaids as well as monotones. The most popular colors are black, reddish and chestnut browns and pine-needle green. The most distinctive are two new shades that are marvelous with brown fur—flagstone gray and smoke blue.

Hats have never had so many surprises in store for us. You've heard about the new berets, of course, and No. 6804 includes two of the smartest, a large cushiony affair to be made in velvet, and a trim little model to match the frock of wool or velveteen. The next best bet is a tricorne, and the latest ones have a delightful Louis XV air about them, accented by cords and cockades. The brimmed hat is better than ever, turned up in back and boasting new height in their deftly tucked or draped crowns. And if you like your hats small and sophisticated you'll be glad to hear that turbans are back, some assuming a pill box shape, others draped East Indian fashion or like tricornes. In lamé or velvet they are perfect with your new restaurant clothes.

Shoes, to jump from one extreme to the other, also reveal the British influence in sturdy oxfords with low comfortable lines for wear with tweeds. The more formal shoes mount the instep in a high, flattering line. And oxfords of crêpe, bengaline or suède are fashion's way of carrying this restaurant furore straight to your toes.

7396   7376

6804 HATS
7405 COLLARS

No. 2

No. 1

7380 7396 7376

7398 7391

7398   7391

7376—Suit. Companion woolens provide smart contrast. Designed for 12 to 46. For 16—2⅜ yards 54-inch plain, 1⅛ yard plaid, 2⅞ yards 39-inch lining. Width 1⅜ yard.

7396—Coat. With the flattery of a fur pouch collar. Designed for 12 to 46. For 16—3¾ yards 54-inch fabric, ½ yard 54-inch fur cloth, 3⅛ yards 39-inch material for lining coat.

6804—Hats. Your new hat should be a beret. Designed for 21½, 22, 22½, and 23 inches. For 22, No. 1, ⅝ yard 39-inch material; No. 2, 1 yard 39-inch material.

7405—Collars and Sleeves. Bring last season's coat up-to-the-minute! Designed for 14 to 42. For 16—No. 1, ½ yard 54-inch fur cloth; No. 2, ½ yard 54-inch fur cloth.

7398—Frock. Designed for 12 to 48. For 16—2½ yards 54-inch material, ¾ yard 39-inch contrasting for belt, ½ yard for collar and cuffs. Width about 1⅛ yard at lower edge of frock.

7391—Frock. Top off your wool frock with satin. Designed for 12 to 50. For 16—2¾ yards 54-inch material, 1 yard 39-inch contrasting to trim. Width about 2¼ yards at lower edge.

Examples of the sloping hats of the late 1930s, Pictorial Review, October 1934.

WOOL

7395

7390

7368
FOR BEGINNERS

7384—Larger-Hip Frock. A dramatic
white jabot and a cleverly-contrived slim
skirt create slender distinction for the
important figure. Designed for 35 to 51.
For 41—4⅛ yards 39-inch material, 1
yard 39-inch contrast. Width about 1⅝
yard at the lower edge of frock.

7388—Larger-Hip Frock. Sweeping
around the neck in a symmetric swirl,
this jabot daringly subtracts inches from
full hips. Designed for 35 to 51. For
41—4½ yards 39-inch material, 1⅜
yard 39-inch contrast. Width about 2⅜
yards at the lower edge of frock.

7390—Frock. A soft scarf swings with
casual bravado around the neck of this
slim wool frock with its double diagonal
lines and don't overlook the new button
treatment. Designed for 14 to 48. For
16—3¼ yards 36-inch material, 1 yard
39-inch contrast. Width about 1½ yard.

7395—Frock. The mode for contrast finds
exciting expression in this light-topped
frock with its provocative neck-treatment.
The fulness at the elbow is very smart.
Designed for 12 to 44. For 16—1⅝
yard 54-inch material, 1¾ yard 39-inch
contrast. Width about 1⅝ yard.

7368—Frock. There's sophistication in
the clean-swept lines of this sleek dark
frock dashingly accented by a white
jabot. Note the smart plain set-in sleeves.
Designed for 14 to 48. For 16—2½
yards 54-inch material, ½ yard 39-inch
contrast. Width about 1¾ yard.

East, West, wool's best—for every wear under the sun. The
current mode of simplicity combined with elegance is interpreted
in the modern manner by slim, straight lines expressed in fabrics
of bewildering loveliness.

And the greatest of these is wool! But a new wool, different
from any you have ever seen in the past. . . . There are soft
smooth wools and sheer transparent wools as cobwebby as the
stuff of which dreams are made. There are sturdy tweedy and
hairy fabrics. And every cable from Paris mentions wonderful
novelties—Lelong's beaded woolens, Vera Borea's wool-mixed
moire. Mainbocher sponsors rough bouclettes, Worth likes hairy
woolens for evening wraps and Chanel makes frocks of double-
faced wools, plain on one side and plaid on the other, with fringe
to make them very sporting.

LARGER-HIP
7388

LARGER-HIP
7384

Examples of the sloping hats of the late 1930s, Pictorial Review, October 1934.

171

Hat styles continued to evolve during the 1940s, despite the wartime shortages. Besides being a banner of individuality, hats have also been a great morale booster. The shortage in materials made small creative hats the rule. Larger hats came into vogue with the new look of 1947 and balanced out the full skirt. Permanent waves and the smart new short hairstyles made an impact on the hat styles of the period.

The cartwheel hats in straw for summer have always been popular, Vogue, 1943.

BOOK No. 208

PRICE 10 CENTS

fascinating Toppers

Fascinating Toppers, a pattern book for making your own hat with J. & P. Coats Knit-cro-sheen, 1944.

Becoming Designs

A FEMININE FLATTERY . . . in a Toque made entirely of delicate flowers and leaves. Wired ring at back for secure fit. Height-giving mesh bow. Colors: Pink, Aqua, Lime Green, Purple Violet or White—ea. with black veil; Light Blue with navy veil. Ship. wt. 14 oz. State color.
HC 5462—Fits 21½ to 23 in. 3.98

B NEW PROFILE BERET of imported lustrous synthetic Straw Braid. Grosgrain ribbon and braid trim. All Black; Black with white ribbon; Brown with beige; Navy with ice blue; Toast Tan with brown; White with black. Ship. wt. 1 lb. State color.
HC 5463—Fits 21½ to 22¼ in. 3.98
HC 5464—Fits 22½ to 23¼ in. 3.98

C CUSHION BRIM POSTILLION of shiny synthetic Straw Braid. Attractive pleated grosgrain motif centered with novel ornament. Grosgrain band, bow. Colors: Black, White or Navy—each with matching trim; Toast Tan with brown; Red with black; Gray with navy. Ship. wt. 14 oz. State color.
HC 5465—Fits 21½ to 23 in. 2.98

D BECOMING MUSHROOM BRIM BONNET of shiny imported rough Straw Braid. Attractively trimmed with wide grosgrain ribbon band, looped bows. Colors: Black, Navy, Red or White—ea. with matching trim; Toast Tan with turf tan. Ship. wt. 2 lbs. 2 oz. State color.
HC 5466—Fits 21¾ to 22¼ in. 2.98
HC 5467—Fits 22½ to 23 in. 2.98

E PRETTY HALF-HAT TEMPLET of lustrous Cellophane Braid. Garland of flowers adds face-framing flattery. Wired felt ring in back. Mesh veil. Colors: Black, Navy, Med. Blue, Red, Lime Green or White—ea. with white flowers; Black with pink flowers. Ship. wt. 14 oz. State color.
HC 5468—Fits 21½ to 23 in. 2.55

F POPULAR ROLLED-BRIM PORK-PIE of good New Wool Felt. Creased crown, grosgrain band and streamers. Colors: All Black, Navy, Gray, Red, Coffee (lt. brown) or White; Med. Blue with navy ribbon; White Sand with brown. Ship. wt. 12 oz. State color.
HC 5470—Fits 21½ to 22¼ in. 2.55
HC 5471—Fits 22½ to 23¼ in. 2.55

G FLATTERING BUMPER BERET of imported lustrous synthetic Straw Braid. Cluster of soft flowers and grosgrain ribbon at side. Headband at back for secure fit. Colors: Black, Navy, White or Red—each with white flowers; Toast Tan with tea rose. Ship. wt. 14 oz. State color.
HC 6472—Fits 21½ to 23 in. 2.98

H GRACEFUL PILL BOX of shiny synthetic Straw Braid. Soft ruffle effect in back, attached to wired ring which insures snug fit. Grosgrain bows. Colors: All Black or Navy; Red or White, ea. with black veil; Med. Blue with navy; Toast Tan with brown. Ship. wt. 14 oz. State color.
HC 5473—Fits 21½ to 23 in. 2.98

J ATTRACTIVE BUMPER of lustrous Cellophane Braid. Femininely flattering net ruffle, with contrasting color edging. Back headband for comfortable fit. Colors: Black, Navy, Brown or White—ea. with matching ruffle; Med. Blue or Red, each with navy. Ship. wt. 14 oz. State color.
HC 5474—Fits 21½ to 23 in. 2.55

K CREASED CROWN CLASSIC of New Wool Felt. A budget priced casual in bright and basic Spring colors. Perfect with all your casual clothes. Has matching felt hat pin. Colors: Black, Navy, Med. Blue, Gold, Red, Coffee (lt. brown), Gray or White Sand. Ship. wt. 14 oz. State color.
HC 5475—Fits 21½ to 23 in. 1.75

HATS ON THIS PAGE shipped from Chicago. Mail order direct to Chicago using the special Blue Order Form and Blue Envelope. Allow postage from Chicago. To speed delivery we ship by fast overnight air service to your mail order house, then direct to you by parcel post. (See Page 167.)

174 WARDS PO

Various styles available from Wards catalog, ranging in price from $1.75 to $3.98, 1947. These styles may not be high fashion, but they are certainly representative of what the average woman in the late 1940s would have been wearing.

The sculptured fashion of the early 1950s was a stabilizing effect after World War II. Women were once again involved in style, and as stated in *Vogue*, hats were "emphatically feminine." The role of hats changed quietly, becoming an important element in the overall image. There was a new market in the under-25 age range. The large picture hats were worn back on the head with a more open look, exposing the brow. Evening or cocktail hats were more of a coiffure, but less of a hat … mere veiling, a velvet bow or one large flower.

We enter the 1960s with two of the strongest looks, which were bright psychedelic, and light hearted. Fashion etiquette did not demand hats as in previous decades, consequently the millinery business suffered a decline. Simple designs were mass produced and less expensive for a declining market. The highly teased bouffant hairstyles of the 1960s made wearing hats difficult, if not impossible, as they would perch atop high puffy hairstyles. The "horticultural" hats with a mass of flowers were colorful and capricious.

Determining the Era

ecause so many styles repeat themselves, it can be confusing to determine the exact age of your hat. Many sources can be called upon, and even experts can be baffled by some hats. May I recommend looking at a great number of hats to start with, either in vintage stores or at antique shows to get the feel of an era. There are wonderful books on the subject of hats. Museums of fashion are excellent sources for information with documentation. If at all possible, look at old magazines and books of the period. By carefully examining the lines you can clearly see the relationship between the fashion illustration of 1845 below and the photos that follow.

Hand-colored fashion plate from November 1845, Illustrated London and Paris Fashion Magazine. Courtesy of Beth Bown.

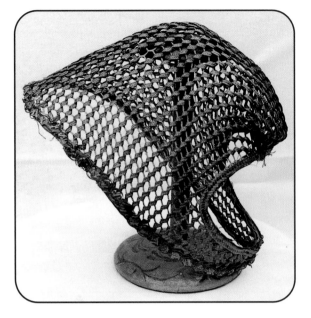

Open-weave straw bonnet of the mid 1840s, trimmings have been long since removed. It is a great example of the style, and in wonderful condition for the age.

Buckram and net over wire frame of the mid 1840s. It may at one time have had a silk covering that has been removed.

A bonnet of the 1840s that is original, wire frame and buckram base, covered with silk, and long ribbon ties, side view.

Back view, tailored self-fabric bow with curtain or havelock. *Above hats courtesy of Beth Bown.*

Becoming familiar with construction details will also help in determining the era of a hat. The hats of the 1920s usually have linings unless they have been removed. Look for evidence of threads. What kind of label does it have? The two examples below are delightful and imaginative labels from cloches of the 1920s.

Straw cloche of the 1920s, sewn in circular pattern, worn down on the head. *Courtesy of Beth Bown.*

Inside of straw cloche with peach lining and label showing elf lifting hat-box lid, "La-Von" of Paris and New York, with front clearly marked.

Attractive peach and green cloche of the 1920s in faille and straw; typical was the brimless deep crown. *Courtesy of Beth Bown.*

Inside view of peach and green cloche with the lining intact and a lovely label of a lady in a hat, "Landsco" of New York and Paris.

Whether you collect hats or wear them, you have a great number to choose from. It is rare to find two alike! There is the cloche, fedora, homberg, tricorn, sailor's cap, bonnet, pillbox, beret, cartwheel, toque, and toy toppers … always remember the aji, or "essence of previous owners."

Olive drab silk bonnet with rolled and padded brim, artificial flower trim, ruched crown and havelock or curtain in back with silk ribbon ties, early Victorian. $200.00 – 250.00. *Courtesy of Beth Bown.*

Black cotton prairie bonnet with stitched brim and ruffle, one of the few pieces from my family with a history. It was my Aunt O'Zelia, age 94, from South Carolina, who sent this piece to me years ago when she heard I was collecting "old clothes." In the letter which accompanied this bonnet she said, "If I had known anyone would have been interested in these old things, I would have taken better care of them. Was in the attic, where you can see the mice got into it (the back was eaten for a mouse dinner)." This bonnet belonged to her mother, who was my great-grandmother, and a young woman in 1870. This is a good example of why alerting family members to your desire to protect and save history is important. And why we, as caretakers, should learn about protecting and documenting the pieces we have under our care for future generations. $55.00 – 75.00.

An elaborate black cotton crocheted bonnet, called a fascinator, with black silk ribbon trim on top and ties under the chin, dating to mid-Victorian. $65.00 – 75.00.

Great example of slat bonnet with extra long havelock to protect the side and back of neck, black cotton with extended brim, created by stitching 8" pieces of cardboard or thin wood at intervals to make the brim rigid for the ultimate sun protection, mid-Victorian. $110.00 – 145.00.

Black silk faille padded bonnet with short havelock trimmed with silk ribbon, folded ribbon trim along the front, lined with silk, original ribbon ties, probably used in winter, dating to mid-Victorian. $55.00 – 75.00. *Courtesy of Dolores Palermo, Barntique Village, Moriches, NY.*

Back view with beaded passementerie, ribbons, and small hat pin.

Widow's bonnet fits high and to the back of the head, always black, however can be trimmed with a variety of materials, dating to mid-Victorian period. $110.00 – 135.00.

Inside view showing style of lining and label which reads "Madam Albert, Imported Millinery, Chicago" (the lettering has begun to wear), labels for hats of this vintage are rare.

High fashion, dark teal velvet hat, small brim trimmed with black soutache and egret feathers, dating to late Victorian. $135.00 – 165.00.

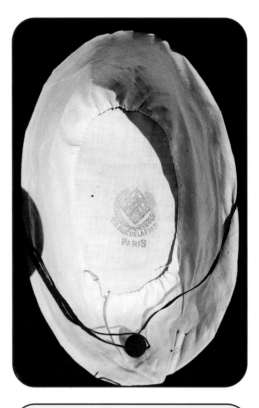

Inside view showing typical style of lining in white cotton, the cord and button which fits around the back of head to secure hat in place, and the label which reads "23 Rue DeLaPaix, Paris."

Lovely black straw with cranberry silk ribbon trim and gathered facing along the inside of brim, small ostrich plumes, black velvet bow in back and beaded trim at the edge of brim, note the cord and button similar to the photo above right, dating to late Victorian. $100.00 – 125.00.

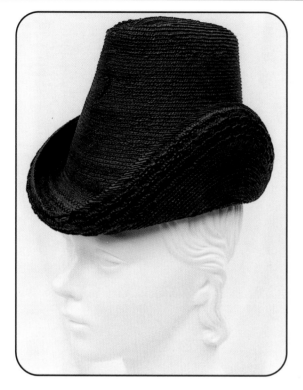

Classic Gibson black straw boater with grosgrain ribbon band, inside leather headband, and the label "Yacht," dating to 1900. $110.00 – 135.00.

Wonderful example of black straw flowerpot hat, no trims and very tailored, no lining or label, dating to mid-Victorian. $100.00 – 125.00.

Inside view of above with label, "Yacht."

Large elliptical brim spring green velvet hat decorated with everything: velvet artificial flowers, ostrich plumes, metallic veiling, and cut steel bauble; small crown, no label – the designer should have signed this one! Dating to early 1900s. $150.00 – 200.00.

An ethereal pink silk lingerie hat, with self fabric folded roses, ruched and gathered around a wire frame. For the creative woman, this type of hat was often made at home from directions in ladies' magazines, dating to early 1900s. $175.00 – 225.00.

Lovely white woven horsehair adorned with delicate white tulle, silk ribbons, and artificial flowers, label printed inside crown reads "Anaconda Copper Mining Co., Mercantile Dept., Hamilton, Montana," dating to early 1900s. This is one of my favorite pieces, which I got early in my collecting career while living in Missoula, Montana. The Anaconda Copper Mining Company, one of the world's largest producers of copper at that time, is located in Anaconda, which was a flourishing area with many wealthy families. $175.00 – 225.00.

Delicate black tulle-covered wire frame with horsehair-edged brim, trimmed with egret feathers, dating to early 1900s. $175.00 – 225.00. *Courtesy of Beth Bown.*

Black silk wide-brimmed hat on wire frame that has been wrapped with black tulle and ribbons, trimmed with velvet flowers and bow in back, dating to early 1900s. $200.00 – 250.00. *Courtesy of Beth Bown.*

Midnight blue velvet large Edwardian hat, trimmed with black ostrich plumes, no label, dating to early 1900s. $165.00 – 185.00.

Extravagantly large black sheared beaver Edwardian hat, 23" diameter, trimmed with willow ostrich plumes, dating to 1910. $260.00 – 310.00.

Striking black velvet Edwardian hat with black and white woven grosgrain ribbon on crown, no label, dating to early 1900s. $130.00 – 150.00.

Stunning large Edwardian in shades of rust and brown, trimmed with pheasant feathers and large velvet rosette in front, large crown to accommodate the Gibson girl hairstyle, dating to ca. 1910. $200.00 – 250.00.

Simple brown velvet toque style with narrow brim and a vertical ostrich plume to the back, dating to mid to late teens. $95.00 – 125.00.

Inside view of photo above right, showing the style of lining common in pre-war hats, and the label which reads, "BeeHive Dept. Store, Astoria, Oregon." This hat was purchased from Persona Vintage Clothing of Astoria, Oregon.

Elegant metallic lace over purple velvet with beaded passementerie around the crown, purple velvet covering edge of brim, dating to mid-to-late teens. $200.00 – 225.00.

Makes Any Hat Fit Any Head

It's a DeLeon Bandeau

Does entirely away with hat pins. Holds any hat comfortably yet firmly in any desired position, regardless of head-dress. Adjustable to any size hat and can be easily inserted in less than ten seconds—no sewing—no stitching.

Ideal for Bobbed Hair

Bobbed hair—thin hair—large hat—small hat—it's all the same to the DeLeon Bandeau. Nothing else like it—thousands of enthusiastic users. Satisfaction guaranteed.

If your milliner or dealer cannot supply you, send us 25c with dealer's name and we will send one promptly, postpaid. State color, black or white.

DeLeon Bandeau Co.
2117 Locust Street
St. Louis, Mo.

Dealers—See your jobber. If he can't supply you, write us, giving jobber's name.

Makes Any Hat Fit Any Head

Classic black satin Renoir style, dipped brim and ostrich plume to one side, inside a small label sewn into the headband reads, "Pat. date 1915, DeLeon, made in U.S.A.," referring to the interior drawstring cord in a casing for perfect fit! $150.00 – 200.00.

Ad for the DeLeon bandeau that makes any hat fit any head, patented in 1915.

Brown cotton driving hat, large soft crown to accommodate hairstyle of the day, visor brim in front with very sheer silk veiling, a tab and button to hold it in place when not in use, dating to Edwardian period of horseless carriages. $110.00 – 135.00.

Another view showing veiling in down position.

Warm brown pleated horsehair with narrow brim and interesting crimped rayon fan over front of hat, accented with rhinestone trim, lined, no label, dating to mid teens. $100.00 – 125.00.

Gold-tone metal hair accessory, Egyptian influence from the discovery of the King Tut's tomb, adjustable to the head and position desired, embossed side medallions with ornamentation of pearls, turquoise beads, and jeweled drop; worn in the 1920s. $175.00 – 200.00.

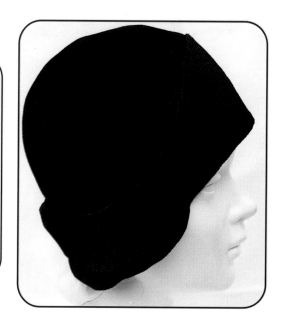

Dark navy fur-felt helmet cloche with very deco design detail around the lower edge, unlined, two labels: "Copy of Original Colette Goupy, 10 Rue de Castiglione, Paris"; and, "Harry Fink & Company, N. Y., Paris, Los Angeles." 1920s. $95.00 – 125.00. *Courtesy of Beth Bown.*

Classic blue felt cloche, smooth fitting and narrow brim with lovely grosgrain ribbon band and deco trim, dating to the 1920s. $75.00 – 95.00.

Fine peach straw cloche with hand-stitched lavender felt brim, turned up on one side with felt bow in back; worn in the 1920s. $85.00 – 100.00.

Inside view showing the typical lining of the 1920s period hat and the label reading "The May Co., Los Angeles."

Outrageous metallic lace cloche on wire frame with large butterfly including double wings and antennae on the front, unlined, label reads "Collins, Los Angeles," dates to 1920s. $175.00 – 200.00.

Side view to show the fit of the metallic lace butterfly cloche.

Rust-colored molded felt, lined, gros-grain ribbon trim with metallic ornament in back; this hat might have been a remodeled cloche, dates to the 1930s. $55.00 – 75.00.
Courtesy of Beth Bown.

Brown felt toy hat with aqua velvet trim and matching aqua feathers that curve around the face, back band of brown wired felt to hold hat in place, dating to the 1930s. $75.00 – 95.00.

Real leopard toy hat with brown cording in loops at the back and a brown cord band to hold hat in place, dating to the 1930s. $85.00 – 100.00.

Small olive green felt hat, showing proper placement of the back band which is trimmed with pinked bows of same felt, dating to the 1930s. $40.00 – 60.00.

Small olive green felt hat, showing front view with proper placement and use of back band, label reads "Berkshire," dating to the 1930s. $40.00 – 60.00.

Black felt stylized feather with pink feather trim curved to the face; fits close to the head, label reads "Bedell, New York," dating to 1940s. $55.00 – 85.00.

Ecru lacy straw broad brim summer hat, shallow crown with grosgrain ribbon band and ivory artificial flower accent in front, dating to late 1930s. Purchased from Persona Vintage Clothing, Astoria, Oregon. $55.00 – 75.00.

Red straw broad brim summer hat with shallow crown, accented with red polka-dot grosgrain ribbon band and bow, dating to 1940s (gift, Ms. Camelli). $45.00 – 65.00.

1940

Black soft woven straw type material with black silk jersey back band that knots and drapes in the back, dating to early 1940s. $55.00 – 75.00.

Black woven straw-type material on main part of hat that is creatively folded in an asymmetrical fashion with cream faille fabric and back band, label reads "Bedell, Paris, New York," dating to 1930s. $55.00 – 75.00.

Left side view showing bow and fan fold of asymmetrical hat.

Another great asymmetrical topper designed in brown felt, with veiling, no label unfortunately, dating to the 1940s. $75.00 – 95.00.

Left side view showing the series of self fabric bows and upswept design.

Front view showing the creative aerodynamic line.

Magenta felt with front detailing of same felt, matching hat pin, veiling, dating to the 1940s. $65.00 – 85.00.

White sheared plush, black quills for accenting the marvelous design, label reads, "Madame Suzy, Paris," dating to the 1940s in original hat box. $95.00 – 105.00.

Classic black felt with feather cockade to one side, label reads, "An Original Caspar-Davis," gift of I. Camelli, dating to 1940s. $55.00 – 75.00.

"Bee with beehive hat," natural straw in cone shape with red rhinestone bee, feathers, and velvet trim, label reads "Hattie Carnegie," dating to the 1940s. $145.00 – 165.00.

Right view showing design details.

Close-up of red rhinestone bee.

Dramatic plush velvet in champagne, assymetric brim pinned back in front, lined in black velvet, trimmed with brush and rhinestone pin, label is "Daral, 5 W. 42nd St., New York." Great example of the new look from the late 1940s. $95.00 – 125.00. *Courtesy of Beth Bown.*

Wedgewood blue velvet broad brim with blue and white ostrich plumes covering crown and wide brim, label reads "Lilly Dache," dating to the 1950s. $135.00 – 165.00.

Detail of inside construction and "Lilly Dache" label.

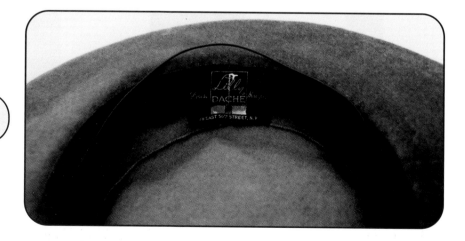

Narrow brim edged with spring green velvet and veiling, crown covered with artificial pansies, gift of Robyn Starr Dezendorf, dating to 1950s. $45.00 – 55.00.

Pink heavy lace motif and pearl trim cover this brimless hat, with faux feather trimmed with same lace, hat box from the Klara Alma Hat Shop, Astoria, Oregon, which might have sold a hat like this in the 1950s. $25.00 – 35.00.

White synthetic straw, flat crown, reverse brim, label reads "Valerie Modes," dating to the 1950s. $20.00 – 35.00.

Rose petals in velvet, label reads "Mr. Rickey Original," soft-fit hat dating to the 1960s, gift of I. Camelli. $25.00 – 35.00.

Impressive black feather "crown," label reads "styled by Jack McConnell, N.Y.," with original hat box, dating to the 1960s. $45.00 – 65.00.

Satin turban style with shades of deep blue, purple, green, and aqua, label reads "Haggarty's," dating to the 1960s. $20.00 – 35.00.

Pillbox, woven in silver and gold textured synthetic with veiling, labels reads "Miss Sally Victor," dating to the 1960s. $25.00 – 40.00.

Natural straw with red, blue, and yellow silk flowers on crown and cascading down the back, label reads "Miss Dior," dating to the 1960s. $60.00 – 75.00.

Natural straw on crown with pastel pleating in shades of lavender, green, and cream silk, self fabric bow in back, label reads "Schiaparelli," dating to the 1960s. $69.00 – 85.00.

Oversized black fox pillbox, Russian influence, large hatpin to secure in place, label reads "Schiaparelli," with original hat box, dating to the 1960s. $130.00 – 165.00.

Voluminous crinkled black fabric leaves, fondly referred to as the cabbage leaf hat, label reads "Mr. John," dating to the 1960s. $45.00 – 65.00.

Very soft cream plush wide brim with brown velvet bow on front and inside brim, stamped in crown "Made in France," dating to the 1960s. $45.00 – 65.00.

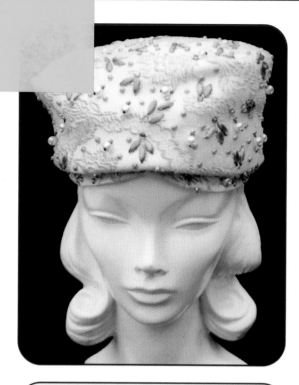

Cream brocade pillbox, gold studding and pearl trim, label reads "Christian Dior," dates to the 1960s. $65.00 – 85.00.

Natural straw loaded with very large red silk poppies for real impact, label reads "Leslie James," dating to the 1960s. $65.00 – 85.00.

Pink and red silk cabbage roses adorn a 3" wide headband style, label reads "Sonni, California," dating to the 1960s. $45.00 – 60.00.

Classic pillbox hat with matching handbag in cut velvet, dating to 1960s. Set, $55.00 – 75.00.

Umbrella hat, indispensable in the north-west for protection from rain, elastic band around head holds securely in place, folds down like umbrella when not in use. $20.00.

Expandable orange nylon hat for rain or shine folds up neatly into zippered bag, which reads "The Pop Top, Official Mount St. Helens Observer Hat, May 18, 1981." $20.00.

Page from H. O'Neill & Co. Fall and Winter Catalogue, 1890 – 91, with typical small late Victorian hats. Note the plumage and whole birds used for trim.

Variety of delightful and whimsical hat stands, usually in wood; note the blue hat stand to the left has a charming character with a brush and the gray hat stand to the right with brush has a mirror finish on the base with Scottie dog image. The brushes were used to clean or dust hats gently. In front of the hat stands is another hat brush, "Compliments of The Alberta Millinery" in Portland, Ore. Just in front, to the left of the hat brush, is a wee hat tape measure, a store advertisement gift, from the early 1900s. *Courtesy of Beth Bown.*

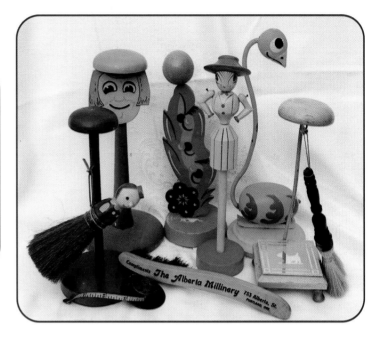

Marvelous wooden hat block, used in blocking hats into their final form by steaming the felt or straw and letting it dry on the block. *Courtesy of Beth Bown.*

Detail showing all the various components of the hat block and how they fit together.

Parasol Party. A party of thirteen parasols, tasseled, tatted, and beribboned.

Photo Credit: © 2000 Chris Bryant

The old saying, "Everything old is new again" may be appropriate for the twenty-first century as we reflect back on the use of parasols. A tanned skin in Victorian times meant a woman must have been of the working class. Maintaining the illusion of upper class status was achieved by use of a parasol whenever outside to protect skin from tanning. Once an accessory that shielded a lady from the sun to assure her position in the elite society, we may find the parasol useful again. Not so much to show our social status, but to ensure healthy skin, shielding us from the damaging rays of the sun. The sun worshipping days are over, but although smart women are not exposing themselves unnecessarily to the sun for the sake of a tan, they may not be willing to accessorize with a parasol in the twenty-first century.

In the early part of the nineteenth century parasols were larger than the later "Victoria parasols" for carriages. The sticks of these early parasols were heavier and usually made of wood, the ribs made of cane or if more expensive, whalebone. The color of the cover was usually plain, though plaids could be seen. Covers were of course hand stitched until the invention of the sewing machine in 1843 by Howe. An excellent example of this early parasol is seen in the photo on the top left of page 215, which can be documented to circa 1820. This period was marked by a more utilitarian parasol.

During the first part of Queen Victoria's reign, in the early 1840s, a lady's face was defended against the sun by way of her hat's brim, optional veiling, and a parasol. The period through the 1860s is marked by the smaller parasols with slender sticks, usually of the folding style. These folding parasols could easily be carried and used while riding in a carriage. Often parasols of this

> ### "Fashion is a kind of communication. It's a language without words."
>
> *Helmut Lang*

era also had a tilt feature that allowed the parasol to move so as to shade the face from different angles. Parasols of this era showed more elaborate details, as they were on display, so to speak, in the carriages. It was an opportunity to communicate one's status and, no doubt, served as a means of flirtatiously shielding one's face from the opposite sex as well.

Fashionable novelties in work and dress, Godey's Lady's Book, October 1856.

FASHIONABLE NOVELTIES IN WORK AND DRESS.

WHITE BASQUINE.

WE have met with many novelties lately that will no doubt be of interest to our numerous lady readers; and we shall therefore endeavor to give a slight sketch of them, hoping they may be useful by suggesting hints for the employment of their active needles and tasteful ingenuity; and perhaps also enable those who have no superabundance of money to fashion some elegant and useful articles of the female toilet, that in this country are generally beyond the reach of limited means.

We would recommend all those who have sufficient leisure to make *basquines*, or jackets, of white material, *jean*, *piqué*, or marcella (such as worn for gentlemen's waistcoats), but not of too thick a material of this kind; and being careful that the *plain* bodice of the same should mount high up to the throat, and have the *basques* deep, and rounded, and sloped up to the front, as in the pattern given. This bodice is most elegant when trimmed with tolerably wide frills, edging the sleeves of *broderie Anglaise* (open cut work on thick jaconet), and a collar or small frill round the throat of the same description. The bodice should be closed up the front, and have no other trimming besides a dozen or so of raised mother-of-pearl buttons, passed through well-made button-holes. This *basquine* is not only elegant, but an economical *toilette*, and suited to all.

Basquines of the same make, but in black *glacé* silk, are also very elegant; they should be trimmed with frills of black lace (see cut), with dropping black buttons, or, what is more novel, enamelled buttons, gold *plaque* or steel, or best gilt, enamelled with green or blue, which is both a novel and graceful finish to this useful part of a woman's dress, and will enable her to change her muslin or other skirts at pleasure.

Over low bodies (for evening or dinner wear) a *basquine* of clear black *tulle grenadine*, as seen in our cut (only open in front), is highly fashionable. The material may be rendered very beautiful by being crossed over (in the lozenge pattern adopted by quilters) with soft black chenille, and edged with deep silk fringe, mixed with the same material, which the fair worker can make herself with a little ingenuity. She must place her sleeve or bodice flat on a frame or table; cross the threads of chenille at equal distances, one over the other, fastening them at the points where they intersect each other; and after this is evenly done, she can finish the sewing on her hand. The border can be varied, as in the

THE BEDOUIN D'ÉTÉ.

[From the establishment of G. BRODIE, 51 Canal Street, New York.   Drawn by L. T. VOIGT, from actual articles of costume.]

THIS garment has obtained much favor; it is unique in style, and its capaciousness has rendered it very popular.   The one we illustrate is made of a light summer tissue.   Its peculiarity consists in the mode in which the stuff falls down the back, it being the angle which would, if it was fitted to the figure, be cut away; the stuff being simply folded straight up the back.

We give the above as a variety, but the fashion, *par excellence*, is of course some of the various laces which we mentioned in our last.

Small fashionable parasol trimmed with lace, Godey's Lady's Book, August, 1860.

Dainty parasol with ruffle illustrated in Godey's Lady's Book, January, 1871.

In 1840 metal ribs of tubular steel were patented by Hollands of England, and later redesigned in 1850. Until this new patent the ribs had been made of cane or whalebone. Finding a parasol with cane may also mean that it was a less expensive parasol, not necessarily dated earlier, simply because the metal frame was more expensive initially. The solid steel ribs were primarily made for umbrellas, with Fox's patent for the U-section in 1852. A parasol with whalebone ribs is uncommon after 1870. Parasol length for the period 1835 to 1865 was on average 22 to 28 inches, with a cover diameter of 16 to 22 inches.

During the mid ninteenth century the small folding parasol was the most favored because it could easily be folded and stored when not in use. The wooden stick was hinged with a short metal tube which slid over the joint to keep it rigid, as shown in the center photo on page 216. Another hinged aspect of the parasols for this time was the tilt top, allowing the parasol to tilt at the top of the stick. Most folding stick parasols will date before 1865. A rarely seen "Sylphide" parasol, patented in 1844, had a spring at the end of the handle so the parasol could be closed with one hand.

The *Englishwoman's Domestic Magazine* of 1862 states, "For occasions when a full-dress parasol is required, nothing is so suitable and distinguished as black or white lace made up over a bright coloured or white parasol." The deep fringed awning disappeared in the 1860s. Among the more unusual were feather-covered or feather-trimmed parasols. It is unlikely that many would survive to today, but a feather-trimmed parasol is illustrated below left.

Ocasionally a square parasol is found, but the usual shape is the dome shape as in the figure below right.

Feather-trimmed parasol with rows of ribbon ruching as illustrated in Godey's Lady's Book, May, 1871.

The classic dome shape of parasols, with a great deal of ornamentation as illustrated in Godey's Lady's Book, May, 1871.

Another very somber and serious lady with what appears to be a parasol with a looped handle of wood and a lace flounce, probably black again. The costume is very similar, but the parasol is a different style from left photo, more of a walking parasol. Back of the photo is printed "T. A. Dunlap, Photographer, Bloomfield, IA. Negatives preserved." (I wonder if they are?)

Rare and somewhat faded photo of lady with small carriage parasol in closed position, probably black. These parasols are often mislabeled as children's parasols, because of their size. Back of the photo reads (in pencil) "Mrs. John Wilson, 3 – Columbia Avenue, Astoria, Oregon," the photographer was Mrs. Emelia Olsen.

By 1866 we see a change in parasol style as stated in the 1866 *Queen*, "The sticks are much shorter than formerly and the handles extremely thick." The handles decorated with animal forms were popular in the 1870s, and into the 1880s we see natural knobbed and gnarled handles of wood. The 1870s and 1880s saw the deep lace awning as ornament for the covers which also had ruched trimmings. The middle period of 1865 to 1885 parasols are slightly longer with average length being 25 to 30 inches, with 20 to 25 inch diameter covers.

In the 1890s we see an interest in the linings with puffed or ruched chiffon and silk muslin. We also see the parasol covers become larger and the sticks become longer and slimmer, on average between 36 and 40 inches.

Tintype of two ladies with parasol, "leg-of-mutton" sleeves date the photo to early 1890s.

Mischievous-looking lady dressed to go with satchel, umbrella, and purse. Notice the coat has the tiered cape effect and is very fitted. The Illustrated American, October 1893.

THE FASHION DEPARTMENT
CONDUCTED BY
GRACE MARGARET GOULD

Parasol Embroidery Made Beautiful

A handsome effect can be obtained by placing one of our number 219, 3¾ in.; 220, 3½ in.; 207, 3¼ in. Old English, 241, 3 in.; 307, 3¼ in. Script, or 1253 3 in.; 1254, 4 in. Block letters on a parasol and embroidering over with silk or cotton. Many pretty color combinations will suggest themselves, all of which the most inexperienced sewer can produce by the use of REIS' FOUNDATION LETTERS. They require no "stamping" or "filling in" — you save time, work and expense.

Don't ask for Embroidery Forms, Padding Letters, etc. Say "give me REIS' FOUNDATION LETTERS"—the only kind that are guaranteed to retain their shape and appearance and to be absolutely washable. Sold in Art Departments everywhere. Send for Booklet and Free Sample of your Initial.

G. REIS & BRO.
644 Broadway, New York

REIS' FOUNDATION WASHABLE LETTERS FOR HAND EMBROIDERY

Small ad for parasol embroidery; and an illustration for a graceful afternoon frock and parasol, from the fashion department of *Woman's Home Companion*, August 1910.

No. 1566 — Bib Waist With Guimpe

Pattern cut for 32, 34, 36 and 38 inch bust measures. Price of pattern ten cents

No. 1567 — Flounce Skirt With Slashed Tunic

Pattern cut for 22, 24, 26 and 28 inch waist measures. Price of pattern ten cents

Paul Wurstenberg

A GRACEFUL AFTERNOON FROCK FOR SUMMER
DEVELOPED IN PLAIN AND DOTTED FOULARD

Copyright, 1910, by The Crowell Publishing Company

Real photo postcard from early 1900s taken along the boardwalk of Seaside, Oregon, showing the ladies with simple black umbrellas to be used rain or shine.

Delightful real photo postcard dated February 27, 1911, written in pencil, "I don't suppose you know who this is but it is me. I just got through singing Little Brown Jug. Lovingly, Ida." Note her light-colored parasol and large hat with extreme buckle decoration.

Real photo postcard of a confident lady with what looks like a floral cloth parasol, small purse, and T-strap shoes with large brimmed hat. An accessory rich photo! Courtesy of Beth Bown.

Even into the 1920s women continued to use parasols for defense against the sun, though the use was mainly for the sake of fashion as more and more young women were taking an active role in society and sports. The printed cotton or linen parasol was more popular than the silk variety of the earlier era. The Oriental influence of the earlier decade also heightened the demand for paper parasols, as shown in fashion magazines.

our attention in its lacquer red and deep yellow color scheme, with yellow piping on the bodice.

Mah-jongg, of course, is present in a printed linen top with a plain plaited linen skirt. Glass buttons, which are very much "in," attach the skirt in a new step formation, and a grosgrain bow is at the right side. Run in the tucks of a white batiste frock are narrow pastel-shaded ribbons. From top to hem the colors are orchid, blue, silver, gray, silver, white, white, orchid, blue, silver, gray, silver, blue and orchid. Dark-blue grosgrain is run through the waist casing.

A simple chemise frock of white cotton crêpe has embroidered red rings and red piping outlining the lace insertion on bodice, while next to it a pink cotton crêpe has threads in the much-liked Roman stripe effect trimming bodice and skirt. At left above, a perfect example of a daytime frock is of coral crêpe, with white organdie plaitings and a box-plaited skirt. A fetching coat of embroidered white linen is bound with orange and worn over a white linen skirt.

Lace frocks are seen in every assemblage of well-dressed women, and the cream Alençon one

in center, over white net, is particularly lovely. Cream chiffon cascades at left side of skirt.

The cyclamen-pink linen second from right with white linen bands and cyclamen grosgrain tie would create attention anywhere. Left to right trimming is very new, and so are the white glass buttons. Beneath a white eyelet embroidered linen a rose crêpe de chine slip shows faintly. At one side the crêpe falls in a plaited cascade.

These sketches are shown here for their news value, and no patterns are offered. You will find dresses made on similar lines in your local shops.

Variety of parasols shown, in upper left is a sheer voile or silk, a printed paper parasol, a lace trimmed style, and dangling from the arm of the lady in the floral tunic is a short handled style in closed position. The Ladies' Home Journal, July 1924.

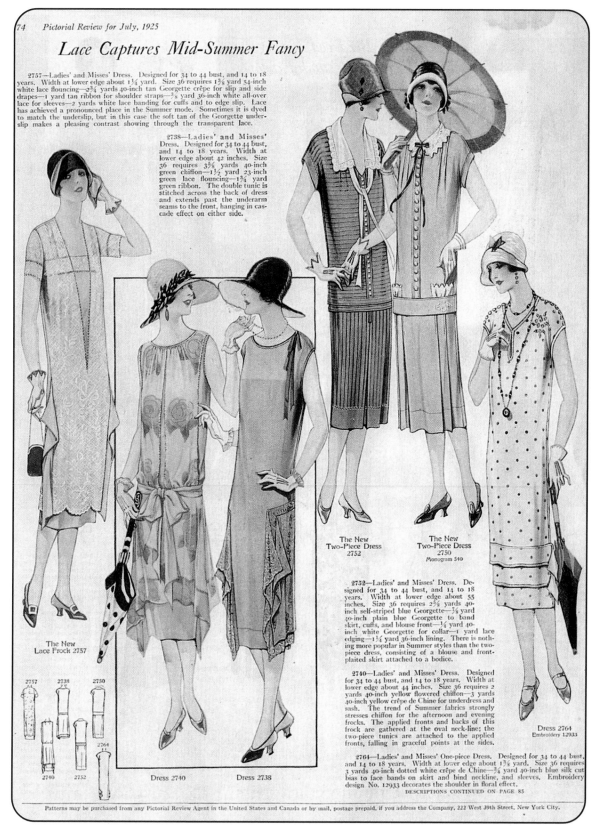

Lace Captures Mid-Summer Fancy

2757—Ladies' and Misses' Dress. Designed for 34 to 44 bust, and 14 to 18 years. Width at lower edge about 1¾ yard. Size 36 requires 1⅜ yard 54-inch white lace flouncing—2¾ yards 40-inch tan Georgette crêpe for slip and side drapes—1 yard tan ribbon for shoulder straps—⅜ yard 36-inch white all-over lace for sleeves—2 yards white lace banding for cuffs and to edge slip. Lace has achieved a pronounced place in the Summer mode. Sometimes it is dyed to match the underslip, but in this case the soft tan of the Georgette underslip makes a pleasing contrast showing through the transparent lace.

2738—Ladies' and Misses' Dress. Designed for 34 to 44 bust, and 14 to 18 years. Width at lower edge about 42 inches. Size 36 requires 3⅝ yards 40-inch green chiffon—1½ yard 23-inch green lace flouncing—1¾ yard green ribbon. The double tunic is stitched across the back of dress and extends past the underarm seams to the front, hanging in cascade effect on either side.

The New Lace Frock 2757

The New Two-Piece Dress 2752

The New Two-Piece Dress 2750 Monogram 549

Dress 2740

Dress 2738

Dress 2764 Embroidery 12933

2752—Ladies' and Misses' Dress. Designed for 34 to 44 bust, and 14 to 18 years. Width at lower edge about 55 inches. Size 36 requires 2⅝ yards 40-inch self-striped blue Georgette—⅜ yard 40-inch plain blue Georgette to band skirt, cuffs, and blouse front—¼ yard 40-inch white Georgette for collar—1 yard lace edging—1¼ yard 36-inch lining. There is nothing more popular in Summer styles than the two-piece dress, consisting of a blouse and front-plaited skirt attached to a bodice.

2740—Ladies' and Misses' Dress. Designed for 34 to 44 bust, and 14 to 18 years. Width at lower edge about 44 inches. Size 36 requires 2 yards 40-inch yellow flowered chiffon—3 yards 40-inch yellow crêpe de Chine for underdress and sash. The trend of Summer fabrics strongly stresses chiffon for the afternoon and evening frocks. The applied fronts and backs of this frock are gathered at the oval neck-line; the two-piece tunics are attached to the applied fronts, falling in graceful points at the sides.

2764—Ladies' and Misses' One-piece Dress. Designed for 34 to 44 bust, and 14 to 18 years. Width at lower edge about 1⅝ yard. Size 36 requires 3 yards 40-inch dotted white crêpe de Chine—¾ yard 40-inch blue silk cut bias to face bands on skirt and bind neckline, and sleeves. Embroidery design No. 12933 decorates the shoulder in floral effect.
DESCRIPTIONS CONTINUED ON PAGE 85

Patterns may be purchased from any Pictorial Review Agent in the United States and Canada or by mail, postage prepaid, if you address the Company, 222 West 39th Street, New York City.

Lovely color summer fashion illustration with three parasols shown, two in closed position and the flatter style of the Oriental influence, either in paper or silk. Also of note are the glove and hat styles shown. Pictorial Review, July 1925.

Storage and Care

f your collection includes parasols or umbrellas, you have very fragile collectibles. Obviously they were used in their day, in the sun or rain which will take their toll on fabric. Now 75 – 100 years later the fabrics have become even weaker due to time. It is very risky to open these old parasols to full extension. The silk or other fabric will surely split when tension of this kind is put on the fabric. It is recommended that parasols and silk umbrellas are stored in the closed position and never fully extended. They should be stored in acid-free tissue, or washed cotton pillow cases work well too. They are lovely to have on display, but please take care that they are not damaged by opening them fully.

There are two ladies I would like to make note of who collected parasols for us to enjoy today. Their collection was kindly loaned to me to photograph by their grandniece, Signe Johnson of Salem, Oregon. Because of their fragile nature only some of the collection was included in the chapter heading photo, Parasol Party. The hand-painted china ball parasol belonged to Ruby Alice. Susan Pearl's parasol had her name engraved on the gold handle. They were two sisters who never married, and lived their entire lives at 600 Northwest Third Street in Abilene, Washington, in an Italianate Victorian built by their father in 1886. Knowing they carried the two parasols pictured, I've included their photos.

Two sisters, Ruby Alice Johntz, wearing a lovely large hat of the Edwardian era, and Susan Pearl Johntz with thick braided hair.

Top view of folding parasol, blue/brown plaid cotton cover, pinked edge, hand stitched, 26" diameter top.

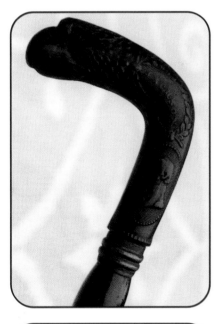

Inside view showing the hand stitching, wooden ribs and a piece of twill tape stitched in place with the name "Paula L. Clark" hand written.

Close-up of the handle with the name "Decatur" lettered and the profile of another man. Possibly this parasol was a commemorative souvenir of the "Jackson-Decatur debates," which dates the parasol to before 1820. The larger size and hand stitching would indicate that it was made before 1840. Historically significant. $510.00 – 720.00.

Close-up of the handle with a very detailed eagle on the end and the name "Jackson" lettered with a profile of a man in relief.

Tilt top, small folding parasol in black cotton sateen, with a row of self fabric ruffles and silk fringe, cover measures 25" in diameter, wood handle with ball, 25" in length, early-Victorian. $95.00 – 125.00.

Two examples of parasols in closed position, both are black cotton with pinked edges; one handle is extended and one is folded, early-Victorian. $79.00 – 99.00.

Small folding parasol in open position, black cotton sateen cover aged to almost dark green, pinked edge, lined in ivory cotton, lovely twisted wooden handle, early-Victorian. $110.00 – 135.00.

Small folding parasol, delicate black Chantilly lace over ecru silk liner, 26" diameter; handle is twisted tortoise, 25" in length, early-Victorian. $135.00 – 155.00.

Small folding parasol in cobalt blue silk with black lace ruffles and small woven button trim, cover measures 22" diameter, carved wood hand with embellishments is 20" in length, early-Victorian. $210.00 – 235.00.

Cobalt blue parasol in closed position.

Black silk lace parasol, cover is 50" diameter, lined with black silk, wood with hand-painted lady on porcelain and embossed brass handle, 37" in length, late Victorian. $260.00 – 300.00.

Parasol in closed position, lined with yellow silk, matching silk ribbon bow to embellish handle with end that is an enameled green vine with yellow bud handle, 38" in length.

Ivory silk parasol with hand-painted floral design in shades of yellows and greens, given as a wedding gift to Minnie Muriel Morse in 1914 by one of her bridesmaids. $275.00 – 300.00

Ecru lace parasol with ivory silk lining, gathered ecru silk ribbon at the base of the metal tipped ferrule, carved wood handle, Edwardian era, gift of founding family in Astoria, OR. $250.00 – 275.00.

Close-up view of parasol, ivory tips with ivory ring to hold parasol closed, ruched silk trim on handle which measures 37" in length.

White linen parasol with white embroidered iris and butterflies, cover measures 40" in diameter, wood handle with iris embossed silver end measures 37" in length, Edwardian era. $175.00 – 200.00.

Close-up detail of parasol handles.

Ivory cotton parasol with floral embroidery and cutwork, scalloped edge finished with buttonhole stitch, gathered ribbon at the base of the ferrule, wood handle with curved end, 38" in length. $150.00 – 200.00.

Pink dot patterned silk jacquard cover, lined, pinked edge, bamboo handle with brass embossed end, 35" long. $150.00 – 165.00.

Black lace cover, burgundy sateen lining, twisted wood handle, 36" long, early 1900s. $195.00 – 225.00.

Closed position of parasol above with tasseled ring attached by cord for closure.

Ecru linen with tatted edge, plain wood handle with original tassel, 38" in length, early 1900s. $155.00 – 175.00.

Black silk umbrella cane, may have been a gentleman's, rigid cover telescopes down, early 1900s. $55.00 – 65.00. Very practical cane/purse; cane is lightweight bamboo and purse is a heavy cotton ticking, early 1900s. $95.00 – 110.00.

Very thin pale lavender silk parasol with ivory embroidered flowers, silk is very delicate and split in some places, 1920s. $25.00 – 35.00.

Inside view of wooden ribs and mechanism, bamboo handle.

Three paper parasols, quite colorful, wood ribs and mechanism, two in closed position, 1920s. $39.00 – 49.00.

Two umbrellas, both black: partially open is a classic Edwardian period silk with two tucks on the cover, original tassel, wood handle measuring 42"; the closed umbrella is similar with original tassel and a beautifully detailed handle with mother-of-pearl inlay. $65.00 – 85.00.

Grouping of three umbrellas: open plaid rayon, closed green rayon with nicely painted wood handle, and floral cotton with incised wood handle and cord, 1940s. $35.00 – 55.00.

Grouping of six colorful umbrellas: two in open position have plain covers with patterned linings, both original tassels, 1950s. $19.00 – 35.00.

Grouping of three umbrellas: two in open position are plastic, the black and white polka dot with clear panel is the classic bubble umbrella of the 60s, measures 33", the smaller black and white paisley measures 21", in closed position is the umbrella at left with patterned lining, 1960s. $19.00 – 35.00.

riginally known as pockets, the purse as we know it today has evolved, chameleon-like. Unlike other accessories, shoes or gloves for instance, the purse does not have to fit any particular body or size. It has an unlimited variety of forms. The purse is also made of every kind of material such as long-lasting leather, rich beading, or embroidery on silk and velvet, rigid plastic or shell, or woven macramé twine and palm leaves.

The early bags or pouches carried any number of necessary items from important papers and documents for men, to lace-making and sewing implements for women. It was uncommon for women to use cosmetics, except in the privacy of their boudoir at home. Special bags were made to carry snuff or tobacco, medicines, sachets, keys, or fans. Rarely did one carry money, so much was done on the barter system in the medieval times. Throughout the middle ages and the Renaissance, specifically designed bags called "almoners," which were suspended from the belt, carried gold coins that were distributed to those in need.

As the demand increased, by the sixteenth century, guilds were established solely devoted to the making of purses and bags. The first of these bags for women were called pockets and were usually made of cloth attached with a tape or tie around the waist, under the skirt. The needlework skills of the maker were often displayed with various crewel or fancy embroidery techniques. Over time men's clothing evolved to incorporate pockets, thereby eliminating the need for detached bags which tended to be inconvenient. For women the use of pockets went the other way, becoming an attractive and decorative accessory.

These pockets were not designed to carry money, and became such important feminine accessories that they were often mentioned in wills. As the need for a receptacle for money arose, a flat envelope style developed called a pocketbook. The slender silhouette of the early 1800s made it impossible to have hidden pockets under the skirts and a bag was fashioned as stated in an 1804 London journal, "While men wear their hands in their pockets so grand, the ladies have pockets to wear in their hand."

The reticule became indispensable and was often called an "indispensible." These small bags, gathered with a drawstring of ribbon or cord, were made of many materials such as satin, silk, or velvet. The reticule was trimmed with anything the imagination could supply, including gold bullion, beads, ribbon embroidery, and sequins. The term "ridicule" was a satirical term given by the French. The reticule when worn suspended from the belt, as was the custom, was known as a chatelaine. Chatelaines can be differentiated from other types of purses because of the hook attachment (see left photo on page 227). Purses that were hand carried then became known as handbags.

The fashionable reticules of the early 1800s were made of the same fabric as the dress. Bead embroidery was becoming popular, as well as hand-painted silks and velvets, thereby showing a woman's skill and creativity. Although the drawstring reticule was the most common, the use of framed bags came into use as early as 1820. Piping as a finishing detail for the seams was quite common from 1830 – 1850. Reticules with bright-colored wool work known as "Berlin work" was in vogue for several decades from 1840 – 1870. The synthetic dye known as aniline dye was discovered in 1856 by a young English chemist, Sir William Perkin. This dye changed the color palette for fashionable embroidery threads and fabrics.

> *"Lucy Locket lost her pocket, Kitty Fisher found it, Not a penny was there in it, Only ribbons round it."*
>
> *Old Rhyme*

Jewel Bags. Glittering jewel tones in beaded bags.

Photo Credit: © 2000 Chris Bryant

A LADY'S WORK, OR CARRIAGE BAG.

(See blue Plate in front of Book.)

Materials.—Twelve skeins of black, three shades of scarlet, three shades of green, and three shades of puce Berlin wool; six skeins of each will be required.

WITH black make a chain twenty-two inches in length. Work three rows in double crochet with black, before commencing the pattern. Work on one side only, detaching the wool at the end of the row; and in working with two colors change the wool in the middle of the stitch.

1st pattern row (black and scarlet).—4 black, *, 2 scarlet, 2 black, 8 scarlet, 2 black; repeat from*, and finish with 4 black.

2d.—2 black, *, 2 scarlet, 2 black, 8 scarlet, 2 black; repeat from *, and finish with 2 black.

3d. (mid. scarlet).—4 black, *, 2 scarlet, 4 black, 4 scarlet, 4 black; repeat from *, and finish with 4 black.

4th. (lightest scarlet).—4 black, *, 2 scarlet, 2 black, 8 scarlet, 2 black; repeat from *, and finish with 4 black.

5th.—Like 4th.
6th.—Like 3d.
7th.—Like 2d.
8th.—Like 1st.

This completes one pattern. Repeat the pattern with shades of green and black, and with puce and black, till there are two stripes worked with each color; then work a third scarlet, stripe, and finish with three rows of black. Fold and crochet the sides together, and work two rows round the top with black wool. Line with scarlet or green silk. Insert two or three small pockets in the inside, mount on a clasp about eleven inches wide, and cover a thick cord with black velvet for the handles. Our fair readers will find this a very useful and convenient bag for many purposes.

CROCHET PURSE.

A lady's work, or carriage bag, made with twelve skeins of black, three shades of scarlet, three shades of green, and three shades of puce Berlin wool; six skeins of each will be required. "Our fair readers will find this a very useful and convenient bag for many purposes." Complete directions are given in Godey's Lady's Book, July 1856.

LADY'S NETTED PURSE

Materials.—A skein of scarlet gossamer netting silk, a little vert-islay and white netting silk; six skeins of gold thread, No. 1; French trimmings; steel netting mesh, Nos. 14 and 17. Ivory gauge.

BEGIN with four stitches, and fine mesh, close into a round, and net two in every stitch. Of the eight thus worked, four will be long and four short stitches. Do two in every short stitch, and one in every long. Continue to work round and round in this manner, always increasing by netting two in every short stitch (which occurs four times in each round) until there are sixty stitches altogether. Then do sixty-four rounds without any increase. Take the mesh No. 14, and do one round with it.

Resume the fine mesh; net the second long stitch, drawing it through the first; then the first. Continue all round in the same way.

Do two plain rounds, and again repeat from the one with the large mesh, finishing with six plain rounds instead of two.

A lady's netted purse is also shown in the year 1856 with drawstring and tassel, Godey's Lady's Book, September 1856.

HANDKERCHIEF RETICULE.

This little article is extremely sparkling and effective when worked; it is a small bag or reticule, just sufficiently large to contain the handkerchief and scent-bottle, and is very convenient when visiting, for evening wear, or when going to any place of public amusement. The design is worked on fine canvas, in various colored wools, and gold and steel beads.

The following are the arrangements: The centre diamond is a gold star on a crimson or scarlet ground, the diamond having an outline of steel beads. The scrolls round have an outline of steel beads, filled in with gold color. The escalopped circle is also in steel beads, the ground within being black. The remainder of the ground is a brilliant green, the scrolls being the same as those within the circle—namely, a steel bead outline, filled in with gold color. The two sides are united together, the joins being hidden either with a gold cord or a gold and steel bead alternately, nearly close to each other. A set of small gilt or steel rings must be sewn on to the top, for the cord to pass through. Three handsome tassels—one at each side and one at the bottom, selected to match in color with the bag—complete this article, which will be found a very satisfactory production of the Work Table when completed.

Early photograph of couple, lady with bustle dress holding very small purse with cord or chain handle. What could have been in that small accessory?

A handkerchief reticule "is extremely sparkling and effective when worked; it is a small bag or reticule, just sufficiently large enough to contain the handkerchief and scent-bottle, and is very convenient when visiting, for evening wear, or when going to any place of public amusement. The design is worked on fine canvas, in various colored wools, with gold and steel beads." Godey's Lady's Book, September 1860.

No. 366.—Ladies' Chatelaine Bag.

This is one of the finest premiums we have ever been able

to offer for a small club of subscribers. The bag is made of fine Black Kid, full leather lined, with oxidized nickel trimmings and clasp. Its size is 5½x6 inches, exclusive of the chatelaine. It will be found most convenient for shopping and calling; indeed the chatelaine bag is now all the rage with ladies. We will send this Chatelaine Bag by mail, postpaid, also THE PEOPLE'S HOME JOURNAL for one year, upon receipt of only **Seventy-five Cents ;** or we will give the bag *free* to any one sending us a club of **Four** subscribers for one year at 35 cents each or **Eight** subscribers at 25 cents each. Or we will send the Bag post-paid, without subscription to the paper, upon receipt of 50 cents.

First mesh bag made by Mr. Whiting in 1892.

Whiting & Davis Golden Anniversary purse of 1926, retailed for less than $10.00.

Ad for subscribers to receive this black kid, full leather lined chatelaine bag, "indeed the chatelaine bag is now all the rage with ladies," The People's Home Journal, December 1894.

The metal mesh bags have always been extremely popular, and continue today as a collectible. Wade & Davis Co., starting in 1876 as a jewelry firm, is the oldest continuously operated purse company in the United States. Charles Whiting started as an errand boy at 9¢ an hour in 1880, and developed the technique for the first mesh bag, which he made completely by hand in 1892. By 1896 he became a partner, changing the name to Whiting & Davis. These mesh purses were made by hand by women as a cottage industry, with as many as 100,000 individually soldered links. What started out as a New England home industry grew into big business with the invention of the mesh machine in 1909.

The Mandalian Manufacturing Co., founded in North Attleboro, Massachusetts, in the early twentieth century, also made metal mesh purses. If you have a Mandalian purse it can be dated from early 1900s to 1940, when the company was bought out by Whiting and Davis. The Whiting & Davis Co. remained in the family of Charles Whiting until 1962 when it was sold. In 1992 it changed hands again and is now part of WDC Holdings Co. Several prominent designers were brought to Whiting & Davis, including Paul Poiret in 1929 with brighter colors, and Elsa Schiaparelli in 1937, changing the look to a more functional bag. The original prices ranged from $6.00 to $75.00.

The beautiful beaded bag made its first appearance in the late 1700s. Often designed with a drawstring closure, these bags had an infinite variety of themes, colors, and styles. In the early ninteenth century, Venetian bead knitting reached its peak of popularity in which a lady would carefully string the colors of glass or metal seed beads onto her crochet thread according to her pattern. Once all the beads were strung she would begin to crochet or knit a bead into each stitch, as the bag developed the pattern could be seen. Obviously the solid-color bags were the easiest to make, and perhaps were the beginner's patterns. Looking at the intricacy of floral or scenic patterns, you recognize the true artistry, technical complexity, and visual sophistication of these bags.

Wild Rose and Forget-me-not Chatelaine Bag Design No. 69.

By Mary Ward Shuster.

A novelty in the line of chatelaine bags has a pretty floral design of wild roses and forget-me-nots, with their leaves, worked in colored beads on a background of white crystal beads. The bag is oval in shape and measures, when completed, eight inches from clasp to bottom of fringe and about five inches across.

> *For those interested in creating their own beaded bag, a pattern for a floral beaded chatelaine from Home Needlework Magazine, April 1902.*

HOME NEEDLEWORK MAGAZINE.

The reverse or back of the bag may be worked solid in white beads or in plain crochet with white silk. The bottom and sides are finished with a heavily twisted fringe of white glass beads. A bright silver clasp top looks best with the bag, and the lining should be white suede.

White Purse Twist is used for working and the beads are strung in the order given below. As so many beads are difficult to handle it will be a good plan to string, say, half way through on one spool and the remaining beads on the other.

Commence with a chain of 48 stitches, turn, and work back along both sides of this chain, with a bead in every stitch. This closes the bottom of the bag without seaming. Now work the pattern according to diagram shown by Fig. 49. If the directions for stringing have been carefully followed each bead should come exactly in the position marked on diagram.

For stringing one side of bag :—

275 white, 2 light green, 37 white, 1 light green, 22 white, 1 light green, 13 white, 1 light green, 23 white, 1 light green, 8 white, 1 light green, 6 white, 1 light green, 8 white, 1 light green, 3 white, 1 light green, 7 white, 1 light green, 4 white, 1 light green, 6 white, 2 light green, 11 white, 1 light green, 1 white, 1 light green, 9 white, 1 light green, 6 white, 1 light green, 4 white, 2 light green, 2 white, 1 light green, 2 white, 1 light green, 8 white, 1 light green, 4 white, 1 light green, 5 white, 1 light green, 16 white, 2 light green,

WILD ROSE AND FORGET-ME-NOT CHATELAINE BAG DESIGN No. 69.

9 white, 1 light green, 6 white, 1 light green, 4 white, 1 light green, 3 white, 1 dark green, 1 white, 1 dark green, 8 white, 1 light green, 5 white, 1 light green, 3 white, 1 light green, 1 dark green, 21 white, 1 light green, 8 white, 1 light green, 6 white, 1 light green, 3 white, 1 light green, 4 white, 1 dark green, 1 white, 1 dark green, 2 white, 1 dark green, 5 white, 1 dark green, 6 white,

1 light green, 2 white, 1 dark green, 24 white, 1 light green, 3 white, 1 light green, 3 white, 1 light green, 1 white, 1 light green, 3 white, 1 light green, 1 white, 3 white, 4 white, 4 dark green, 1 white, 1 dark green, 6 white, 1 dark green, 1 white, 2 dark green, 3 white, 1 dark green, 1 white, 1 dark green, 26 white, 2 light green, 4 white, 1 light green, 2 white, 2 light green, 2 white, 1 light green, 1 white, 1 light green, 7 white, 1 dark green, 4 white, 2 dark green, 6 white, 1 dark green, 1 white, 1 dark green, 4 white, 1 dark green, 1 white, 1 dark green, 6 white, 1 light green, 18 white, 1 light green, 4 white, 1 light green, 3 white, 1 light green, 1 white, 1 light green, 4 white, 6 light green, 7 white, 6 dark green, 5 white, 2 dark green, 5 white, 1 dark green, 2 light green, 4 white, 1 light green, 17 white, 2 light green, 3 white, 1 light green, 5 white, 4 light green, 1 dark green, 3 white, 1 dark green, 1 white, 1 dark green, 1 white,

FIG. 49. DETAIL OF PATTERN, BAG No. 69.

- ● Signifies Dark Green Beads.
- ○ Signifies Pink Beads.
- ✕ Signifies Light Green Beads.
- ⊘ Signifies Blue Beads.
- ⊗ Signifies Dark Red Beads.
- □ Signifies Yellow Beads.
- ⊙ Signifies Light Red Beads.

1 light green, 2 white, 1 dark green, 2 light green, 5 white, 2 light green, 4 white, 1 light green, 5 white, 4 dark green.

3 white, 1 dark green, 5 white, 3 light green, 1 dark green, 3 white, 1 light green, 7 white, 1 light green, 17 white, 2 light green, 2 white, 2 light green, 2 dark green, 9 white, 1 dark green, 2 white, 1 dark green, 1 light green, 2 white, 2 dark green, 9 white, 1 light green, 7 white, 3 dark green, 2 white, 5 dark

green, 5 white, 3 light green, 1 dark green, 2 white, 1 light green, 4 white, 1 light green, 2 white, 1 light green, 20 white, 1 light green, 1 dark green, 1 light green, 1 white, 1 light green, 1 dark green, 7 white, 1 light green, 1 white, 1 dark green, 2 white, 4 dark green, 3 white, 3 light green, 10 white, 3 light green, 1 white, 1 dark green, 7 white, 2 dark green, 1 white, 3 blue, 1 white, 2 dark green, 2 white, 1 light green, 2 white, 1 light green, 3 white, 1 light green, 1 white, 1 light green, 19 white, 1 light green, 1 dark green, 2 light green, 1 dark green, 1 light green, 4 white, 3 light green, 1 white, 1 dark green, 1 light green, 6 dark green, 3 light green, 14 white, 1 light green, 1 white, 1 dark green, 9 white, 4 blue, 1 dark green, 2 white, 1 dark green, 1 white, 1 light green, 3 white, 1 light green, 2 white, 2 light green, 21 white, 1 light green, 1 dark green, 1 light green, 1 dark green, 1 light green, 2 white, 3 light green, 1 dark green, 1 light green, 1 white, 2 dark green, 1 light green, 5 white, 1 light green, 2 white, 2 light green, 11 white, 1 light green, 5 white, 1 light green, 6 white, 4 blue, 1 dark green, 2 white, 2 dark green, 4 white, 1 light green, 2 white, 1 light green, 19 white, 5 light green, 2 dark green, 1 light green, 2 white, 1 light green, 1 dark green, 2 light green, 1 white, 2 dark green, 2 white, 2 light green, 4 white, 1 light green, 3 white, 1 light green, 10 white, 1 light green, 6 white, 2 light green, 1 white, 1 light green, 2 white, 3 blue, 1 light green, 1 dark green, 3 white, 1 dark green, 4 white, 1 light green, 2 white, 1 light green, 20 white, 1 light green, 5 dark green, 1 light green, 1 white, 1 light green, 1 dark green, 3 light green, 2 dark green, 5 white, 1 light green, 3 white, 1 light green, 13 white, 1 light green, 9 white, 4 dark green, 1 white, 3 light green, 1 white, 2 dark green, 1 white, 1 dark green, 1 white, 2 light green, 2 white, 1 dark green, 2 light green, 22 white, 3 light green, 1 dark green, 1 white, 1 light green, 1 dark green, 3 light green, 1 white, 1 dark green, 32 white, 2 dark green, 2 white, 1 dark green, 8 white, 2 dark green, 3 white, 1 dark green, 1 white, 1 dark green, 27 white, 1 light green, 1 dark green, 1 light green, 1 dark green, 4 white, 1 dark green, 31 white, 1 dark green, 3 white, 1 dark green, 3 white, 1 light green, 5 white, 2 dark green, 4 white, 2 dark green, 22 white, 7 light green, 2 dark green, 1 light green, 1 white, 2 dark green, 2 white, 1 light green, 37 white, 2 light green, 2 white, 1 light green, 3 dark green, 4 white, 1 dark green; 22 white, 1 light green, 7 dark green, 1 light green, 1 dark green, 2 white, 2 dark green, 2 light green, 40 white, 2 light green, 3 white, 1 dark green, 4 white, 1 dark green, 2 white, 2 dark green, 1 light green, 18 white, 4 light green, 1 dark green, 1 light green, 3 white, 2 dark green, 49 white, 1 dark green, 1 white, 3 blue, 1 white, 3 dark green, 2 white, 1 light green, 18 white, 2 light green, 2 dark green, 1 light green, 2 white, 1 light green, 1 white, 1 dark green, 47 white.

2 light green, 2 white, 5 blue, 29 white, 1 light green, 2 white, 1 dark green, 2 white, 1 light green, 1 dark green, 2 white, 1 light green, 1 dark green, 2 light green, 36 white, 3 light green, 1 dark green, 1 white, 1 light green, 3 blue, 1 dark green, 26 white, 2 light green, 1 white, 1 light green, 2 white; 1 dark green,

2 white, 1 dark green, 2 light green, 41 white, 1 dark green, 1 light green, 2 dark green, 1 white, 2 light green, 1 blue, 2 dark green, 28 white, 1 dark green, 3 white, 1 dark green, 1 white, 1 dark green, 1 white, 1 dark green, 2 light green, 34 white, 2 light green, 5 white, 2 dark green, 3 white, 1 light green, 2 dark green, 2 white, 1 light green, 2 dark green, 25 white, 1 dark green, 1 white, 1 dark green, 1 white, 1 dark green, 1 light green, 1 white, 1 light green, 1 dark green, 1 light green, 35 white, 1 light green, 1 white, 1 light green, 5 white, 3 light green, 1 white, 1 dark green, 2 white, 1 light green, 1 dark green, 1 light green, 15 white, 1 light green, 4 white, 1 light green, 6 white, 2 dark green, 1 white, 1 dark green, 3 white, 2 light green, 36 white, 1 light green, 3 white, 1 dark green, 1 white, 3 blue, 1 light green, 3 dark green, 1 white, 1 dark green, 1 light green, 5 white, 2 light green, 1 dark green, 8 white, 1 light green, 1 dark green, 1 light green, 2 white, 2 light green, 2 white, 1 light green, 2 white, 2 dark green, 1 white, 1 dark green, 40 white, 2 dark green, 2 white, 1 dark green, 2 white, 4 blue, 1 dark green, 2 white, 1 dark green, 6 white, 2 light green, 1 dark green, 10 white, 1 light green, 1 dark green, 1 light green, 1 white, 1 light green, 1 dark green, 2 white, 2 light green, 1 white, 2 dark green, 1 white, 1 dark green, 42 white, 1 dark green, 1 white, 1 dark green, 2 white, 4 blue, 1 dark green, 2 white, 1 dark green, 3 white, 1 dark green, 2 white, 1 light green, 1 dark green, 1 light green; 11 white, 1 light green, 1 dark green, 2 light green, 1 dark green, 1 light green, 1 white, 1 light green, 1 dark green, 2 light green, 44 white, 4 dark green, 3 white, 3 blue, 3 white, 1 dark green, 1 white, 1 light green, 1 white, 1 dark green, 1 light green, 1 white, 1 dark green, 1 light green, 10 white, 4 light green, 1 dark green, 1 light green, 1 dark green, 1 light green, 1 white, 1 light green, 1 dark green, 5 light green, 44 white, 2 dark green, 1 white, 1 dark green, 4 white, 1 light green, 1 white, 1 dark green, 1 white, 1 light green, 1 white, 1 light green, 1 dark green, 1 white, 1 dark green, 12 white, 1 light green, 5 dark green, 1 light green, 1 white, 1 light green, 1 dark green, 1 light green, 2 dark green, 1 light green, 43 white, 7 dark green, 4 white, 1 light green, 1 dark green, 1 light green, 3 white, 1 light green, 1 dark green, 14 white, 4 light green, 1 dark green, 1 light green, 1 white, 1 light green, 2 dark green, 3 light green, 2 white, 4 light green, 1 dark green, 2 light green, 33 white, 1 dark green, 5 white, 4 dark green, 3 white, 1 dark green, 1 light green, 4 white, 3 dark green, 2 light green, 12 white, 3 light green, 1 dark green, 1 white, 1 light green, 1 dark green, 2 light green, 2 white, 3 light green, 1 dark green, 1 light green, 1 dark green, 1 light green, 38 white, 2 dark green, 4 white, 2 dark green, 1 white, 1 dark green, 4 white, 1 dark green, 1 white, 2 light green, 1 dark green, 16 white, 1 light green, 1 dark green, 1 light green, 1 dark green, 1 light green, 2 white.

2 light green, 1 dark green, 1 light green, 2 dark green, 3 light green, 38 white, 1 dark green, 4 white, 1 dark green, 2 white, 2 dark green, 2 white, 1 dark green, 1 white, 1 dark green, 16 white, 4 light green, 3 dark green, 2 light

green, 47 white, 3 dark green, 2 white, 1 dark green, 1 white, 1 dark green, 14 white, 2 light green, 2 dark green, 4 light green, 2 dark green, 3 light green, 2 dark green, 3 light green, 1 dark green, 2 light green, 48 white, 2 dark green, 1 white, 2 dark green, 18 white, 1 light green, 4 dark green, 1 light green, 1 dark green, 1 light green, 2 dark green, 2 light green, 1 dark green, 1 light green, 53 white, 1 dark green, 2 white, 3 dark green, 3 light green, 12 white, 6 light green, 1 white, 5 light green, 1 white, 1 light green, 1 dark green, 1 light green, 52 white, 1 dark green, 2 white, 1 dark green, 1 white, 1 dark green, 2 light green, 12 white, 4 light green, 2 white, 1 light green, 1 white, 2 light green, 2 dark green, 1 light green, 8 white, 1 light green, 33 white, 1 light green, 13 white, 1 dark green, 2 white, 1 dark green, 20 white, 1 dark green, 1 white, 1 dark green, 1 white, 1 light green, 1 dark green, 2 light green, 1 dark green, 1 light green, 6 white, 1 light green, 35 white, 1 light green, 12 white, 1 dark green, 1 white, 1 dark green, 21 white, 1 dark green, 1 white, 1 dark green, 1 white, 1 light green, 1 dark green, 1 light green, 2 white, 1 dark green, 1 white, 5 dark green, 36 white, 2 light green, 4 white, 3 blue, 1 white, 3 blue, 2 white, 1 dark green, 21 white, 1 dark green, 1 white, 1 dark green, 1 white, 1 light green, 1 dark green, 1 light green, 2 white, 2 dark green, 1 light green, 4 white, 3 light green, 33 white, 1 light green, 1 dark green, 3 white, 4 blue, 1 white, 4 blue, 1 white, 1 dark green, 17 white, 4 light green, 1 dark green, 2 light green, 1 white, 1 light green, 1 dark green, 1 white, 1 dark green, 1 white, 1 dark green, 2 white, 1 light green, 3 white, 1 light green, 2 white, 1 light green, 32 white, 1 light green, 1 dark green, 1 light green, 2 white, 9 blue, 2 white, 2 blue, 2 white, 2 blue, 12 white, 1 light green, 3 dark green, 2 light green, 1 white, 1 dark green, 3 white, 1 dark green, 43 white, 1 light green, 1 dark green, 1 light green, 2 white, 4 blue, 1 white, 4 blue, 1 white, 3 blue, 1 white, 3 blue, 10 white, 2 light green, 1 dark green, 1 light green, 1 dark green, 2 light green, 1 white, 2 dark green, 2 white, 2 dark green, 43 white, 1 light green, 1 dark green, 1 light green, 4 white, 1 blue, 1 white, 1 yellow, 1 white, 1 blue, 3 white, 7 blue, 8 white, 2 light green, 2 dark green, 2 light green, 1 dark green, 1 light green, 2 white, 1 dark green, 3 white, 1 dark green, 1 white, 3 light green, 36 white, 1 light green, 2 white, 2 light green, 1 dark green, 1 light green, 2 white, 4 blue, 1 white, 4 blue, 3 white, 1 blue, 1 yellow, 1 blue, 10 white, 5 light green, 1 white, 1 dark green, 1 light green, 2 white, 2 dark green, 2 white, 1 dark green, 2 white, 1 light green, 1 dark green, 2 light green, 4 white, 1 light green, 29 white, 2 light green, 1 white, 2 light green, 1 dark green, 1 light green, 2 white, 9 blue, 1 white, 7 blue, 13 white, 1 light green, 1 dark green, 4 white, 1 dark green, 2 white, 1 dark green, 3 white, 1 light green, 1 dark green, 2 light green, 2 white, 2 light green, 5 white, 1 light green, 19 white, 1 light green, 4 white, 1 light green.

1 white, 1 light green, 1 dark green, 2 light green, 2 white, 4 blue, 1 white, 4 blue, 1 white, 3 blue, 1 white, 3 blue, 13 white, 2 light green, 5 white, 1 dark

green, 1 white, 1 dark green, 1 white, 1 dark green, 1 white, 2 light green, 1 dark green, 2 light green, 1 white, 1 light green, 1 dark green, 4 white, 2 light green, 16 white, 1 light green, 1 white, 1 light green, 5 white, 1 dark green, 2 light green, 1 dark green, 1 light green, 4 white, 3 blue, 1 white, 3 blue, 1 white, 1 dark green, 1 white, 2 blue, 1 white, 2 blue, 14 white, 1 light green, 6 white, 1 dark green, 2 white, 1 dark green, 3 white, 2 light green, 1 dark green, 1 light green, 1 white, 1 light green, 1 dark green, 1 light green, 3 white, 2 light green, 10 white, 1 light green, 6 white, 1 light green, 6 white, 1 light green, 1 dark green, 1 light green, 1 dark green, 1 light green, 5 white, 1 dark green, 5 white, 1 dark green, 29 white, 1 dark green, 1 white, 1 dark green, 4 white, 2 light green, 1 dark green, 2 light green, 1 dark green, 1 light green, 2 white, 1 light green, 1 dark green, 2 light green, 6 white, 4 light green, 1 white, 1 light green, 4 white, 1 light green, 6 white, 1 light green, 1 dark green, 1 light green, 1 dark green, 1 light green, 1 white, 2 light green, 2 white, 1 dark green, 1 white, 3 blue, 1 white, 3 blue, 24 white, 2 blue, 1 white, 2 blue, 1 white, 2 light green, 1 dark green, 1 light green, 3 white, 1 dark green, 1 light green, 1 dark green, 2 light green, 1 white, 1 light green, 1 dark green, 2 light green, 6 white, 1 light green, 3 white, 1 light green, 2 white, 3 pink, 2 white, 2 pink, 3 white, 1 light green, 1 dark green, 1 light green, 1 dark green, 3 light green, 2 white, 1 dark green, 1 white, 4 blue, 1 white, 4 blue, 22 white, 3 blue, 1 white, 3 blue, 2 white, 1 light green, 2 dark green, 2 light green, 1 dark green, 1 light green, 1 dark green, 2 light green, 1 white, 1 light green, 1 dark green, 2 light green, 2 white, 2 light green, 6 white, 1 light green, 1 white, 4 pink, 1 white, 4 pink, 2 white, 1 light green, 2 dark green, 2 light green, 1 dark green, 1 light green, 2 white, 1 dark green, 1 white, 9 blue, 22 white, 7 blue, 3 white, 2 light green, 2 dark green, 1 light green, 2 dark green, 2 light green, 1 white, 2 light green, 1 dark green, 1 light green, 1 white, 2 light green, 7 white, 1 light green, 1 white, 9 pink, 2 white, 1 light green, 2 dark green, 1 light green, 1 dark green, 1 light green, 2 white, 1 dark green, 2 white, 4 blue, 1 white, 4 blue, 16 white, 2 blue, 1 white, 2 blue, 3 white, 1 blue, 1 yellow, 1 blue, 6 white, 3 light green, 3 dark green, 2 light green, 1 white, 2 light green, 1 dark green, 1 light green, 1 white, 2 light green, 3 white, 4 pink, 2 white, 3 pink, 3 light red, 3 pink, 1 white, 2 light green, 3 dark green, 1 light green, 3 white, 1 dark green, 1 white, 1 dark green, 2 white, 1 blue, 1 white, 1 yellow, 1 white, 1 blue, 2 white, 3 dark green, 13 white, 5 blue, 1 white, 7 blue, 6 white, 4 light green, 1 dark green, 1 light green, 1 white, 2 light green, 1 dark green, 1 light green, 1 white, 2 light green, 3 white, 5 pink, 2 white, 1 pink, 4 light red, 3 pink, 1 white, 1 light green, 1 dark green, 3 light green, 4 white, 2 dark green, 1 white, 4 blue, 1 white, 4 blue, 2 white, 2 dark green, 2 light green, 8 white, 2 light green, 1 white, 1 blue.

1 yellow, 1 blue, 2 white, 3 blue, 1 white, 3 blue, 11 white, 1 dark green, 2 white, 1 dark green, 1 light green, 1 white, 1 light green, 1 dark green, 1 light

green, 3 white, 2 pink, 2 light red, 1 pink, 2 white, 1 pink, 5 light red, 2 pink, 1 white, 1 dark green, 3 pink, 4 white, 1 dark green, 3 white, 9 blue, 2 white, 1 dark green, 3 white, 1 light green, 6 white, 1 light green, 2 white, 5 blue, 2 white, 2 blue, 1 white, 2 blue, 6 white, 5 light green, 2 white, 1 dark green, 1 white, 1 dark green, 2 white, 1 white, 1 light green, 5 white, 1 pink, 4 light red, 2 white, 1 light red, 4 dark red, 1 light red, 2 white, 5 pink, 2 white, 1 dark green, 4 white, 4 blue, 1 white, 4 blue, 3 white, 1 dark green, 12 white, 2 blue, 1 white, 2 blue, 7 white, 1 dark green, 4 white, 1 light green, 5 dark green, 1 light green, 2 white, 1 dark green, 3 white, 1 dark green, 3 white, 5 pink, 3 light red, 3 white, 3 dark red, 1 light red, 2 white, 1 light red, 5 pink, 1 white, 1 dark green, 6 white, 3 blue, 1 white, 3 blue, 4 white, 2 dark green, 16 white, 3 blue, 1 white, 3 blue, 1 white, 1 dark green, 1 light green, 1 white, 7 light green, 5 dark green, 1 white, 1 dark green, 3 white, 5 pink, 2 light red, 3 dark red, 2 white, 1 dark red, 3 dark red, 3 light red, 2 pink, 1 white, 2 dark green, 2 light green, 13 white, 2 dark green, 1 white, 1 light green, 14 white, 4 blue, 1 white, 4 blue, 1 white, 1 dark green, 1 white, 1 light green, 11 white, 2 dark green, 3 white, 3 pink, 4 light red, 4 dark red, 4 yellow, 2 white, 3 dark red, 3 light red, 2 white, 1 dark green, 3 white, 3 light green, 8 white, 1 light green, 1 dark green, 1 white, 1 dark green, 16 white, 9 blue, 2 white, 1 dark green, 14 white, 1 dark green, 2 white, 4 pink, 2 light red, 4 dark red, 6 yellow, 3 dark red, 4 light red, 2 pink, 16 white, 1 light green, 1 white, 1 dark green, 12 white, 1 light green, 3 white, 4 blue, 1 white, 4 blue, 3 white, 1 dark green, 6 white, 1 pink, 3 light red, 3 dark red, 1 white, 2 dark green, 1 white, 4 pink, 1 light red, 4 dark red, 7 yellow, 2 dark red, 2 light red, 5 pink, 4 white, 1 light green, 1 dark green, 4 light green, 3 white, 1 light green, 3 white, 1 light green, 12 white, 3 dark green, 2 white, 1 blue, 1 white, 1 yellow, 1 white, 1 blue, 2 white, 7 dark green, 1 white, 3 pink, 2 light red, 4 dark red, 1 pink, 2 white, 1 dark green, 9 white, 1 dark red, 6 yellow, 2 dark red, 1 light red, 6 pink, 3 white, 2 light green, 1 white, 1 light green, 1 dark green, 1 light green, 4 white, 1 light green, 4 white, 1 light green, 10 white, 1 dark green, 3 white, 1 blue, 1 white, 4 blue, 4 white, 1 light green, 2 white, 3 pink, 1 light red, 4 dark red, 3 pink, 1 light red, 1 dark red, 1 white, 4 dark green, 3 white, 1 light red, 4 dark red, 3 yellow, 1 white, 1 light red, 5 pink, 4 white, 1 light green, 1 dark green, 2 light green, 1 dark green, 1 light green, 6 white, 1 light green, 3 white, 1 light green, 10 white, 1 light green, 3 white, 9 blue, 3 white, 2 light green, 2 white, 3 pink, 1 light red, 2 dark red, 4 pink, 2 light red.

2 dark red, 4 white, 1 dark green, 2 pink, 2 light red, 4 dark red, 1 white, 3 dark red, 11 white, 1 light green, 1 dark green, 1 light green, 1 dark green, 5 light green, 6 white, 1 light green, 10 white, 1 light green, 4 white, 1 blue, 1 white, 4 blue, 2 white, 1 light green, 1 white, 1 light green, 2 white, 3 pink, 2 light red, 5 pink, 2 light red, 2 dark red, 3 white, 3 pink, 3 light red, 4 dark red, 3 pink, 2 white, 3 dark green, 2 white, 1 light green, 1 dark green, 1 light green, 3 dark green, 2 light green, 7 white, 2 light green, 15 white, 3 blue, 1

white, 3 blue, 3 white, 1 light green, 3 white, 2 dark red, 2 pink, 2 light red, 5 pink, 2 light red, 3 dark red, 2 white, 2 pink, 2 light red, 3 dark red, 1 white, 3 dark red, 2 light red, 4 pink, 3 white, 5 dark green, 3 light green, 24 white, 1 light green, 4 white, 1 dark green, 9 white, 2 pink, 5 dark red, 6 pink, 4 light red, 1 white, 3 pink, 6 light red, 2 dark red, 1 white, 7 light red, 3 pink, 5 white, 1 dark green, 25 white, 1 light green, 3 white, 4 dark green, 9 white, 1 dark green, 3 pink, 5 dark red, 5 pink, 2 light red, 2 pink, 1 dark red, 6 pink, 5 light red, 1 white, 8 light red, 2 pink, 3 white, 2 light green, 2 dark green, 6 white, 2 light green, 16 white, 2 light green, 2 dark green, 2 light green, 3 white, 6 light green, 1 dark green, 2 white, 3 pink, 1 light red, 3 dark red, 3 yellow, 6 pink, 1 dark red, 6 pink, 5 light red, 2 white, 5 light red, 4 pink, 1 white, 3 light green, 2 dark green, 2 white, 2 dark green, 2 light green, 2 dark green, 1 light green, 18 white, 1 dark green, 3 white, 1 light green, 4 white, 4 yellow, 5 pink, 2 dark red, 1 white, 3 pink, 1 white, 2 pink, 3 light red, 1 pink, 2 white, 1 pink, 3 light red, 4 pink, 1 white, 3 light green, 2 dark green, 1 light green, 3 white, 1 light green, 2 dark green, 1 light green, 19 white, 3 dark green, 10 white, 1 dark green, 2 light green, 3 white, 4 pink, 3 white, 2 dark red, 5 pink, 3 dark red, 4 white, 6 pink, 2 white, 2 pink, 2 light red, 2 pink, 3 white, 2 light green, 2 dark green, 1 light green, 2 dark green, 1 light green, 2 white, 1 light green, 2 dark green, 4 light green, 15 white, 1 dark green, 2 white, 1 light green, 2 light green, 7 white, 1 dark green, 1 white, 2 light green, 3 white, 3 pink, 2 white, 2 light red, 3 dark red, 3 pink, 3 dark red, 1 light red, 4 white, 6 pink, 3 white, 2 pink, 1 light red, 2 pink, 2 white, 2 light green, 1 dark green, 1 light green, 1 dark green, 1 light green, 2 white, 1 light green, 1 dark green, 1 white, 2 dark green, 3 light green, 11 white, 1 light green, 3 white, 1 light green, 2 white, 1 light green, 5 white, 1 light green, 1 dark green, 1 white, 2 light green, 7 white, 2 pink, 1 light red, 4 dark red, 1 white, 3 dark red, 2 light green, 4 white, 6 pink, 3 white, 5 pink, 2 white, 1 light green, 1 dark green, 2 light green, 1 dark green, 1 light green, 1 dark green, 1 light green, 2 light green, 1 dark green, 2 light green, 1 dark green, 1 light green, 1 white, 1 light green, 1 dark green, 2 light green, 12 white, 1 light green, 3 white, 1 light green, 7 white, 1 light green, 1 dark green, 1 light green, 5 white, 1 light green, 7 white, 3 pink, 2 light red, 2 dark red, 1 white, 3 pink, 3 light red, 5 white.

4 pink, 5 white, 3 pink, 3 white, 2 light green, 1 white, 1 light green, 1 dark green, 3 light green, 2 white, 1 light green, 1 dark green, 1 white, 2 light green, 1 dark green, 2 light green, 9 white, 1 light green, 2 white, 1 light green, 7 white, 1 light green, 1 dark green, 1 light green, 10 white, 4 pink, 1 light red, 2 dark red, 1 white, 4 pink, 1 light red, 7 white, 1 dark green, 5 white, 4 light green, 2 white, 2 light green, 4 white, 31 white, 3 light green, 1 dark green, 1 light green, 1 white, 2 light green, 3 white, 2 light green, 2 white, 2 light green, 1 dark green, 1 light green, 1 white, 1 light green, 7 white, 1 light green, 10 white, 2 light green, 11 white, 5 pink, 1 light red, 1 dark red, 1 white, 4 pink, 2 light red, 6 white, 1 dark green,

1 white, 4 dark green, 4 light green, 6 white, 1 light green, 1 dark green, 1 light green, 11 white, 3 light green, 30 white, 2 pink, 1 white, 1 pink, 1 light red, 1 dark red, 1 white, 4 pink, 1 light red, 7 white, 1 dark green, 2 white, 1 dark green, 1 dark green, 9 white, 1 light green, 1 dark green, 1 light green, 13 white, 1 light green, 31 white, 1 pink, 1 light red, 1 dark red, 2 white, 3 pink, 7 white, 2 light green, 3 white, 1 dark green, 2 white, 1 dark green, 5 light green, 3 white, 2 light green, 32 white, 6 light green, 5 white, 1 dark green, 3 white, 1 dark green, 3 white, 3 light green, 5 white, 1 light green, 3 white, 1 light green, 1 dark green, 3 white, 3 light green, 5 white, 1 light green, 31 white, 2 light green, 2 dark green, 2 light green, 2 white, 2 dark green, 4 white, 1 dark green, 2 white, 2 light green, 1 dark green, 2 light green, 4 white, 2 light green, 2 white, 2 light green, 1 dark green, 42 white, 3 light green, 1 dark green, 1 light green, 2 dark green, 6 white, 1 dark green, 2 white, 2 light green, 1 dark green, 1 light green, 6 white, 1 light green, 2 white, 2 light green, 1 white, 1 dark green, 2 white, 4 light green, 35 white, 1 light green, 2 dark green, 1 light green, 8 white, 1 dark green, 1 white, 1 light green, 1 dark green, 2 light green, 9 white, 2 light green, 2 white, 1 dark green, 4 light green, 31 white, 3 light green, 1 dark green, 1 light green, 1 dark green, 1 light green, 9 white, 1 dark green, 1 light green, 1 dark green, 2 light green, 9 white, 1 light green, 3 white, 1 light green, 1 dark green, 5 white, 3 light green, 23 white, 1 dark green, 1 light green, 1 white, 1 dark green, 1 light green, 10 white, 2 dark green, 11 white, 1 light green, 2 white, 2 light green, 1 white, 1 dark green, 2 light green, 1 white, 3 light green, 22 white, 2 light green, 1 dark green, 1 light green, 1 white, 1 light green, 1 dark green, 1 light green, 8 white, 1 light green, 1 dark green, 1 light green, 1 white, 1 dark green, 2 light green, 11 white, 2 light green, 2 white, 3 dark green, 1 light green, 1 dark green, 2 light green, 1 white, 3 light green, 7 white, 2 light green, 1 dark green, 1 light green, 1 white, 1 light green, 1 dark green, 2 light green, 10 white, 2 light green, 3 white, 2 light green, 3 dark green, 1 light green, 15 white, 1 light green, 1 dark green, 2 light green, 2 white, 2 light green, 8 white, 1 light green, 1 dark green, 2 light green, 1 white, 2 light green, 1 dark green, 1 light green, 10 white, 2 light green, 3 white, 2 light green, 1 white, 2 light green, 1 dark green, 2 light green, 12 white, 3 light green, 13 white, 1 light green, 1 dark green, 1 light green, 3 white, 3 light green, 11 white, 1 light green, 3 white, 2 light green, 3 white, 1 light green, 1 dark green, 1 light green, 10 white, 1 light green, 16 white, 2 light green, 4 white, 2 light green, 16 white, 5 white, 1 light green, 25 white, 1 light green, 6 white, 1 light green, 131 white.

Materials : Two ¼ ounce spools Corticelli Purse Twist, White 1190. Four bunches Crystal Beads, and the following Colored Beads : 655 Dark Green, 965 Light Green, 130 Dark Red, 155 Light Red, 210 Pink, 325 Blue, 37 Yellow. The Purse Twist costs 50 cents per spool, and the beads 25 cents a bunch. The Clasp Top costs $2.50.

The tapestry and needlepoint bags of the early twentieth century are much sought after by collectors. There is an important difference between these two types of work, which is often confused. The early tapestry bags were made from machine woven cloth, or possibly hand woven. The needlepoint, as well as the smaller petit point, was worked on a fine canvas where the pattern or color was individually stitched. These are considered works of art of the finest tradition, sometimes consisting of up to 3,000 stitches per square inch. They almost look as if they were woven! These exquisite petit point bags were often imported from Austria.

The early tapestry bags were sometimes remade from earlier pieces of tapestry hangings. If the bag was made in the late 1800s with a metal frame, it is possible that the cloth used was actually recycled from an earlier peri-od. Then some tapestry bags were made from cloth that was designed specifically for bags. It becomes a mystery to be unraveled. The most reliable way to date a purse of this type is to study the frame for any markings; even today some pretty believable copies are being made. One is wise not to assume it is an authentic antique until the piece has been carefully studied.

A woman's skill in needlework was the mark of a refined woman. She could study and practice the arts, whether it be lace-making, needlepoint, crocheting, cross-stitch, or quilting. Despite running a household, the lady of the house took great pride in her needlework. Magazines of the day reflected this interest and almost every issue had new patterns to work or patterns that could be ordered for as little as 10 cents, such as the two examples.

CROCHET AND TATTING   Series No. 9

FIGURE 4

Venetian Lace Crocheted Bag
Cordonnet Cotton Nos. 3, 5, 15, White or Ecru

1st row. 6 ch, 1 s into the 1st ch to close ring.

2d row. 6 ch, 1 d into the ring, * 3 ch, 1 d into ring; repeat from * 6 times, 3 ch, 1 sl st into the 3rd ch.

3d row. 1 ch, * 4 s over the next 3 ch; repeat from * 7 times, 1 sl st into the 1st s.

4th row. 6 ch, 1 d into the 2nd s, * 3 ch, 1 d into the 2nd s; repeat from * 14 times, 3 ch, 1 sl st into the 3rd of the 6 ch.

5th row. * 10 ch; turn, 2 s into the 2nd and 3rd ch, 5 d into the next 5 ch, 1 s into the next ch, 1 sl st into the last ch; turn, 1 ch, 1 s into the 1st d, 1 ch, 1 s into the 3rd d, 1 ch, 1 s into the 5th d, 1 ch, 1 s into the last s, 1 sl st into the ch; turn, 1 s into the sl st, 1 s into the s, 5 d into the next 5 st, 1 s into the s, 1 sl st into the 1st ch, 1 sl st into the same 1st ch, 3 s over the next 3 ch of the 4th row, 11 ch, 1 s into the 4th ch to form a p, 8 ch, skip 1 ch, 7 s into the next 7 ch, 4 ch, 1 s into the 1st ch to form a p, 7 s into the next 7 ch, 3 s over the next 3 ch of the 4th row; repeat from * 8 times.

6th row. Work 10 sl st along 1st petal, * 11 ch, 1 s into point of next bar, 11 ch, 1 s into point of next petal; repeat from * 8 times.

7th row. * 3 s into the 1st 3 ch, 4 ch, 1 s into the 1st ch to form a p, skip 1 ch, 3 s into next 3 ch, 1 p, skip 1 ch, 3 s into next 3 ch, 1 s into next s, 1 p, 1 s into the same s, 3 s into the next 3 ch, 1 p, skip 1 ch, 3 s into the next 3 ch, 1 p, skip 1 ch, 3 s into the next 3 ch; repeat from * 8 times. Work another motif and join the two together by working the p of last point as follows: 1 s into the s over the bar, 2 ch, 1 s into the p of the point of the first made motif, 2 ch, 1 s into the 1st ch to form a p, 1 s into the same s. There are four motifs which make the band for the bag. Work two more motifs and join them as explained. For the top of band.

8th row * 1 s into the p of middle point of motif, 11 ch, 1 s into the 3rd p, 5 ch, 1 s into the next p, 19 ch, 1 s into the 2nd p, 11 ch, 1 s into the 2nd p, 5 ch, 1 s into the next p, 5 ch, 1 s into the 2nd p of the next motif, 5 ch, 1 s into

6

Directions for Venetian Lace Crocheted Bag, from Woolco cotton threads, Woolworth Co., early 1900s.

Pu
femin
wome

Clear and gold micro-beaded reticule with metallic rings for drawstring chain, subtle Art Nouveau design, measures 9½" x 6½" with 1" lattice fringe, early 1900s. $200.00 – 300.00.

Burgundy cloth reticule with couched metallic cord, design on both sides, turquoise stone embellishment, measures 6" long by 3" wide, cord handle and metallic tassel, late 1700s. $375.00 – 400.00.

Brown crocheted bag with cut steel bead design, beaded fringe, two metal rods at the top with small chain attached, measures 9" by 2½", mid-Victorian, purchased in London in 1986. $125.00 – 145.00.

Assortment of six miser's bags, crocheted or knitted, plain or with cut steel bead design, some with tassels, all have double rings to separate sides and keep coins secure, average measurement is 13½" to 17" in length, dating from early 1800s to 1860s. $85.00 – 115.00. Note unusual beaded card motif and unusually petit 6" aqua silk bag with gold rings and beads. $115.00 – 195.00.

Large and lovely Art Nouveau bag in vibrant colors of orange, gold, blue, green, lavender micro-beaded drawstring style, measures 11½" x 8½" with 2" tri-color twisted fringe, dating to early 1900s. $395.00 – 495.00.

Pastel micro-beaded bag in rug pattern of blue, pink, green, gold; pink and white enamel frame with pink cabochon kissing closure; long link chain, bag is lined with pocket and mirror, measures 9½" by 7½" with 1½" twisted tri-color fringe, dating to early 1900s. $495.00 – 595.00.

Assemetrical floral pattern, micro-beaded in shades of blue, aqua, green, gold, and browns on black background, embossed metal frame with kissing closure and chain, measuring 11½" x 7½" with 3" lattice fringe, dating to early 1900s. 300.00 – 500.00.

Black beaded background with stylized floral pattern in clear beads, drawstring closure, twisted 1½" fringe, measures 10" by 8½", early 1900s. $475.00 – 550.00. *Courtesy of Hampton Antiques.*

White beaded background with stylized floral pattern in iridescent black beads, sterling silver filigree frame and original chain, measures 9½" x 8", early 1900s. See next photo for the same pattern in reverse colors. $550.00 – 650.00. *Courtesy of Hampton Antiques.*

Metallic gold and silver beaded bag in diamond pattern, metal frame with push-button closure, original peach silk lining with delicate ribbon rose trim, two pockets, a small beveled mirror, measures 7¾" x 5½" with 2½" bead fringe, early 1900s. $195.00 – 275.00.

Close-up of frame and bead design; note the small strands of beads twisted over the frame to cover the sewing holes.

Metallic gold, silver, and pink abstract design in micro beads, pale yellow silk lining with original tiny coin purse attached, small cloth label reads "Made in France," floral embossed metal frame stamped "Made in France," double chain, dating to early 1900s. $200.00 – 450.00.

Micro-beaded scenic purse from Venice, original lining and pocket, cloth label reads "Made in Italy, hand knitted," mosaic frame, measures 7½" x 5" with 1½" twisted tri-color bead fringe, purchased originally from T. A. Chapman Co., Milwaukee by Mrs. H. J. Droppers (name is engraved on inside frame), dates to early 1920s. $425.00 – 550.00.

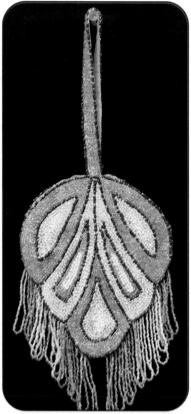

Dainty dance bag in pink and white beading, beaded hand strap, silk lined, measures 5½" by 4¾" with 2" fringe, 1920s. $125.00 – 145.00.

Deep blue carnival glass beaded wrist bag with long beaded loops and tassel, measures 5" by 3½", matching beaded, tasseled belt, measures 68" in length, early 1900s. Set, $225.00 – 275.00.

Figural beaded bag with peacock resting on column, rose accents, both sides the same, embossed metal frame and chain, measures 7" x 6¼" with 2½" twisted bead fringe. $350.00 – 450.00.

Variety of gold beaded bags: top, round in amber colored central swirl pattern, measures 5" with 2½" beaded fringe (note the one red signature bead); right, gold bugle beaded with embossed metal frame, measures 6½" x 6" with 2" fringe; left, gold shag in three tiers of looped fringe, filigree frame, measures 7" by 4½", 1910 – 1920s. $100.00 – 150.00 each.

Variety of colors: top, lime green with vertical loop fringe, embossed and filigree frame, measures 6" x 8"; right, royal blue diamond shaped bag, lined and attached to two plastic rings which slip over the arm for dancing, measures 6" x 6" with 3¼" looped beaded fringe; left, orange beaded with loop fringe below the frame, measures 8" x 7", 1910 – 1920s. $125.00 – 185.00 each.

Black beaded clutch with cut-steel beaded floral design, curved top with zipper closure, lined with small pocket, label reads, "Handmade in Belgium," ruffled effect on bottom, measures 6" x 8½", 1940 – 1950. $35.00 – 55.00.

Copper colored bead design over tapestry type cloth with embossed gold washed frame, small ring-pull and push-button closure, double handle with small bow detail on each side, measures 10" x 11", 1940s. $45.00 – 75.00.

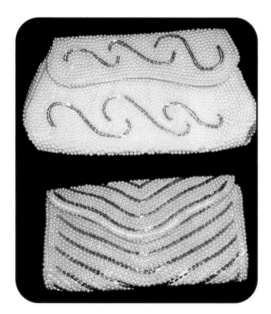

Two examples of small pearl clutch bags with silver bugle bead design, both snap closures and "Made in Hong Kong" labels, average measurement 4" x 7", 1950s. $15.00 – 35.00 each.

Three examples of evening clutch bags: top, blue velvet faux weave design with zipper closure and jeweled zipper pull, measures 5" x 9"; gold sequin and beaded envelope style clutch bag with snap closure, lined with pocket, measures 4½" x 8"; white beaded clutch bag with kissing closure, satin lined, "Made in Hong Kong," late 1950s – 1960s. $15.00 – 20.00 each.

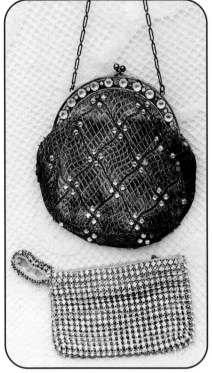

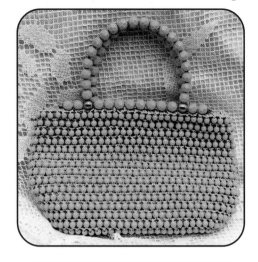

Rhinestone evening bags: top, rhinestones are set with prongs on silver woven fabric (tarnished), rhinestone embellished metal frame, elongated chain indicates 1920s or earlier, measures 6" x 6"; bottom, very glittery rhinestone clutch bag with small loop carrying handle, top zipper closure, rhinestones are set with prongs, measures 3½" x 5", 1930s. $75.00 – 125.00 each.

Lime green plastic beaded handbag with double handle, lined, measures 7" x 10½", 1950s. $10.00 – 15.00.

Austrian figural fine petit point of lady and gentleman in field surrounded by garlands, enameled and jeweled frame, amethyst cabochon push-button closure, original lining, measures 7" x 7", dating to early 1900s. $300.00 – 400.00.

Reverse side depicting a castle with bridge over stream through a field with trees and bushes, garland embellishes the outside edges, notice the frame is simpler on the back than the front.

Art Nouveau tapestry bag in brown tones with fabulous silver frame depicting lady with flowing hair and outstretched arms on both sides, chain handle, measures 6¾" x 8", 1910 – 1915. $200.00 – 275.00.

Two examples of tambour embroidery, probably French: top, curve-top black faille with pastel tambour embroidery, jeweled closure on frame, two jeweled links in chain, measures 4¾" x 3", early 1900s; bottom, envelope clutch bag with pastel tambour embroidery on black faille, snap closure, measures 5½" x 7¾", 1930s. Smaller bag, $125.00 – 220.00; clutch bag, $75.00 – 100.00.

Interior detail of smaller bag above, showing silk lining with two shirred pockets, one for the coin purse and one for the small round beveled mirror.

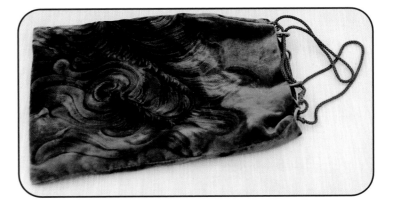

Drawstring turquoise silk velvet bag with feather design on front, small rings with cord for handle, lined, measures 9" x 7", early 1900s. $55.00 – 85.00.

Macrame cord bag with original red and blue silk ribbons, cord fringe and handle, lined in pink cotton, handmade, measures 11" x 5½", early 1900s. $45.00 – 75.00.

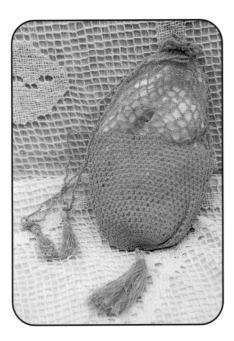

Dainty pink cotton crochet bag, open pattern on top, with crocheted cord and tassels, measures 8" x 7", early 1900s. $25.00 – 45.00.

Two examples of ecru cotton crochet bags, both unlined: left, "pineapple" design with ball fringe and ball tassels, measures 9" x 8", right, filet crochet design, measures 8½" x 8½", early 1900s. $35.00 – 75.00.

Arts and crafts linen purse in primary colors of embroidery, plain gold-tone frame and chain handle, lined in cotton, measures 7¼" x 8¼", 1910 – 1920. $65.00 – 100.00.

Art Deco geometric brocade evening bag in green tones with elaborate flip-up closure of stylized leaves, frosted glass embellishment, stamped on lining, "Florence DeGorog," original comb and mirror, 1930s. $130.00 – 175.00.

Black crocheted gimp purse attached to a hinged plastic frame that has birds on each side, measures 9" x 11", a style that was often made at home by kit, late 1930s – early 1940s. $25.00 – 45.00.

Drawstring dark green felt purse, scalloped edge, cut out three-dimensional flowers attached with embroidery and beads, measures 14½" x 14", 1940s. $25.00 – 35.00.

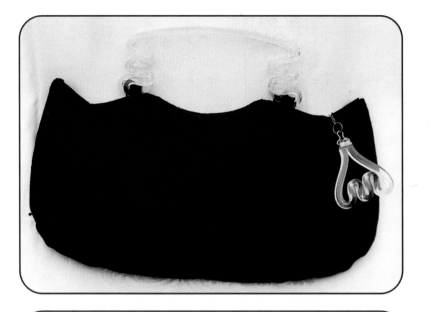

Black corded handbag with decorative Lucite double handle and zipper pull, measures 7½" x 15", 1940s. $55.00 – 95.00.

Charming floral cloth purse with Bakelite frame, self fabric loop handle attached to clasp, lined, with matching coin purse and mirror holder, measures 9" x 8", 1940s. $35.00 – 55.00.

Reversible rose/cream cotton rayon purse with crystal frame, self fabric double handles, never used, "new-old" with original hangtags, measures 7" x 9", late 1940s – early 1950s. $45.00 – 65.00.

Crocheted drawstring bag in gray and cranberry cotton thread, measures 9" x 12", handmade, 1940s. $15.00 – 25.00.

Similar to bottom right photo page 247, crocheted in metallic thread with colored wooden beads, drawstrings has metal tips, 1940s. $15.00 – 25.00.

Gold cotton crocheted drawstring bag, long cord with crocheted tassels on the ends, inside tag reads "Chateay, hand made crochet, Made in China," measures 12" x 11", retro bag dating to 1960s – 1970s. $15.00 – 20.00.

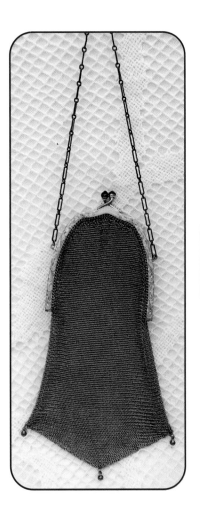

Gold-wash mesh purse with etched gold cathedral dome frame, kissing clasp set with sapphire cabochons, frame etched with "Etta M. Walker, Bloomington, Ill." on one side and the makers mark, "Whiting & Davis Co., soldered mesh," numbered 6021 on the other side of frame, three metal drops on bottom, measures 6½" x 4", 1910 – 1920s. $200.00 – 300.00.

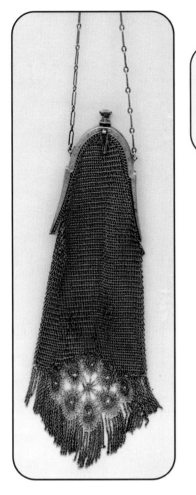

Gold mesh bag with etched cathe-dral dome frame, turn lock clasp, marked "Whiting & Davis Co.," embellished with open lace pattern and fringe, measures 8½" x 4", dates to 1910 – 1920s. $195.00 – 250.00.

Mesh compact-purse, etched compact measures 4" x 2½" includes mirror, space for coins, powder compartment, attached mesh measures 4" x 6" with open lace effect fringe, some damage to mesh, 1920s. $95.00 – 145.00.

Variety of Whiting & Davis mesh bags: top, gold finish, plain frame, measures 5" x 4½"; left, silver finish with small rhinestones on frame, measures 5" x 6"; bottom, white enamel mesh with gold frame and rhinestone flip-up clasp, measures 5" x 5", 1920 – 1930s. $55.00 – 85.00 each. (Added to my collection in memory of my dear friend, Donna Rae).

Silver mesh bag with lovely Art Nouveau frame marked "German silver," measures 6½" x 5", 1910 – 1920s. $75.00 – 95.00.

Enameled metal mesh bag with stylized birds and floral design, pointed fringe, cathedral embossed frame marked "Mandalian Mfg. Co.," measures 7¾" x 3½", 1920s. $225.00 – 265.00.

Silver-tone mesh bag with coral, green, and black enameled deco design, mesh fringe, interesting silver frame marked "Whiting & Davis," measures 6½" x 4", 1920s. $185.00 – 245.00.

Silver mesh bag, lined, marked "Whiting & Davis" with original box, measures 4½" x 4½", 1920s. $75.00 – 145.00.

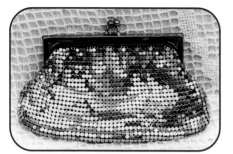

Gold-tone finish mesh coin purse, snap closure, marked "Whiting & Davis," measures 3" x 5½", lined, with extension chain for key, 1920 – 1930s. $30.00 – 60.00.

Interior view with detail of extension chain that pulls out for key and automatically retracts.

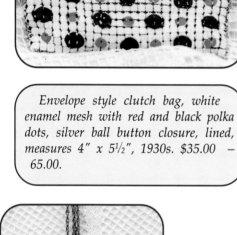

Envelope style clutch bag, white enamel mesh with red and black polka dots, silver ball button closure, lined, measures 4" x 5½", 1930s. $35.00 – 65.00.

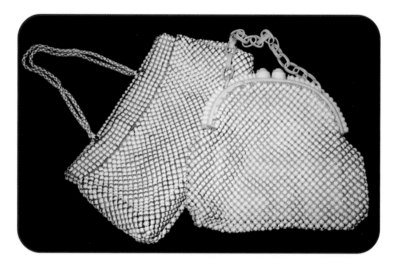

Two examples of alumesh handbags: left, large aluminum beadlite enamel mesh with zipper closure, double alumesh handle, navy lining with inside pocket, measures 6¼" x 11", label reads, "Alumesh Bags, Whiting & Davis Co.," 1940s; right, aluminum beadlite enamel with decorative celluloid frame and chain handle, measures 9½" x 7¼", label reads "Whiting & Davis Co., 1930s. $45.00 – 85.00 each.

Large scale gold-tone mesh pouch purse with loops and long chain handle, lined, label inside marked "Whiting & Davis," measures 9" x 8", 1960s. $25.00 – 35.00.

Black leather handbag with intricate turn lock clasp, rigid handle, inside is written, "M. Uzafovage, Tacoma, Wa.," measures 4¼" x 9", early 1900s. $35.00 – 65.00.

Black smooth leather, metal frame is hand painted with flowers, flip-up clasp, single handle, measures 11" x 10", 1930s. $40.00 – 65.00.

Two examples of arts and crafts leather handbags: top, leather envelope style, floral design imprinted with snap closure, maker "Bosca Built" stamped inside on pocket, top strap handle, whip-stitched with leather lacing, measures 5¼" x 8¾"; bottom, leather handbag with gold-tone frame and turn-lock pull, embossed floral design, leather strap handle with leather lacing, measures 7" x 6½", 1915 – 1920s. $110.00 – 165.00.

Brown alligator purse with real baby alligator head and legs on front flap, snap closure, adjustable shoulder strap, measures 6" x 9", 1940s. $75.00 – 95.00.

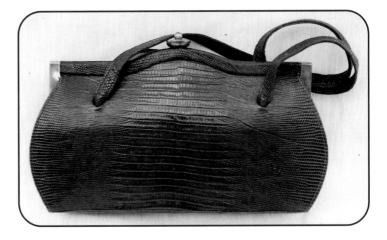

Brown lizard rigid purse with double handles, gold-tone clip closure, measures 5½" x 10¼", 1950s – early 1960s. $55.00 – 85.00.

Two examples of snake skin handbags: top, classic 1950s shape with single handle, inside pocket, label reads "Andrew Geller," measures 7¼" x 10½"; bottom, rigid box purse with single strap handle, top clip closure, measures 6" x 7½" 1940s. $65.00 – 150.00.

Mustard suede handbag, with double handles, zipper top closure, measures 7" x 12", 1960s. $25.00 – 45.00.

White faux leather with black paten trim, adjustable handle, snap closure on flap, measures 8½" x 10", 1960s. $15.00 – 35.00.

Satchel style leather handbag with multicolored jungle animals, zipper closure, double handles, measures 9" x 10½", 1980s. $15.00 – 20.00.

Two examples of vinyl handbags: top, forest green, gold-tone frame with clip closure and single handle, divider inside with pocket, measures 10" by 11½"; bottom, pink with gold-tone frame, clip closure, black rayon lining with zippered pocket, stamped "Theodor California," measures 4½" by 13½", 1960s, $15.00 – 30.00.

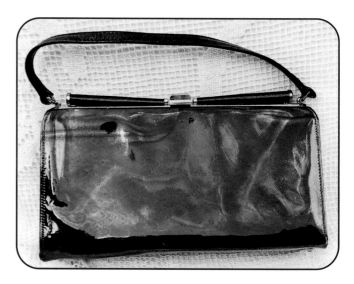

Iridescent vinyl handbag, clip closure, single handle, measures 6" x 1¾", 1960s. $15.00 – 25.00.

Beige plastic hatbox style purse, four metallic decorations with rhinestones on front, clip closure, rigid handle, "Wilardy" stamped on hinge, measures 7½" x 7¼" x 3½", 1950s. $125.00 – 145.00.

Rigid box style purse with black plastic top and molded handle, silver and gold-tone metallic basketweave sides, measures 8" x 4¼" x 3¾", 1960s. $75.00 – 85.00.

Rigid metallic basketweave purse, metallic handle, lined in black rayon, measures 9" x 8", 1960s. $55.00 – 65.00.

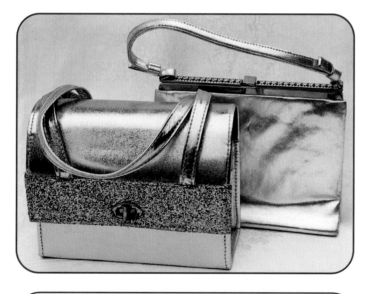

Two examples of evening bags: front, gold box-type bag with gold glitter on front flap, twist button closure, double handles, measures 7" x 8"; back, silver with rhinestone and silver frame, single handle, marked "After Five," measures 6¼" x 8¼", both 1960s. $15.00 – 35.00.

Beige rigid bucket-type purse with blue/green jeweled and sequined peacock motif, faux leather trim, double handles, twist button closure, wood bottom, measures 10¾" x 12" x 3½", 1960s. $15.00 – 25.00.

Floral tapestry type fabric on rigid handbag, gold-tone frame, single handle, label reads, "Vendi, Made in USA," measures 8" x 12½" x 4", 1960s. $15.00 – 45.00.

Rigid plastic clutch bag resembling a folded magazine reads, "1978 Spring/Summer Home Improvements" showing a backyard garden, white leather strap wraps around and snaps for closure, black rayon lining, measures 5" x 12", late 1970s. $29.00 – 45.00.

Cut velvet multicolor design, gold-tone frame with clip closure, long chain can double, measures 9" x 8½" 1980s. $10.00 – 19.00.

Two examples of shell purses: right, mother-of-pearl with silver filigree trim, red silk compartments (found with the blond lock of hair inside), measures 3" x 2½"; left, polished mussel shell purse with small silver hinge on bottom, clasp and tiny chain, divided into three inner compartments, probably a seaside souvenir purse, measures 4½" x 2", late Victorian. $55.00 – 75.00.

Three examples of vanity bags: front, black enamel double necessaire with gold-tone trim and carrying chain, push button closures open both sides, measures 2½" x 3½" x 1½"; top right, gold-tone/rhinestone sunburst designed minaudière, push button closure opens two compartments, small carrying chain, measures 3½" x 5½"; top left, gold-tone basket weave minaudiére, attached lipstick holder, snake carrying chain, measures 3" x 4", 1940s. $55.00 – 110.00.

Detail with vanity bags in open position showing the compartments for powder, money clip, mirror, comb, and hankies.

258

Photo Credit: 2000© Chris Bryant

Stepping Out in Style. Captivating hosiery and shoes made for dancing.

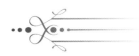

*I*f you only had the ruby red sequined shoes worn by Dorothy in the *Wizard of Oz*, you would have known that you have always had the power. If you only had a pair of glass slippers (with the tiniest feet in the kingdom) you would have Prince Charming. Shoes have given the illusion of power. And shoes have also meant constraint and restriction. Just ask a Venetian lady in the 1600s how fast she could run in a chopine. These pedestal-type shoes meant walking on platforms that might range from 6 inches to the ridiculous height of 30 inches, not exactly what is meant by being put on a pedestal. Or ask a Chinese lady of the 1800s how far she could walk in the embroidered satin lotus shoes, three inches long, common for the ladies of high society who had their feet bound at an early age to retain the much sought after delicate small foot. Shoes have always made a fashion statement, even though it may not have been what we wanted to hear.

As we move into a new century, let us step back in time to the mid-1800s, and imagine a woman shopping for a pair of shoes. Her skirts were long with layers of petticoats, or perhaps a hoop. If she was of the leisure class she would have ridden in a carriage, therefore would not have been concerned about mud on the train of her skirt or her shoes. But most women would have been walking along unpaved or dirt roads that were wet and muddy, certainly not sidewalks as we know them today. Her requirements for footwear would have been fairly simple, something to keep her clean and dry. Probably the most common footwear would be the low-heeled black boot, high buttoned or laced up. It was practical, keeping her feet clean and dry as she worked and walked to most destinations.

The lady of leisure, however, may have selected a satin pump with beaded ornamentation for her social obligations. Less practical, and worn for indoor functions, her shoes would be shoes of beauty. Or, perhaps a special shoe was needed for her wedding day. These shoes have not stood the test of time as readily as the more common black leather boot that we frequently see.

It was due to the Rational Dress Reform Movement of 1880 that women began to take a serious look at their tight-laced, restrictive clothing. This included the footwear of the time, which brought the lower heel into favor. Beads were used on everything in fashion during the late Victorian period, including bead-embroidered shoes. By 1888 and the disappearance of the bustle, hems were shortened to the ankle, which brought shoes more into focus. Subdued colors in natural tones were popular. As women became more active with sports such as croquet, tennis, and bicycling, their shoes became more practical.

> *"Give a girl the right shoes and she can conquer the world."*
>
> *Bette Midler*

Fancywork, October 1906.

American Lady SHOE

$3.00
$3.50
$4.00

Here is a pump worthy to grace the foot of the daintiest American Lady. Smart enough to set off the smartest tailored gown — dainty enough to perfectly harmonize with the daintiest summer dress. Comfortable enough to please the most tender foot, and like every other

American Lady Shoe

durable enough to please the most economical.

This shoe is No. 6209 — a tan Russia Calf pump with bow of same leather. It is made on the stylish Worth last and has a light welt sole and Cuban heel.

You will find this and many other attractive styles of the American Lady Shoe in our handsomely illustrated booklet. Write for free copy today.

HAMILTON, BROWN SHOE CO., St. Louis

Ladies' Home Journal, June 1908.

$3.00
$3.50
$4.00

o→ *No slipping here*   ▷→ *No bulging here*

A SHOE *should* fit perfectly in whatever position the foot assumes. In a pump there are two tendencies which a shoemaker finds it almost impossible to overcome. These are the slipping at the heel, and the bulging along the top edge. These faults do not exist in the

American Lady SHOE

because the pumps are made on special pump lasts. These lasts are specially designed to produce a comfortable *clinging* pump.

Note the perfectly straight lines (edges) in the small shoe illustrated — then see how perfectly the pump clings to the foot — even when the foot is bent forward in a walking position, as in the larger illustration.

This ankle strap pump is one of this season's newest creations,— the Hebe last. Made in two leathers No. 6241, patent leather with turned sole, and No. 6242 in the swell new Suèdes—London smoke, black and tan, with light welt sole.

The American Lady Shoe, although a leader in fashions, has never sacrificed the fitting qualities for which it is famous. If you have had difficulty in getting a stylish shoe that would fit you and be perfectly comfortable, try the American Lady Shoe.

The latest shoe fashions are fully illustrated in our beautiful new booklet. Send for a free copy today.

Hamilton, Brown Shoe Company,
St. Louis   Boston

Ladies' Home Journal, June 1909.

HOME COMPANION

PUT YOUTH INTO YOUR STEP

Style 28

Foot happiness and foot health are assured when you wear the most famous and easiest shoe ever produced—the

Dr. A. Reed
CUSHION SOLE SHOE
for WOMEN

Don't Endure Foot Troubles

The weight of the body and the constant jar and jolt on the feet in walking, combined so often with the wearing of ill-fitting shoes, are responsible for two-thirds of the foot troubles of womankind.

Letters testifying to the wonderful merits of the Dr. A. Reed Cushion Sole Shoe for Women, on file at our office, are the best proof that the

"Built-In" Lamb's Wool Cushion

invented and patented by Dr. A. Reed, will benefit you as it has thousands upon thousands of others.

It makes a smooth and easy bed, which readily conforms to the shape of the foot. It permits the weight of the body to be evenly distributed, promotes circulation, is a non-conductor of heat and cold; and prevents friction, which is the common cause of corns and bunions.

Style 56-B

The Dr. A. Reed Cushion Sole Shoe has an abundance of style that will appeal to every woman of culture. It is as pleasing to the eye as it is comfortable to the foot.

Write us today for the name of our dealer in your town and "My Lady's Boots"—a beautiful booklet in colors, containing valuable style information, illustrations of our latest models and suggestions for the proper care of the feet.

Showing the "Built-In" Lamb's Wool Cushion

John Ebberts Shoe Co.
202 Clinton St., Buffalo, N.Y.

Exclusive Makers of the Dr. A. Reed Cushion Sole Shoe for Women

Woman's Home Companion, August 1910.

The Delineator, October 1913.

RedCross Shoe
"Bends with your foot"
Trade Mark

Model 317. The newest of the new! Patent leather, long vamp. Spanish-Louis heel.

Model 315. A very dressy plain-toe model of dull kid. Just the shoe for evening wear and very special occasions

Two every-day mistakes in buying shoes

Which have you been making?

WOMEN everywhere have told us of these mistakes—told us they always made them before they found the Red Cross Shoe.

Some made the mistake of sacrificing style to gain that comfort which a tender foot demands.

But most made this mistake—they denied themselves some degree of comfort to have their foot well dressed and *chic*.

Style or Comfort — which of these have you been sacrificing needlessly?

Needlessly, because the Red Cross Shoe combines in highest degree these two great footwear qualities. Tanned by a special process that retains all the natural flexibility of the leather, the snuggest-fitting, most fashionable model in the Red Cross Shoe bends with your foot like a perfect-fitting glove bends with your hand. You will walk with an ease and pleasure you have never known before in a shoe that will be everywhere admired.

Go to your nearest Red Cross dealer and see the smart Fall and Winter models in all the latest leathers and materials. Prices, $3.50 to $5.00.

Write today for the Red Cross Style Book
This book tells what will be worn in shoes this season, and shows the correct models for every occasion and every purpose. Write for your copy today. Address the Krohn-Fechheimer Company, 503-515 Dandridge Street, Cincinnati, Ohio.

Mail Orders
If there is no Red Cross dealer in your town, write for Style Book and we will give you the name of a nearby dealer, or tell you how to order direct. We have fitted 50,000 women by mail and guarantee to fit your foot.

Model 310. Smart walking boot of dull calf with the popular medium low heel.

Look for this trade mark on the sole.

King Edward had a major influence on fashion the first decade of the twentieth century. This period is remembered for ultra feminine fashions, the light and lacy look. The shoe styles of the Edwardian period also lightened up with the new colors of sand, beige, bronze, gray, and taupe. The new turned or reversed calf, chamoised buck or antelope leathers proved very popular in the first two decades. This suede finish was also applied to lamb, goat, and kid for shoes. The dance craze, specifically the tango, had begun in 1912 and was responsible for the fancy beaded and bejeweled slippers of this period. Often evening shoes were of the same fabric as the gown, or simply black or bronze satin with cut-steel, jet, marcasite, or rhinestone buckles.

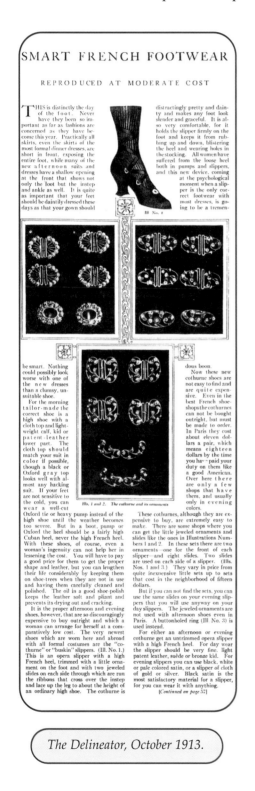

The Delineator, October 1913.

Ladies' Home Journal, September 1915.

Ladies' Home Journal, June 1918.

Pictorial Review for September, 1922

Bellas Hess & Co.
Announce That YOUR Copy of the New Fall and Winter Catalog is Now Ready

Send for it NOW! It's FREE

Latest and Best New York Styles —Lowest Prices in America!

Our fur Scarf 29M11 $11.98

Compare These Prices

Our Waists from	98c up
Our Dresses from	$1.98 up
Our Suits from	$9.98 up
Our Coats from	$5.98 up
Our Sweaters from	98c up
Our Boys' Clothing from	$1.98 up
Our Girls' Dresses from	98c up

And a complete line of all other wearing apparel at Money-Saving Prices

Stylish Embroidered Dress

Dress $6.98

35M10 All Wool Velour Dress

Genuine Dyed Fox Scarf

$2.89 Goodyear Welt Postage FREE

The Flapper Mahogany Calf Goodyear Welt

241 Styles of Shoes in Our New Fall & Winter Style Book—Latest Lasts~Big Values!

$2.98 Goodyear Welt Postage FREE

$2.65 Goodyear Welt Postage FREE

Lowest Prices in Country

Genuine Kid, Brown or Black Genuine Goodyear Welt

Genuine Kidskin Genuine Goodyear Welt

24-Hour Service **Bellas Hess & Co** Satisfaction or Your Money Refunded
WASHINGTON, MORTON & BARROW STS
NEW YORK CITY, N.Y

BELLAS HESS & CO., New York City, N. Y.
Gentlemen:—Please send me your FREE Catalog of New York's Latest Styles.
NAME
STREET
TOWN   STATE

Sport shoes for summer were white buck or linen. For tennis and yachting women wore a flat rubber-soled white canvas tie shoe. About 1915 the white buckskin shoes were strapped with black or brown leather — and the saddle oxford was the new fashion. Women were becoming more active as they sought the right to vote, and their shoes reflected this trend with less restrictive slip-on styles.

World War I created a scarcity in leather, leaving only suede and patent leather for the civilian shoes. Rising hem-lines meant the shoe would be more visible and shoe styles even more important. The neutral tones gave way to color-matching an ensemble, and we see aqua, lime green, and salmon tones in the 1920s. The variety of styles and colors meant more shoes in the wardrobe, instead of the basic black work boot and brown leather day shoe. It was also during this period that we see gracefully curved Louis heels encrusted with rhinestones, that could often be purchased separately to replace the self heel.

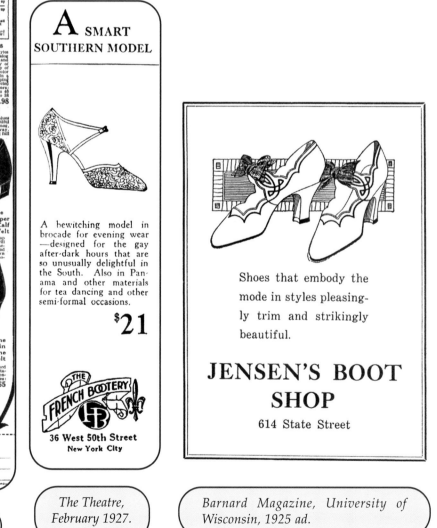

A SMART SOUTHERN MODEL

A bewitching model in brocade for evening wear —designed for the gay after-dark hours that are so unusually delightful in the South. Also in Panama and other materials for tea dancing and other semi-formal occasions.

$21

THE FRENCH BOOTERY
36 West 50th Street
New York City

Shoes that embody the mode in styles pleasingly trim and strikingly beautiful.

JENSEN'S BOOT SHOP
614 State Street

Pictorial Review, September 1922.

The Theatre, February 1927.

Barnard Magazine, University of Wisconsin, 1925 ad.

Foot Saver Shoes

keep the feet young
and the ankles slender

The Maritza

The Chase

ALL women are young in the summer sunlight. All feet are younger in Foot Saver Shoes ⸱ ⸱ ⸱ Their charming individual designs are expressions of the youthful spirit of the mode, the spirit of the smartest Summer costume ⸱ ⸱ ⸱ But Foot Saver Shoes mean so much more. They mean *young, slim ankles,* curving to youthful contours beyond ⸱ ⸱ ⸱ For they conceal a patented in-built construction that equalizes the movement of the muscles ⸱ ⸱ ⸱ Over-development is impossible. With strain eliminated, the lines of ankle and leg are modified, refined to suave contours of natural grace ⸱ ⸱ ⸱ And feet flawlessly shod, perfectly fitted, released from fatigue, are exuberantly young.

Send for Free Style Booklet and Name of Your Nearest Dealer

The Delineator, August 1928.

AT YOUR FEET

Two types — practical shoes that are now "sensible" in the smartest way, and the new trimmed shoes which believe in being pretty

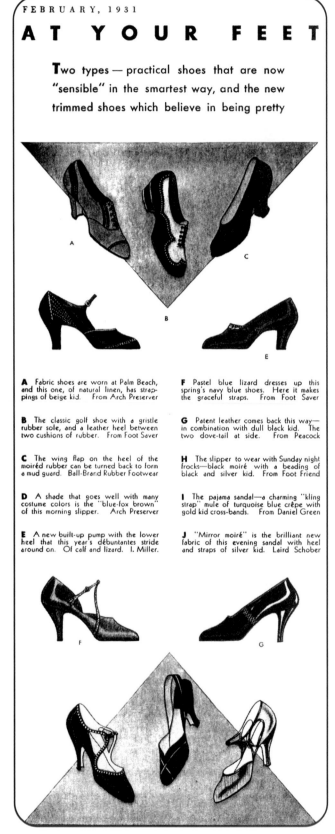

A Fabric shoes are worn at Palm Beach, and this one, of natural linen, has strappings of beige kid.   From Arch Preserver

B The classic golf shoe with a gristle rubber sole, and a leather heel between two cushions of rubber. From Foot Saver

C The wing flap on the heel of the moiréd rubber can be turned back to form a mud guard. Ball-Brand Rubber Footwear

D A shade that goes well with many costume colors is the "blue-fox brown" of this morning slipper.   Arch Preserver

E A new built-up pump with the lower heel that this year's débuntantes stride around on. Of calf and lizard. I. Miller.

F Pastel blue lizard dresses up this spring's navy blue shoes. Here it makes the graceful straps. From Foot Saver

G Patent leather comes back this way— in combination with dull black kid. The two dove-tail at side.   From Peacock

H The slipper to wear with Sunday night frocks—black moiré with a beading of black and silver kid. From Foot Friend

I The pajama sandal—a charming "kling strap" mule of turquoise blue crêpe with gold kid cross-bands. From Daniel Green

J "Mirror moiré" is the brilliant new fabric of this evening sandal with heel and straps of silver kid. Laird Schober

The Delineator, February 1931.

Along with the imaginative variety of shoe fashion in the 1920s, coordinating purses, gloves, and shoes became important in women's attire. In the mid twenties the Charleston dance fad was all the rage, creating the shoe of the same name, which had two eyelets laced with a ribbon that tied. Exotic fabrics and designs followed, metal tissues in gold and silver being very popular for evening. More innovations followed with the platform backless shoes, and shoes of plaited or woven rafia in bright colors for the beach. Open-toed sandals became the play shoe of 1934, with wedge soles appearing in 1937.

McCalls, March 1937.

Mademoiselle, April 1942.

Mademoiselle, April 1942, most styles $7.95.

Mademoiselle, April 1942 ad with "duty-ful work to win" appeal for WWII.

Mademoiselle, April 1942, early Tweedies ad.

Mademoiselle, April 1942, early DeLiso Debs ad.

In 1943 the World War II restrictions rationed two pairs of new shoes a year per person. Since military use claimed 40 percent of the leather, leather shoes were limited and soles were thinner. Because of these wartime restrictions, a successful synthetic sole made of cotton fiber, reclaimed rubber, and plastic was developed which outlasted the best rubber soles.

Reptiles and Platforms

LEADING STYLES THIS YEAR are luxurious reptiles deftly styled and expertly crafted for season after season wear; and new, higher platforms coordinated with beautiful leathers to set each other off to best advantage.

GENUINE LIZARD HANDBAG

[F] SMART COMPANION FOR LIZARD SHOES... Skillfully fashioned from imported skins carefully selected for beauty and durability. Top handle style. Envelope closing has gold-color metal lift lock. Softly shirred front. Inside zipper compartment. Frame coin purse. Roomy. Lined. Other handbag selections on Pages 212 through 216. Abt. 11 x 6 inches. Ship. wt. 1 lb. 6 oz. Price includes 20% Federal Tax.
20 C 4441T—Brown only 28.50

WIDTH EXPLANATION FOR THESE TWO PAGES

Width AAA ....Extra Narrow
Width AA ....Very Narrow
Width A ....Narrow
Width B ....Medium Narrow
Width C ....Medium

Be sure the style you want comes in your correct width and size. If you are not sure of your shoe size, turn to Page 226 for How to Measure Instructions. All the shoes on this page are mailed to you from Chicago. Send your order to and allow postage from Wards nearest Mail Order House.

[G] GENUINE LIZARD ENVELOPE PUMP. The distinction of fine reptile styled with smart simplicity in every line — a perfect combination for your day and date-time best. Rich Mahogany Brown, Black or brilliant Red Lizard is light weight, yet amazingly sturdy. Leather sole, 2⅝-inch heel.
Width AA in Whole and Half Sizes: 6 to 9.
Width B in Whole and Half Sizes: 5 to 9.
Ship. wt. 1 lb. 3 oz. State width and size.
23 C 1052T—Brown.
23 C 1053T—Black.
23 C 1054T—Red............Pair 9.95

[K] PLATFORM SANDAL. Platform is really high... with a slim ankle strap that winds 'round your ankle. In Black Patent Leather with a patent covered platform or Black Suede Leather with a Suede Leather covered platform. Leather sole. 3-in. heel.
Width AAA in Whole and Half Sizes: 6 to 9.
Width AA in Whole and Half Sizes: 6 to 9.
Width A in Whole and Half Sizes: 5½ to 9.
Width B in Whole and Half Sizes: 4½ to 9.
Ship. wt. 1 lb. 5 oz. State width and size.
23 C 1063T—Black Patent.
23 C 1064T—Black Suede......Pair 15.95

[H] GENUINE LIZARD ENVELOPE SANDAL designed in striking colors... Mahogany Brown, brilliant Red or sparkling Emerald Green. Skillfully cut low vamp complements and sets off the genuine Reptile that keeps its shape and retains its sparkling glow. Flexible leather sole, slim 2⅝-inch heel.
Width AA in Whole and Half Sizes: 6 to 9.
Width B in Whole and Half Sizes: 5 to 9.
Ship. wt. 1 lb. 2 oz. State width and size.
23 C 1055T—Brown.
23 C 1056T—Red.
23 C 1057T—Green..........Pair 9.95

[L] PLATFORM PUMP. The classic sling Pump with a new Genuine Reptile covered platform. Platforms have always been noted for their flattery. Black Suede Leather or Black Plastic Patent that won't crack or peel, each with a Black Reptile covered platform. Buckle at side is adjustable. Flexible leather sole and 2⅜-in. heel.
Width AA in Whole and Half Sizes: 6 to 9.
Width B in Whole and Half Sizes: 4 to 9.
Ship. wt. 1 lb. 4 oz. State width and size.
23 C 1062T—Black Suede.
23 C 1061T—Black Plastic Patent..Pr. 9.95

[J] GENUINE LIZARD CROSSBAND. Its open-to-the-air style co...and sets off fine reptile ma...best advantage. Made in mello...Brown, Brilliant Red or de...Blue Lizard that is lightweight...ple, yet holds its shape and...glow. Leather sole, 2¼-in...Width AA in Whole and Half Si...Width B in Whole and Half Siz...
23 C 1058T—Med. Brown. Ship. w...
23 C 1059T—Red. State width, si...
23 C 1060T—Navy..........Po...

[M] HIGH-CUT AND SOPHISTICAT...higher platform to underscore...beauty. Note clever way perfor...and accent vamp. Soft Calfsk...Brown or Black...each with...ered platform. Leather sole. 2¼...Width AAA in Whole, Half Siz...Width AA in Whole, Half Siz...Width A in Whole, Half Sizes:...Width B in Whole, Half Sizes:...Ship. wt. 1 lb. 5 oz. State width...
23 C 1066T—Brown.
23 C 1065T—Black..........P...

1947 Wards catalog, platform ankle strap retailing for $15.95.

269

The 1950s produced the 4" stiletto, the extreme in narrow pointed toes, and the dainty "spring-o-lator." The rebellious 1960s lowered the tottering heel of the previous decade; and according to *The Observer* in 1968, "Sensible shoes and fashionable shoes no longer mean two different things." The Dr. Scholl's wooden base slip-on sandal appeared in 1969. It was the early 1970s that brought back the platform shoe to the extreme, a decidedly clunky look. The most profound change in style was the sports shoe of the 1980s, worn everywhere and with anything, even to the office, replacing the earlier feminine look of classic pumps. One can only guess what strides will be made in shoe fashion this next century!

> *"The shoe fits ... and we can finally wear it."*
>
> *Mayde Lebensfeld, foot specialist*

Notes

* *

- One pair of Dorothy's red sequined shoes from *The Wizard of Oz* sold for $165,000.00.
- By the time you were one year old, your foot was half of its adult size.
- Each foot has 26 bones, one-fourth of all the bones in your body.
- The average person takes 8,000 steps a day.
- In our lifetime we probably walk about 115,000 miles, half way to the moon.
- In the early 1900s, most kids did not wear shoes, except in cold climates.
- In the 1700s, men were granted a divorce if lured into marriage by a woman wearing high heels.
- In medieval Europe the bride's father gave her shoe to the groom to symbolize the transfer to her new family.
- Old shoes were tied to the bumper of a newly wed couple's car to symbolize fertility.
- The simple inexpensive wooden clog was worn for almost six centuries in northern Europe, until about 1915.
- The basic oxford had 47 variations offered by Buster Brown in 1949.
- The all-leather, laced-up boot of the 1860s cost about $5.50.

Shoes reveal much about us individually and as a culture, whether it is the tiny delicate lotus shoes of the Chinese woman with bound feet, or the laced-up Victorian boot concealed beneath a froth of frillies. Shoes reveal our practical nature as well as our frivolous and fanciful desires. As we accessorize, shoes can be sexy, feminine, and provocative elements. Shoes are also necessary for protection, warmth, and for getting us to our destinations. So what is it about shoes that is almost magical in their transformation of the little girl lost in Oz to the empowered Dorothy who can conquer fear? Why are some shoes just a natural show stopper for the Prince? The shoes that follow are some of my personal favorites, worn by the average woman in America over the past century and a half.

Hosiery

brief word about hosiery. Originally hosiery, utilitarian in nature, was worn in the fifteenth and sixteenth centuries to cover the foot, leg, and all the way to the waist. Stockings came about in 1660 when the lower part was divided from the upper part, creating two stockings. Queen Elizabeth I was the first to wear knitted silk hose.

During the late Victorian era, stockings were often matched to the shade of the gown for evening, and by day white or light-colored hose, generally of a thin lisle. Silk was reserved for the very wealthy. The fine lisle thread was first made in Lille, France; however, the name was taken from the original spelling of an old Flemish town. Lisle is actually combed Egyptian cotton that was made fine and silky by a mercerizing process.

"I have reached an age when, if someone tells me to wear socks, I don't have to."

Albert Einstein

When the bright silk petticoats were popular in shades of purple or red, it was fashionable to have stockings that matched. The Gay Nineties also led to the candy-striped hose, either circling around or in vertical stripes, as well as other patterns.

Starting in the 1880s, sheer black hose was considered de rigueur and most appropriate. This vogue for black held its own until the 1920s, when hemlines began to reveal more leg. It was suggested by a fashion magazine of 1915 that stockings of a delicate stripe would be permissible with the new saddle oxford. It was further suggested that plaid or polka dot stockings with plain shoes would be in good taste. For evening, stockings of gold or silver were worn with the fashionable lamé dance slippers.

Ladies' Home Journal, July 1903, silk embroidered lisle lace hose.

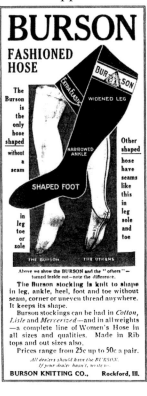

Ladies' Home Journal, June 1901, prices 25 – 50¢ a pair.

Princess Chic

TRADE MARK REGISTERED

SIX STRAP — **FIGURE SHAPER**

Demanded by Present Styles — Perfect Support Perfect Comfort

Gives better results in figure shaping than the new corsets, at a trifle of their cost.

The only device that healthfully supports instead of dragging on the muscles of the back.

At leading stores or direct from the makers if you don't find them.

Price $1.00 for 6-strap as illustrated. 4-strap style, 50c. Colors, black, white and blue. Give waist measure in ordering.

A. STEIN & CO., 319 W. Congress St., Chicago

Ladies' Home Journal, June 1909, Princess Chic garter belt ad.

Real beauty and long wear combine to make Ipswich quality.

And this is the way we get both beauty and service:

We command the skill that can only be acquired by nearly half-a-century of good stocking-making. We are particular to get first-choice cotton with long, strong fibre. We spin our own yarn, knit on the latest machines, and dye the stockings by a costly process that produces rich fast color.

This makes the Ipswich quality that thousands have insisted on for years. See that *you* insist on Ipswich Hosiery if you expect to get such high quality at anywhere near the price.

12½c to 25c a pair for men, women, and children

If your dealer can't supply you write us his name. We'll send you the **handsomest hosiery booklet ever issued**, and we'll see that you get the stockings.

IPSWICH MILLS
Ipswich, Mass.

Ladies' Home Journal, June 1910, Ipswich Hosiery.

The hosiery for women who wish to please

McCallum Silk Hosiery

We make a specialty of matching to any sample in style 153. The best dealers in your city will furnish you the goods within a few days. This is a great convenience, considering the variety of color effects now in vogue.

The best silk hosiery in the world for men, women and children, at prices upward from $1.00.

Send for Booklet "Through My Lady's Ring"

McCallum Hosiery Company
Northampton, Mass.

The Delineator, October 1913, McCallum silk hosiery.

March, 1912

The appearance of a stocking depends as much upon its durability as upon its quality. The neat, trim, attractive appearance of the ankle is more important in this day of short, scant skirts than it was. As the feet become prominent, smart dressing of them becomes necessary.

Gordon HOSIERY

Gordon Hosiery for women (it is made also for men and children) offers at the accepted popular prices unusually attractive stockings in colors to match gowns, or in plain black, in cotton, lisle, silk-and-lisle, and silk, of wonderful sheerness and durability. The reinforced heel and toe and garter hem make Gordon Hosiery wear, while the fineness and delicacy of the weaving and the beauty of the colors make it the most attractive.

"The name of a garment you have worn and tried, is like the name of a friend that you know."

Illustrated catalog sent on request

Brown Durrell Co

Brown Durrell Building
17 West 19th Street, New York
Brown Durrell Building, Boston

Women's Ex-Wide Gordon Silk Hosiery
300Ex Extra Wide Pure Silk, with silk lisle top and sole, high spliced heel, made extra wide, black, white and tan. $1.25
706 Ingrain Thread Silk, wide hem top, cotton sole, made extra wide, black, white and tan. $1.50

Women's Gordon Silk Lisle Hosiery
717 Gauze weight, spliced garter top, high spliced heel, 4-thread toes, black, white and colors. 25c
496 ROUND TICKET* silk lisle, medium weight, wide hem top, 4-thread heel and toe, black, white and tan. 25c
323 Light weight, wide hem top, double sole, high spliced heel, black and tan. 35c
111 Extra Gauze, wide hem top, heavily spliced, black, white and tan. 50c
333 Medium weight, wide hem top, perfection in 50c hosiery, black, white and colors. 50c
515l Medium weight, wide hem top, extra wide, heavily spliced, black, white and tan. 50c

Women's Gordon Silk Hosiery
250 Pure Thread Silk Boot, cotton top and soles, high spliced heel, black, white and colors. 50c
300 Pure Silk, with silk lisle top and sole, high spliced heel, black, white and colors. $1.00
319 Ingrain Thread Silk, silk lisle top and sole, high spliced heel, black, white and colors. $1.00
500 Ingrain Thread Silk, all silk, wide hem top, silk sole, high heel, black, white and colors. $1.50

Men's Half Hose—Silk
173 Thread Silk, cotton sole, black and colors. 35c
176 Light weight, cotton sole, high heel, black and colors. 50c
183 Heavy weight, cotton sole, high heel, black and colors. 50c
190 Medium weight, full-fashioned, cotton sole, high heel, black and colors. $1.00

Men's Gordon Silk Lisle Half Hose
370 Heavy weight, ROUND TICKET,* double sole, high spliced heel, black and colors. 25c
470 Light weight, ROUND TICKET,* double sole, high spliced heel, extra long spliced toe, black, and colors. 25c

Misses' Gordon Hosiery
YL333 Light weight, silk lisle, wide hem top, heavily spliced, black, white and colors. 50c
162 Ingrain Silk, cotton top and sole, high spliced heel, black, white and tan. 25c
777 Misses' fine ribbed, ROUND TICKET,* medium weight, linen spliced heel and toe, black, white and tan. 25c
1610 Misses' fine ribbed, ROUND TICKET,* silk lisle, extra spliced, black, white and colors. 25c

395 Boy's ROUND TICKET,* heavy weight, linen heel and toe, black only. 25c

Infant's Gordon Hosiery
1088 Baby's Gordon Hose, silk lisle, light weight, fine ribbed, black, white and colors. 25c
1086 Baby's Gordon Hose, silk lisle, heavy weight, fine ribbed, black, white and colors. 25c
4120 Baby's Gordon Hose, Cashmere, fine ribbed, pure Australian wool, silk heel and toe, black, white and colors. 25c
41 "Little Queen" Gordon Hose, silk and wool, fine ribbed, black, white and colors. 35c
620 Gordon Thread Silk, ribbed, black, white and colors. 50c

*GORDON ROUND TICKET HOSIERY—The Round Ticket line of hosiery for boys, girls, women and men, stands for the greatest amount of durability possible in 25c hosiery. On the top of each pair of these stockings is a Yellow, Round Ticket, guaranteeing absolute satisfaction to the wearer.

Woman's Home Companion, March 1912, Gordon Hosiery.

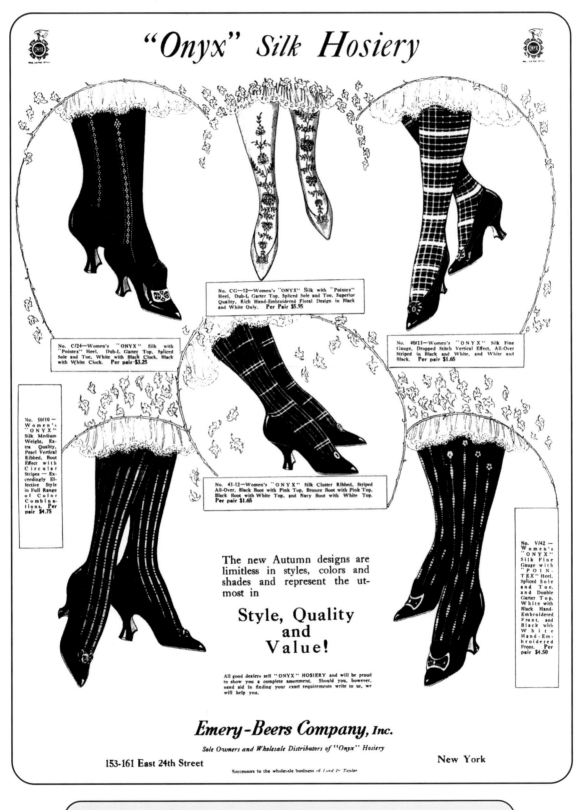

The Theatre, October 1916, Onyx silk hosiery with patterns and embroidery.

Ipswich Hosiery is made for Men, Women and Children
in styles that range in price from 25c to $1.85

One dollar a pair

PEACH, dawn, silver and banana are some of the newest and most fashionable tints in the rainbow range of De Luxe colors, to match or contrast with your frocks and shoes. You've never seen such beautiful stockings as these for a dollar.

On the inside and protecting the lustrous silken surface of these stockings is a smooth lining of long-wearing fibre.

In its texture, fit and flawless knitting, Ipswich De Luxe hosiery is far handsomer and more luxurious than you have ever thought such inexpensive stockings could be. If you don't find them at your favorite store we shall be glad to send you a sample pair. The coupon below is for that purpose.

IPSWICH *De Luxe* HOSIERY

IPSWICH MILLS, Ipswich, Mass. Please send me a pair of your De Luxe Stockings

Size_____ Color_____ I am enclosing a dollar.

Name_____

Address_____

IPSWICH MILLS, Ipswich, Mass.
Lawrence & Co.
Sole Selling Agents
Boston, New York, Chicago, St. Louis, Philadelphia
San Francisco, London, Eng.

Pictorial Review, September 1922, Ipswich hosiery, one dollar a pair.

June, 1927

TO BE WELL-GROOMED

In the matter of husbands ·· there may be some doubt as to the style of the groom. But in the matter of hosiery ·· every bride is certain of her grooming

when she selects McCallum Hose. Glorious, filmy hosiery for the wedding ensemble ·· severely simple styles made beautiful by the sheen and exquisite texture of the silk ·· styles less severe, and to some legs more becoming, show clocking at the sides or lace motifs in front. And for the other costumes of the trousseau there's any shade, there's any style. And they're always beautiful if they are ·· McCallums. The price range of McCallum begins at two dollars.

YOU JUST KNOW SHE WEARS THEM

The sheerest of the sheer, with a dainty openwork clock, in a pale flesh shade, in McCallum No. 278 ·· this is the perfect wedding hose.

For shadings, for style, for prices send for our hosiery booklet, McCallum Hosiery Company, Northampton, Massachusetts.

McCallum
Silk Hosiery

The Delineator, June 1927, McCallum silk hosiery ad.

Onyx ✦ Pointex
Silk Stockings

Lines
Sweeping Gracefully
Above the Heel

Sweet scent of orange blossoms—the majestic measures of the Wedding March. Then the tossed bouquet—laughter—carnival.

Clumsy, indeed, we would be to say that no wedding is successful unless the bride wears Onyx Pointex Silk Stockings.

But we do say that the bride who loves and knows pure silk, and who appreciates the subtle grace of the Pointex heel is among those who *would* have a charming wedding and who *will* remain charming.

The Delineator, June 1927, Onyx Pointex silk stockings.

Nylon was trademarked in 1939, creating a revolution in hosiery. Nylon was more sheer and more durable than silk. However, the World War II shortages in materials caused nylons to be a black market item, and many women actually colored their legs and drew a seam on the back with an eyebrow pencil. As the open-toed sandals and the sling-back pump became popular, so too did the sandal foot hose, without the reinforced toe and heel. Women of the early 1960s were still contending with the girdle and garter belt to hold their stockings, even though they had seamless stretch hose. It was the pantyhose, first patented in 1958 by a firm in France, that eventually eliminated the discomfort of girdles in the 1960s. Pantyhose was essential for the mod British-inspired short miniskirt of the mid-60s.

"*But Darling ...You might change your name some day Too*"

Yes, the name of Bettersilk Hosiery has been changed to Jane Grey Hosiery . . . due to the silk situation, of course. But only their name and the materials from which they are knit are different. For Jane Grey Hosiery is produced with the same meticulous care . . . by the same company that made Bettersilk Stockings famous for beauty and extra wear.

Jane Grey
FORMERLY Bettersilk
HOSIERY

GREY HOSIERY MILLS
Bristol, Virginia

Mademoiselle, April 1942, Grey Hosiery Mills.

Stockings and garter belts made a reappearance in the trend of nostalgic fashion during the late 1900s. As we put our best foot forward in the twenty-first century, we can look to the past for examples of classic feminine accessories.

more hours of wear! sheer runless beauty!
sheerloc™ the runless seamless stocking by

Hanes

U. S. PATENT 2609677 AND CANADIAN PATENT 488987. OTHER PATENTS PENDING.

Vogue, October 1962.

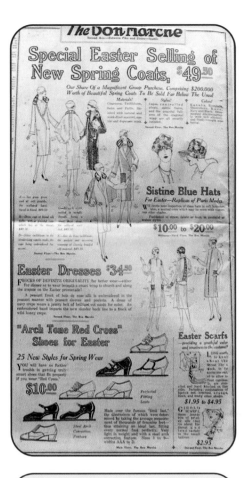

The Bon Marche
Second Ave.—Between Pike and Union—Seattle

Special Easter Selling of
New Spring Coats, $49.50

Our Share Of a Magnificent Group Purchase, Comprising $200,000
Worth of Beautiful Spring Coats To Be Sold Far Below The Usual
Materials!

Sistine Blue Hats
For Easter—Replicas of Paris Modes

$10.00 to $20.00

Easter Dresses $34.50

"Arch Tone Red Cross"
Shoes for Easter

25 New Styles for Spring Wear

$10.00

Easter Scarfs

$1.95 to $4.95

$2.95

Seattle Post Intelligencer ad for
Arch Tone Red Cross shoes on the social
page, September 1925.

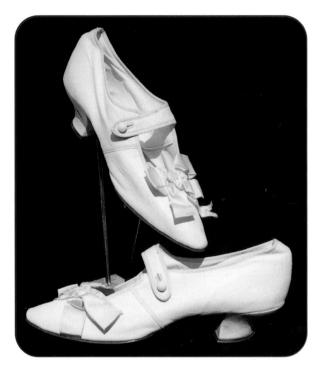

Ivory kid wedding shoes with single button
strap, silk bow and Louis heel, late 1800s. If excellent condition, $95.00 – 115.00.

Pale aqua silk dance slipper with single button strap, Louis heel, late Victorian, shown with
ribbon embellished shoe trees. $85.00 – 100.00.

Ivory silk court shoe with beaded ornamentation on vamps, Louis heel, late Victorian.
If excellent condition, $115.00 – 125.00.

Black suede high button boots, 16 smoke-gray
pearl shank buttons, long narrow toe, Louis heel,
marked inside "J. W. Robinson Co., Los Angeles, Fine
Footwear," early 1900s. $155.00 – 175.00.

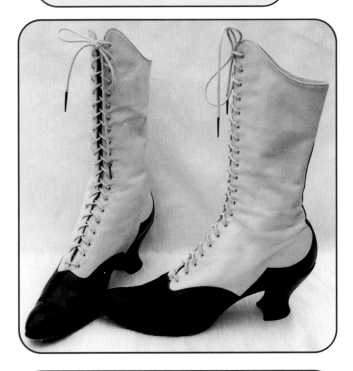

Spectator boot in black leather and ivory canvas,
scoop top, mid calf lace-up, early 1900s. $155.00 – 175.00.

Black work boots, bulldog toe with cap, nine button
closure, flat stacked heel, early 1900s. $45.00 – 65.00.

Gold kid evening shoe with high vamp and cutouts, rounded toe and medium heel, 1910 – 1920s. $55.00 – 75.00.

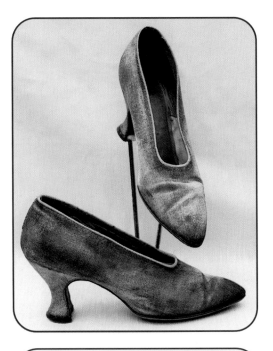

Metallic silver, which has become tarnished, simple court shoe with medium Louis heel, 1910 – 1920s. $55.00 – 75.00.

Black silk evening court shoe with large glittering rhinestone buckles, maker "Cecil, Paris," 1920s. $85.00 – 100.00.

Silver kid evening court shoes, medium heel, shown with "Minuet Dressing for Silver Kid Slippers" and rhinestone shoe jewelry that expands to clip onto shoe for secure fit, 1920s. $45.00 – 55.00 (shoe jewelry), $55.00 – 65.00.

Double bar street shoes, two-tone in black smooth leather and gray suede, gold shank buttons, medium heel, 1920s. $69.00 – 85.00.

Gray-blue moire faille court shoes with small diamante buckle ornamentation on the side, silver welting and heel, 1920s. $45.00 – 55.00.

Aqua moire faille evening shoe with single strap and diamante buckle, medium heel, late 1920 – 1930s. $55.00 – 65.00.

Black satin evening court shoe with rhinestone encrusted heels, 1920s. $90.00 – 105.00.

Seven bar shoe with pearl shank buttons in deep chocolate brown suede, marked "Seymour Troy Original," late 1910s – 1920s. $95.00 – 115.00.

Black silk T-strap with ankle buckle, cut-outs on vamp and ankle, marked on inner sole "Custom made by Newton Elkin, Philadelphia," size 3B hand written on inside, 1930s. If larger size, $65.00 – 75.00.

Multicolor patterned fabric open-toe evening sandal with silver braid trim and heel, diamante buckle on strap, 1930s. $55.00 – 65.00.

Lime green satin and faille ankle strap shoe with gold braid trim and diamante buckle, styled by "Rice O'Neill," 1930s. $55.00 – 65.00.

White ventilated oxford-type shoe for walking or sports, solid Cuban heel, lace-up, marked "Red Cross Shoes," 1930s. $35.00 – 45.00.

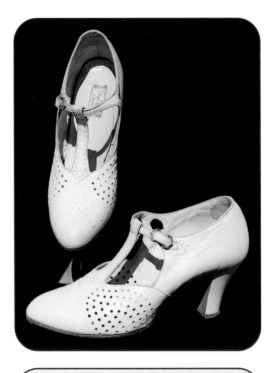

White leather T-strap ventilated day shoe, "Styl-eez" brand, medium heel, 1930s. $40.00 – 50.00.

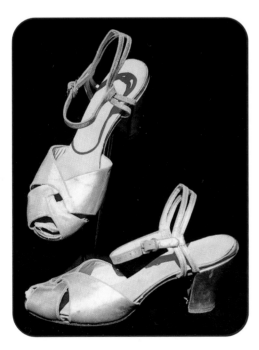

Open-toe evening sandal in gold leather with ankle strap, 1940s. As is, $15.00 – 25.00; excellent condition, $35.00 – 45.00.

Ivory linen shoes with delicate floral cross-stitch on toe, sides, and heel, leather lined, purchased at Persona Vintage Clothing, 1930 – 1940s. $55.00 – 65.00.

Loden green suede day shoe, rounded toe, medium heel with stitched leather bow on vamp, 1930s. $45.00 – 55.00.

Navy faille slip-on day shoe with elastic and leather cross straps for fit, marked "Krippendorf," 1940s. Excellent condition, $45.00 – 55.00.

Black velvet evening sandal with open-toe and ankle strap, 1940s. $55.00 – 65.00.

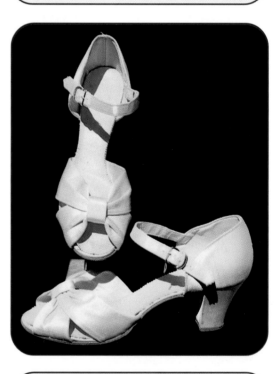

White satin evening dance sandal with ankle strap, medium heel, 1940s. $40.00 – 50.00.

Black suede, high back counter with ankle strap, open toe and sides, 1940s. $55.00 – 65.00.

Brick red felt sandal with ankle strap, sewn bead trim, carved wooden wedge heel with scene, marked "Philippines," may have been a souvenir, gift, Jane Audrey, late 1940 – 1950s. $30.00 – 45.00.

Open-toe sling back spectators in white suede and brown leather, platform, medium heel, marked "Airstep," 1940s. Excellent condition, $45.00 – 55.00.

Green snakeskin platform shoes with open toe and ankle strap, medium heel, 1940s. Excellent condition, $65.00 – 75.00.

Brown alligator open-toe, sling back with narrow strap over the instep, marked "Nordstrom's," 1950s. Excellent condition, $55.00 – 65.00.

Red sling back, T-strap, low heel and open toe, 1940s. $35.00 – 45.00.

Blue polka-dot canvas lace-up sport shoes, rubber sole, marked "Keds," 1950s. $15.00 – 20.00.

Penny loafers in brown leather, 1950s. Depending on condition, $15.00 – 35.00.

Saddle oxfords in beige and brown suede, striped laces, 1950s. $20.00 – 30.00.

Silver and gold glitter stiletto heels, marked "DeLiso Debs," 1950s. $25.00 – 35.00.

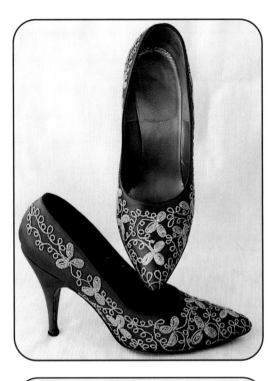

Green satin stiletto heels with metallic gold embroidery, marked "Evins," 1950s. $35.00 – 50.00.

Red satin spring-a-lators with red velvet bow and rhinestone ornamentation, marked "Joseph-Herbert Levine," late 1950s. $45.00 – 55.00.

Pink lace with elastic sling back, marked "Chandlers," late 1950s – 1960s. $30.00 – 40.00.

Snakeskin pumps, medium narrow heel, marked "Andrew Geller," 1960s. $35.00 – 45.00.

Orange silk pump with low narrow heel and self-fabric rosette on vamp, 1960s. $20.00 – 30.00.

Cinderella slippers of the seventies of clear plastic, open toe and sling back with acrylic curved-wedge heel, marked "Kimel," 1970s. $65.00 – 75.00.

Woven natural leather slip-on with high cut-out wedge heel of wood, marked "Stuff, Made in Mexico," purchased and worn by the author in the 1970s. $45.00 – 55.00.

Hippie-era clog, cork platform decorated with orange dots, leather uppers in yellow and aqua, 1970s. $49.00 – 69.00.

Ghillie-style oxford in cream and brown man-made materials, with chunky square heel and platform sole, 1970s. $55.00 – 65.00.

Red patent leather, with steel tipped stiletto heel, silver trim at back of pointed counter, 1980s. $20.00 – 35.00.

Polka-dot fabric shoe, low waist, medium low heel and button-bow trim, purchased and worn by the author in the 1980s. $15.00 – 25.00.

A single platform designer shoe, high waist, open toed with 4" sculptured heel, German designer. Shoes purchased by Stefanie Harman to accessorize bridesmaid ensemble in 1991, original price $140.00. Pair, $85.00 – 95.00.

Retro inspired red leather sling back, open laced with decorative gold-tone eyelets, purchased and worn by the author in the early 1990s. $35.00 – 45.00.

Rose felt slippers with woven ribbon around top, tassels on toe with pinked welting, 1915 – 1920s. $25.00 – 35.00.

Rose felt slippers with faux fur trim, ribbon woven through high vamp, self fabric bow, 1920s. $25.00 – 35.00.

Mauve print felt slippers with faux fur and cut-out felt with tassel on toe, 1920s. $35.00 – 45.00.

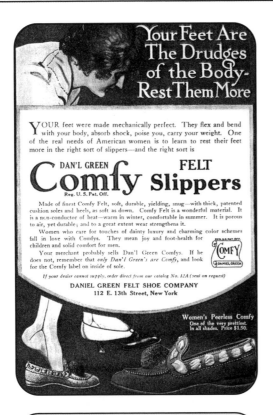

Your Feet Are The Drudges of the Body— Rest Them More

YOUR feet were made mechanically perfect. They flex and bend with your body, absorb shock, poise you, carry your weight. One of the real needs of American women is to learn to rest their feet more in the right sort of slippers—and the right sort is

DAN'L GREEN FELT Comfy Slippers
Reg. U. S. Pat. Off.

Made of finest Comfy Felt, soft, durable, yielding, snug—with thick, patented cushion soles and heels, as soft as down. Comfy Felt is a wonderful material. It is a non-conductor of heat—warm in winter, comfortable in summer. It is porous to air, yet durable; and to a great extent wear strengthens it.

Women who care for touches of dainty luxury and charming color schemes fall in love with Comfys. They mean joy and foot-health for children and solid comfort for men.

Your merchant probably sells Dan'l Green Comfys. If he does not, remember that *only Dan'l Green's are Comfy*, and look for the Comfy label on inside of sole.

If your dealer cannot supply, order direct from our catalog No. 12A (sent on request)

DANIEL GREEN FELT SHOE COMPANY
112 E. 13th Street, New York

Women's Peerless Comfy
One of the very prettiest.
In all shades. Price $1.50.

Ad for Daniel Green Comfy slippers of felt, original price $1.25. Ladies' Home Journal, September 1915.

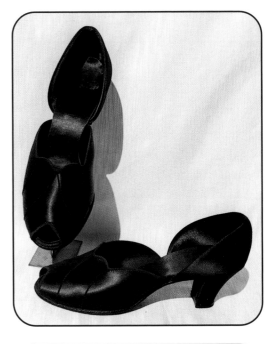

Royal blue satin D'Orsay mule, open toes, medium heel, marked "Daniel Green Comfy Slippers," 1940s. $40.00 – 50.00.

Burgundy satin D'Orsay mules with three gold straps over vamp, 1940s. $40.00 – 50.00.

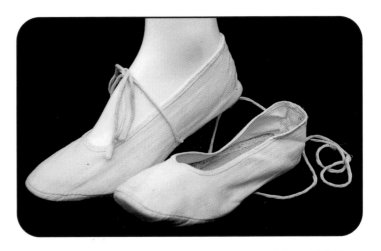

White cotton bathing shoes with fabric sole and string ties to secure, 1910s. $35.00 – 45.00.

Early sport shoes in cream cotton, celluloid button trim, medium heel and rubber soles, marked "Keds," 1910s. $45.00 – 55.00.

Black leather soccer shoes with lace-up closure, 1920s. $25.00 – 35.00.

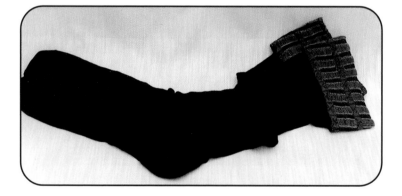

One pair of black fancy rayon stockings with pink and gold designed top edge, early 1900s. $18.00 – 25.00.

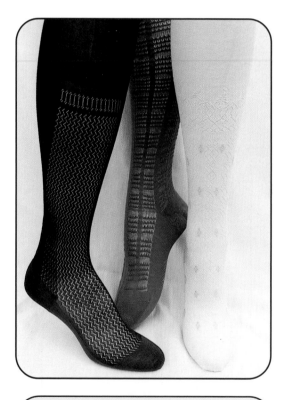

Three styles of cotton hosiery: brown open knit, label reads "Phoenix" brand; rust open knit label reads "Kawmills, Will Wear Well"; white lace with embroidered diamonds and a red "K" sewn onto top; early 1900s. Pair, $25.00 – 35.00.

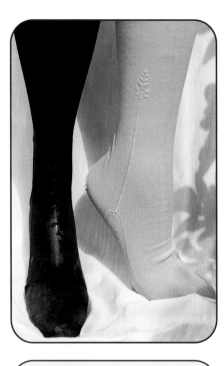

Purple patterned wool stockings, 26" long, early 1900s. $20.00 – 30.00.

Two pair of lisle stockings with ankle design: brown floral embroidery trim on brown; cream embroidered arrow on cream, early 1900s. Pair, $20.00 – 30.00.

Three pair: double seamed with black sole and lovely double point at ankle; cream lace; cream with black butterflies, early 1900s. Pair, $20.00 – 30.00.

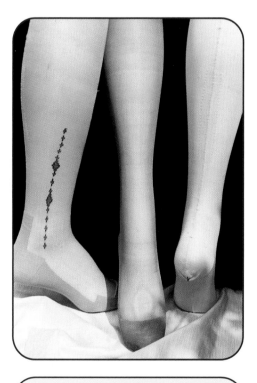

Three pair of stockings in cream, rust, and beige, 1920s – 1930s. Pair, $15.00 – 25.00.

Three pair: nude with black ankle pattern, silver gray, and cream, all seamed and lisle, early 1900 – 1920. Pair, $15.00 – 25.00.

Three pair of Victory Lace, popular during WWII to save materials for
the war effort, in three shades, all
seamed. Pair, $20.00 – 30.00.

Three pair of seamed stockings in
shades of nude, smoke, and black with lovely
seam details, late 1940s – 1950s. Pair,
$15.00 – 20.00.

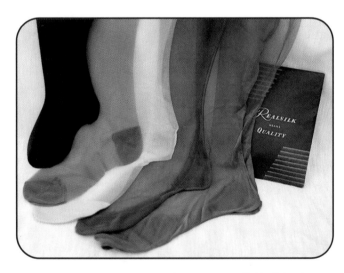

Five pair of stockings from left to right: black stretch
hose; aqua and white nylons; olive seamed; suntan "Real-
silk," which was a brand name, 1950s – early 1960s. Pair,
$10.00 – 20.00.

Seven pair of pastel nylon stockings,
seamed, 1960s. Pair, $10.00 – 20.00.

Six pair of seamless stockings, in various colors, purchased in Paris in 1966. Pair, $10.00 – 20.00.

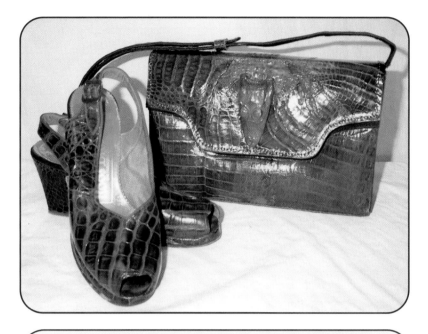

Alligator bag and matching open-toe, sling-back platform shoes of the 1940s. Set, $200.00 – 275.00.

Black and metallic silver shoes and clutch bag for evening, late 1950s. Set, $45.00 – 55.00.

Matching shoes and clutch bag in floral fabric that has tiny pleats, late 1950s. Set, $55.00 – 65.00.

Olive green matching handbag and heels for
daywear, late 1950s. Set, $45.00 – 55.00.

Dark green patent leather shoes and
matching handbag, 1950s. Set, $45.00 –
55.00.

Sling-back shoes and matching handbag of man-made
material in paisley pattern, new-old from the early 1970s
from I. Magnin (purchased from Persona Vintage Clothing,
original price, $73.00). Set, $55.00 – 75.00.

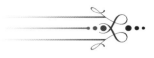

t seems a small postscript is needed to mention the wee accessories for children. The tiny gloves, bonnets, and shoes are so dear, they are often saved and cherished because they hold so many memories. When we see these miniature fashions we cannot but wonder, Who was that small child who wore these dear little shoes or gloves? Did they have a happy childhood, carefree and loved? We would like to know the story of these priceless treasures, a happy story to live on with the little tiny piece of history.

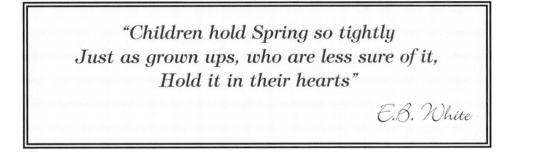

> *"Children hold Spring so tightly*
> *Just as grown ups, who are less sure of it,*
> *Hold it in their hearts"*
>
> *E.B. White*

In the nineteenth century fashions for boys and girls often reflected the fashions of adults. Interestingly enough, some accessories did not follow this trend. Hat styles, for instance, were often worn first by boys, then girls, then adopted into fashion by younger women, eventually being accepted as general fashion.

Real photo postcard of beautiful young girl, hand tinted.

P.S. Petite Size Accessories for children from head to toe.

Photo Credit: © 2000 Chris Bryant

Girls especially mirrored the fashion of their mothers, and were often seen as miniature adults with the dress, bonnet, and other accessories. There was more divergence between the fashion of young boys and their fathers, as evidenced by the tunics and long stockings worn until the age of six or seven. Because of the large amount of black that survives today, we know that children were dressed for mourning. The clothing of the Victorian period does not have the relaxed nature of clothing today, and it truly must reflect the restrictive nature of daily life.

Children's fashion illustrations, Godey's Lady's Book, January 1871.

Fancy costumes for children, Godey's Lady's Book, January 1871.

The hats of the 1840s for small children were usually made of straw or beaver, with round crowns and large brims. By the 1860s we see a variety of styles for children's hats, but most popular was the flat sailor hat with turned-up brim. The styles for boys and girls were often very similar. A broad-brimmed straw hat called the Pamela hat was "first worn only by children and young ladies, but they are now being adopted by ladies of all ages," from the *Englishwoman's Domestic Magazine* in 1865.

Typical young boy's costume with side-button leather shoes, inscribed on the back of photo "Jack Ludford."

Young girl of 10 or 11 years of age in 1880s fashions, with side-button boots.

The 1870s showed the narrow-brimmed straw hat, bound with ribbon and trimmed with ribbons or small feathers. By 1880 the tam-o-shanter with a soft flat crown was the favorite style for little boys and girls as well as the large soft beret. Bonnets for young girls with tie ribbons were always in fashion, as were the soft silk or lace baby bonnets for infants.

School boys wore the round cap, made in sections designed originally for sports such as cricket or football. The naval and the maritime influence was strong in fashion for boys from the 1880s to the turn of the century, both in dress and hat wear. The small sailor hats with turned-up brim were quite popular.

Fading photograph of two young children with hats, ornamented with feathers.

The socks worn by children of the Victorian period were usually white cotton, though black stockings became more usual by the 1880s. Cotton was always worn, but a fine wool did become favored as stated in *Lady's World*, in 1887, "Ribbed cashmere stockings for children have almost superseded cotton."

Infants have always worn small soft booties, either hand knit or hand sewn, especially in the earlier periods.

Small children wore little leather shoes with ankle straps, changing very little from the Mary Janes of modern times. Short boots, buttoned on the side, were also worn by young children. From the early 1860s through the 1870s, boots more often had a front fastening, often a tassel. The laced up boots became more popular by the 1890s. Boots for children began waning after the Edwardian era.

Real photo postcard of young girl sitting on a porch with her doll in a rural or country setting. Notice the crocheted or knitted bonnet, black socks, and very worn boots with a side button.

Two young girls who look as though they might be cousins in similar dresses, perhaps made from the same pattern, both with black stockings and boots. The names on the back of photo are Jessie Davidson Pionke and Esther Weed Bruce.

The tiny parasols or fans used by girls for playing dress-up or with their dolls in a make believe world prepared the way as little girls followed in the footsteps of their mothers. Girls have always wanted to help their moms in the kitchen. We see small size aprons as little girls learn to cook preparing for their role in society. Aprons for children were also worn to protect clothing when they were playing.

Fashion illustrations for young children, The Ladies' Home Journal, June 1909.

Two sisters in matching dresses with black sash. Note their white stockings and black strapped shoes and lovely straw hats with upturned brims, circa 1910.

The Little One From 4 to 10

Designs by Rowena Rice

A WHITE straw bonnet for a child of four is shown just above. It has a ruffle of plaited net edged with lace and faced with rows of lace. A band of light blue moiré ribbon is tied with a bow at each side of the back. The next one is for a little girl of four to six. It is of dull yellow straw, with a wreath of cornflowers and a blue velvet ribbon bow at one side. The third hat is suited for a girl of from six to ten. It is of fine black straw, with clusters of pink roses having alternate bows of light blue ribbon.

THE fourth is a rose hat for a little girl of from six to ten. It is of fine white straw rolled on the left side, trimmed with small pink roses and foliage and a bow of light blue moiré ribbon. The fifth is for a little one of from five to seven, and is made of Mexican straw, trimmed with buttercups, daisies and foliage with a blue bow on one side. The last is a sailor hat appropriate for a child of from six to ten years. It is of black straw with white straw facing, a cherry velvet band and flat stiff bow at the left side.

5244—White is always the prettiest color to use for the children's dresses, particularly for warm days. However, as it shows soil so very quickly it is often more practical to select one of the more serviceable colors for every-day wear. But a dress of sheer, thin material would be better white; while the heavier materials, like linen, poplin or piqué, look just as well in color. For a little girl of four years fine lawn or batiste may be used for this dress, with the square yoke and sleeve trimming of Irish or embroidered insertion bands. Patterns (No. 5244) come in three sizes: 2 to 6 years. Size 4 years requires three yards and a half of 27-inch material.

5250—A dress which is as simple in design as this offers many possibilities: it may be either a play dress or a best dress, depending upon the material of which it is made. For play nothing could be better than checked gingham or chambray, denim or percale in a solid color. But for best use dimity, lawn or batiste, omitting the pocket and the belt at the back. It would be pretty to set in a little lace or embroidered yoke and to make the collar of fine edging. Patterns (No. 5250) come in three sizes: 2 to 6 years. Size 4 years requires three yards of 27-inch material.

Bonnets, shoes, and parasols carried by children from age four to ten, as illustrated in The Ladies' Home Journal, June 1910.

Tucked inside a small shoe box with two tiny pairs of aqua silk baby shoes, I found an envelope with three cents postage, postmarked 1932. On folded yellowing paper, written in pencil was the following:

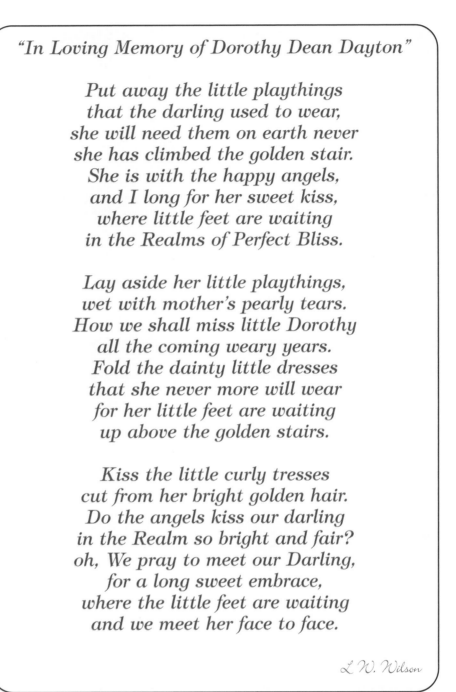

"In Loving Memory of Dorothy Dean Dayton"

Put away the little playthings
that the darling used to wear,
she will need them on earth never
she has climbed the golden stair.
She is with the happy angels,
and I long for her sweet kiss,
where little feet are waiting
in the Realms of Perfect Bliss.

Lay aside her little playthings,
wet with mother's pearly tears.
How we shall miss little Dorothy
all the coming weary years.
Fold the dainty little dresses
that she never more will wear
for her little feet are waiting
up above the golden stairs.

Kiss the little curly tresses
cut from her bright golden hair.
Do the angels kiss our darling
in the Realm so bright and fair?
oh, We pray to meet our Darling,
for a long sweet embrace,
where the little feet are waiting
and we meet her face to face.

L. W. Wilson

The two pairs of tiny aqua silk shoes are pictured on page 322 lower left. We know the sentiment above was appreciated by the parents because the poem, with envelope, has stayed with the shoes all these years. The poem gives the shoes more meaning, and when we see the tiny shoes they certainly help us understand the deep meaning of the poem. It is a poignant reminder of what precious memories a hankie, a pair of gloves, or a small pair of shoes can hold. These fashions in miniature have always been desirable collectibles, perhaps because of the cherished memories and great hopes.

Dainty Picturesque Apparel for the Rising Generation

Pantalet Dress
9270
Appliqué 12629

Bloomer Dress
1092

Suit 1007

Bloomer Dress
1098

Dress 1178

Dress 1169
Appliqué 12564

1178—Girls' and Juniors' One-piece Slip-on Dress. Designed for 6 to 17 years. Size 8 requires 2 yards 54-inch tricotine—1¼ yard braid for trimming collar. This frock of tricotine is both smart and practical for school days. Double box-plaits are formed at the side-fronts and a leather belt holds in the fulness at the waist-line.

9270—Child's Pantalet Dress. Designed for 2 to 8 years. Size 4 requires 2¼ yards 36-inch linen—¼ yard 36-inch contrasting linen for collar, cuffs, and trimming-bands. Appliqué, in design 12629, gives a novel touch to this little pantalet frock. The motifs may be cut from contrasting linen and couched down in blanket, chain, or buttonhole stitches.

1178   1225   9270   1092   1007   1098   1233

1177   1236   1234   1247   1235   1179   1169

Suit 1225

Bloomer Dress
1233
Appliqué 12623

Dress 1177

Bloomer Dress
1179
Embroidery 12623

Dress 1234

Dress 1247

Dress 1235
Embroidery 12596

1177—Girls' Dress. Designed for 6 to 14 years. Size 8 requires 1 yard 54-inch tweed—1¾ yard 54-inch check tweed for skirt—2¼ yards lace for collar—⅝ yard 36-inch lining for underwaist. Tweed makes a practical dress for the schoolgirl.

1225—Boys' Suit. Designed for 6 to 14 years. Size 8 requires 2 yards 54-inch tweed—2¾ yards 36-inch lining for jacket. The suit consists of a jacket and front-closing knickerbocker trousers.

1236—Girls' and Juniors' Dress. Designed for 10 to 17 years. Size 12 requires 3¾ yards 36-inch voile—4 yards grosgrain ribbon. In place of voile the frock could also be developed in silken fabric, such as crêpe de Chine, Canton crêpe, satin or Georgette crêpe.

1007—Boys' Suit. Designed for 1 to 4 years. Size 4 requires 1⅜ yard 36-inch satin—¼ yard 36-inch white satin for collar and applied plait. For more practical wear the suit could be developed in French serge, Poiret twill, corduroy, tweed, or cheviot.

1098—Girls' Bloomer Dress. Designed for 4 to 10 years. Size 8 requires 1¾ yard 54-inch tweed, 6 yards ribbon for trimming.

1169—Girls' One-piece Kimono Dress. Designed for 6 to 12 years. Size 12 requires 1⅝ yard 36-inch taffeta—1¼ yard 36-inch contrasting taffeta for lower section and piping. Appliqué, in design 12564, gives a smart trimming note to this little frock. The design may be cut from contrasting silk and couched down in blanket or buttonhole stitches.

DESCRIPTIONS CONTINUED ON PAGE 89

Patterns may be secured from any Pictorial Review Agent in the United States and Canada or by mail, postage prepaid, ... yo. ... dress the Company, 222 West 39th Street, New York City. Prices 20c to 35c.

Dainty Picturesque Apparel for young children to teens, The Ladies' Home Journal, September 1924.

42   Woman's World for May, 1929

Small Brother and Sister Love to Dress Alike

Some Novel Ideas for Distinctive School, Party and Play Costumes

Designed by SADIE P. LE SUEUR

Jack

Jill

Joe

Joy

Jerry

Julia

Jane

June

Jerome

John

IT ISN'T necessary to be a real twin in order to have a playmate with a matching costume, if one just has a little brother or sister of almost the same size and age.

These unusual brother and sister suits are so designed as to look almost exactly alike and still to be distinctly different as to masculine and feminine details. There is a matching bonnet for each dress and a matching hat for each little boy's suit. Delightful when worn in pairs, these suits are no less attractive when they appear singly.

Jack: Green gingham trousers are buttoned onto a white lawn blouse. Green blanket stitch outlines collar, cuffs and front of blouse where ruffle is attached. A little yellow duck is appliquéd onto trousers with another to match on the blouse. Designed for 6-year size.

Jill: A green gingham dress has white collar and cuffs outlined with green blanket stitch which also goes down front of dress. Green bonnet has white ruffle with a green thread at the edge. A yellow duck is appliquéd onto pocket, with another on opposite side of skirt. A 4-year model.

Joe: A pink gingham suit with white lawn collar and cuffs has a little boy appliquéd and embroidered on blouse front. Pink outline stitch is put around neck and cuffs. Matching pink hat is trimmed with buttons. A crochet edge or coarse narrow lace may be put around collar, cuffs and hat if desired. Designed for 4-year size.

Joy: A pink gingham dress has white lawn collar and cuffs to match *Joe's.* A little girl with blue dress and hair ribbon is appliquéd to front of dress. A pink hat to match has white ruffles around top and brim and white ties. This costume is designed for size 6 years.

Jerry: A one-piece suit of yellow gingham has white collar, cuffs and a yellow hat outlined with yellow buttonholing. Little boy with balloon is appliquéd in place. A 4-year model.

Julia: A yellow gingham dress to match *Jerry's* suit has a little girl with balloon appliquéd on front. Matching yellow bonnet has white ruffle and ties. Designed for 4-year size.

Jane: This white sateen dress and bonnet are finished with pink sateen binding and ruffles. Small pearl buttons trim band on dress front. Design on front is worked in outline stitch. Designed for 6-year size.

John: White sateen makes this one-piece suit. Pink sateen bands finish square neck and sleeves, and pink ruffles trim shoulders and outline front band. Design of boy flying kite is worked in outline stitch on front. A white hat is bound in pink and wears a pink band. Designed for 2-year size.

June: Blue gingham makes a play suit of smock and bloomers. White collar and cuffs are outlined with blue darning stitch and trimmed with ruffles having edges whipped with blue. Red hen and little yellow chickens worked in outline stitch on front. Blue bonnet is bound with white. A 2-year size.

Jerome: A smock and trousers make up this blue gingham suit which has white collar and cuffs like *June's.* Rooster is worked in outline stitch. Blue hat to match. Designed for size 2 years.

Suits and dresses, stamped flat, with floss and appliqués may be secured for $1.00 each from Woman's World, 4223 West Lake Street, Chicago

Very young children with matching bonnets and outfits, Woman's World, May 1929.

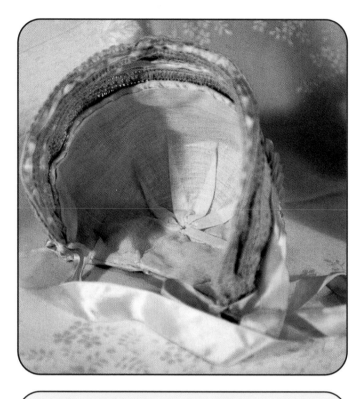

Inside view with decorative pink silk trim inside brim and the cotton lining, no label.

Child's natural straw bonnet with ruched pink silk and pink silk ribbon ties, early 1900s. $165.00 – 175.00. *Courtesy of Persona Vintage Clothing.*

Child's natural straw bonnet with pale yellow silk ribbon bow trim and black velvet lining inside brim, original ties missing, early 1900s. $155.00 – 175.00.

Child's heavy cotton twill cap in light brown with cream band, cord trim and tassel, lined, no label, late 1800s. $98.00 – 118.00.

Child's black straw bonnet with small black ostrich plumes, black lace trim and ribbon ties, early 1900s. $155.00 – 175.00.

Child's black velvet hat, narrow brim with ecru lace along the edge, burgundy silk bow trim on side, 1920 – 1930s. $45.00 – 55.00.

Child's parasol in black cotton, 14" long wood shaft, metal tip and wood handle with hole for tassel, early 1900s. $55.00 – 75.00.

Child's doll parasol in black cotton, 8" long wood shaft, metal tip, and porcelain handle with double tassel, early 1900s. $75.00 – 85.00.

Three examples of petite purses, the top gold-tone metal mesh purse measures 3" in length and could have been for a child; the middle silvertone mesh with the finger ring was probably a lady's dance purse, though a child would have enjoyed it; the lower brass ring mesh measures 3" length and may have been a child's, but more than likely was a woman's dating to the late 1800s. $55.00 – 85.00.

Child's drawstring purse in black velvet with gold-tone studs and tassel trim, 1950s. $15.00 – 20.00.

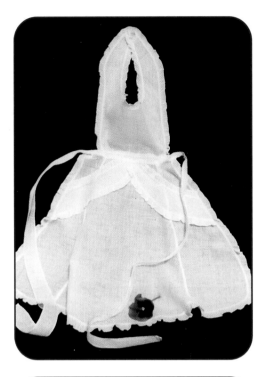

Child's white cotton apron with bib front, narrow ruffled edging all around, two side pockets, measures 18" from front neck to hemline, early 1900s. $20.00 – 25.00.

Child's white cotton bib-front apron with red and blue stripes, the initial L on lower edge, 1920 – 1940. $15.00 – 20.00.

McCall's pattern for children's apron #8956, 1950s.

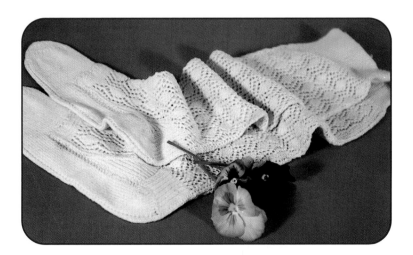

Child's white cotton hand-knit socks in open lace pattern, early 1900s. $27.00 – 37.00.

Child's black leather and fabric shoes, lace-up with black cotton pompons, late 1800s. $65.00 – 75.00.

Child's early leather shoes in brown and black, lace-up with cord ties, mid 1800s. $79.00 – 89.00.

Yellow silk slipper shoes, single strap with button worn with yellow silk dress shown in photo of child. Great example of documentation, gift from daughter who had original photo of her mother wearing the yellow silk dress (and probably shoes since they had always been kept together) dated 1893. Greater value placed on shoes because of condition, color, and documentation, $95.00 – 125.00.

Young child's button shoes, black leather, four buttons with scalloped edge, early 1900s. $75.00 – 85.00.

These shoes belonged to same child as shown on page 320, white kid leather with 11 buttons and lovely scalloped top edge, 1890s. $135.00 – 165.00.

Young child's rose quilted slippers with white rabbit fur trim and silk ribbon ties, early 1900s. Purchased from Persona Vintage Clothing. $45.00 – 55.00.

Young child's black and white two-tone leather button-up shoes, four buttons, tassel missing on one shoe, early 1900s. $50.00 – 65.00.

Black leather lace-up shoes for young child, measuring 3½" on sole, early 1900s. $45.00 – 55.00.

Two pair of handmade aqua silk shoes for infants; embroidered pair of silk tied moccasin style (for a baby boy) and embroidered single strap with button (for baby girl) came in a small box with the stamped envelope, dated 1932, see page 309. Pair, $45.00 – 55.00.

Four child's fans: red paper with floral design on wood sticks, 3¾" in length; ivory colored brisé plastic fan with rabbit design, 2½" length; tiny brisé plastic in pink and blue for a doll, 1¼" in length; brisé plastic deer design with blue guards, 2¾" in length. $10.00 – 15.00 each. Courtesy of Margaret Johntz Johnson Collection.

Single tiny white leather shoe with double button strap and tassel. Priceless.

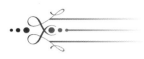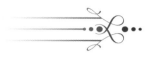

Not the End

The beginning of a new generation who loves dress-up and the nostalgia of vintage accessories.

Olivia Gabrielle Harman, age 3, author's grandaughter.

324

Photo credit: © 2000 Chris Bryant

Drama. Accessories in striking contrast.

325

Photo credit: © 2000 Andrew E. Cier

About the Author

t is a great pleasure for me to open my closets and trunks to share a passion that I have had for many years. It started innocently enough in an antique shop, just before Halloween as I rummaged through a trunk of old clothes. I found two old dresses, and asked, "How much?" "Five bucks each," was the reply.

Since I had majored in home economics and loved sewing my own clothes, I knew that $5.00 each was a pretty good buy, considering how much it would cost to make a costume. Little did I know what was about to begin. With a little research I discovered one piece was a classic 1920s black lace flapper dress lined in peach with a large bertha collar. The second piece was a periwinkle blue silk georgette hobble dress from the early teens, very delicate and in perfect condition. I still have these first two pieces, and of course they were never used as Halloween costumes. A passion for fashion started with these two dresses 25 years ago!

My collection has grown to several thousand pieces, including a vast array of accessories, over the past 25 years. I keep thinking I should quit, but one more piece finds it way into the closet. It has always been a special pleasure for me to share my collection through Nostalgic Fashion Presentations for groups, event promotions, or exhibits, as well as teaching college enrichment classes. My collection has also been a source of inspiration for articles that have been published in *Vintage Fashions* magazine, and then later as a contributing editor for *The Ladies' Gallery* magazine with my own regular column.

The Oregon coast has been my home for the past 20 years, raising one fabulous son, Rhett, who had a mother who was known to "play dress-up" at the drop of a hat! I have been active with our local museums and historical society, as well as a member of the Costume Society of America and the National Button Society. I probably should join Collectors Anonymous while I'm at it! Collectors are a strange lot; fortunately my husband, Tim, has adjusted quite well and is most supportive and understanding.

Although preserving this beautiful art form is my main purpose for writing this book, it is also a special pleasure to pass on information through exhibits and presentations. I feel these authentic fashions and accessories weave a social legacy with a rich cultural heritage, reflecting the changing image and role of women. As collectors we can take on a stewardship role, preserving these priceless garments and accessories for future generations to enjoy.

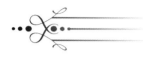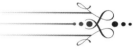

Resources

f you would like to learn more about your collection of accessories, there are many places that you can get additional information. The following are some areas to start your search.

Always begin with the person from whom you received the item. If it is a family purse or hankie or any other accessory, ask family members for information about the person who may have used the accessory. If the item was a gift to you, always ask the donor if they have any information, and be sure to make a note of who the original owner was or where they may have worn the item, or any other details.

If you have purchased the item from a vintage clothier or antique store, ask the store owner if they may have gotten any history with the accessory. Check the Yellow Pages under Clothing, then Vintage for dealers in your area. Most reputable dealers are happy to assist with passing on information that documents the accessory they are selling. I am indebted to Rosetta Hurley of Persona Vintage Clothing who assisted with this book by loaning specific accessories to be photographed, as well as reviewing the values listed.

Rosetta Hurley
Persona Vintage Clothing
100 Tenth Street
Astoria, OR 97103

Persona, a business of 13 years in the small coastal town of Astoria, has an extensive inventory of antique and collectible accessories, as well as clothing for men and women dating back to the late 1800s. The wonderful selection of accessories and the integrity with which they are represented are known by collectors, as well as other dealers. Rosetta has also been a personal friend for the past 15 years and is most helpful and knowledgeable in the field of vintage accessories. She can be contacted at (503) 325-3837; e-mail:rosetta@pacifier.com; website: www.personavintage.com.

As a collector, it is helpful to know the value of your collection. This is especially important in the case of a loss. A very good friend lost her entire collection due to a fire. This is the most dreaded situation a collector can imagine. We all want to be good caretakers, and we all know we need to take precautions to avoid damage and loss. A professional appraisal of your collection will at least offset the loss, even if the specific items cannot be replaced. Check your phone book for appraisers, and ask if they are a member of the International Society of Appraisers. A professional appraiser will be happy to give you references and their credentials.

Bette G. Bell,
ISA, CAAP of Guildmark Appraisals
P. O. Box 952
Edmonds, WA 98020

Bette and her husband Fred have been good friends for well over 20 years. Bette has been a professional appraiser for 14 years in the Seattle area, is a past president of the ISA Northwest Chapter, and has been on the ISA Advisory Council from 1989 to 1992. She has many credits to her name including the many volunteer hours with her local historical society. I am grateful that Bette reviewed the values in this book before publication. She can be contacted by phone (425)775-5650; or e-mail: stashn33@gte.net.

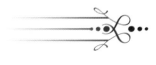

Bibliography

ooks on the subject of vintage accessories are many and varied. Check with your local book store. Books I have found helpful in researching this book include:

Armstrong, Nancy. *A Collector's History of Fans.*
———. *The Book of Fans.*
Buck, Anne M. *Victorian Costume and Costume Accessories.* Bedford: R.Bean, 1984.
Calasibetta, Charlotte Mankey. *Essential Terms of Fashion.* New York, New York: Fairchild Publications, 1986.
Campione, Adele. *Women's Hats.* San Francisco, CA: Chronicle Books, 1994.
Ettinger, Roseann. *Handbags.* Atglen, PA: Schiffer Publishing, 1999.
"Fans," a booklet published to accompany *"Ivory, Feathers and Lace,"* an exhibition of the Museum of London, 1985.
Foster, Vanda. *Bags and Purses.*
Gernsheim, Alison. *Victorian and Edwardian Fashion, A Photographic Survey.*
Holiner, Richard. *Antique Purses.*
Howell, Georgina. *In Vogue.* London, England: Condé Nast Books, 1991.
La Barre, Kathleen and Kay La Barre. *Reference Book of Women's Vintage Clothing: 1900 – 1919.* Portland, Oregon: LaBarre Books, 1990.

Langley, Susan. *Vintage Hats & Bonnets, 1770 – 1970.* Paducah, KY: Collector Books, 1998.
Laver, James. *Costumes Through The Ages.* New York, New York: Simon & Schuster, 1963.
Leventon, Melissa and Stephen de Pietri. *New Look to Now, French Haute Couture 1947 – 1987.* New York, New York: Rizzoli, 1989.
Mayor, Susan. *A Collector's Guide to Fans.*
Moore, Doris Langley. *Fashion Through Fashion Plates, 1771 – 1970.* New York, New York: C.N. Potter, 1971.
O'Keeffe, Linda. *Shoes, A Celebration of Pumps, Sandals, Slippers & More.* New York, New York: Workman, Pub., 1996.
Piecework Magazine, July / August 1999.
Probert, Christine. *Shoes in Vogue Since 1910.* New York, New York: Abbeville Press, 1981.
Rothstein, Natalie, ed. *Four Hundred Years of Fashion.* London, England: Victoria & Albert Museum in association with C. Collins, 1984.
Smith, Desire. *Hats, with Values.* Atglen, PA: Schiffer Publishing, 1996.
Swann, June. *Shoes, The Costume Accessories Series.*
Tortora, Phyllis and Keith Eubank. *A Survey of Historic Costume.*
Wilcox, R. Turner. *The Mode in Footwear.*
Wilson, Eunice. *A History of Shoe Fashion.*

Period Magazines

Barnard Magazine
Fancywork
Godey's Lady's Book
Mademoiselle
McCalls
Pictorial Review
The Delineator
The Ladies' Home Journal
The Theatre

The People's Home Journal
The Englishwoman's Domestic Magazine
The Illustrated American
Sears Roebuck Catalog
Wards Catalog
Woman's Home Companion
Woman's World
World of Fashion
Vogue

Internet Addresses

he Internet holds a vast amount of information available to collectors. The addresses are some I have visited and found helpful. I do not necessarily endorse them other than for information. Each person would have to make an informed decision whether to order merchandise or do business with them. Visiting a site can be entertaining, educational, and may hold some happy surprises!

- www.HamptonAntiques.com
- www.antiquedress.com
- www.designervintage.com
- www.pacificws.com/victorianlady
- www.rrnspace.com
- www.terraworld.net/users/b/bauer/lace
- www.victoriana.com
- www.victorianelegance.com
- www.victorianmillinery.com
- www.vintagesilhouettes.com
- www.personavintage.com

May I suggest museum and guild sites that will also be helpful to the collector:
- www.museumofvintagefashion.org/ or Museum of Vintage Fashion, Walnut Creek, CA
- www.museumofcostume.co.uk/ or Museum of Costume, Bath, England
- www.vam.ac.uk/ or Victoria and Albert Museum, London
- www.fitnyc.suny.edu/museum or Fashion Institute of Technology Museum, New York
- www.hand-fan.org/ or International Fan Collector's Guild
- www.hatsociety.com or The Hat Society, P.O. Box 33362, Austin, TX 78764-0362

By the time this book goes to press, the addresses could have changed, and most assuredly there will be many, many more to explore. Check your local or state historical societies for museums in your area that may have fashion collections. Have fun, this is a good start!

If your local bookstore does not carry this book, you can order an autographed copy from:

- ladies_accessories@excite.com or by writing to Lady With A Past, P. O. Box 601, Astoria, OR 97103 website: www.geocities.com/ladies_accessories.

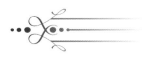

Index

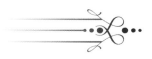

COLLECTOR BOOKS

Informing Today's Collector

For over two decades we have been keeping collectors informed on trends and values in all fields of antiques and collectibles.

DOLLS, FIGURES & TEDDY BEARS

4631	**Barbie Doll** Boom, 1986–1995, Augustyniak	$18.95
2079	**Barbie Doll** Fashion, Volume I, Eames	$24.95
4846	**Barbie Doll** Fashion, Volume II, Eames	$24.95
3957	**Barbie** Exclusives, Rana	$18.95
4632	**Barbie** Exclusives, Book II, Rana	$18.95
6022	The **Barbie Doll** Years, 5th Ed., Olds	$19.95
3810	**Chatty Cathy** Dolls, Lewis	$15.95
5352	Collector's Ency. of **Barbie** Doll Exclusives & More, 2nd Ed.,Augustyniak	$24.95
2211	Collector's Encyclopedia of **Madame Alexander** Dolls, Smith	$24.95
4863	Collector's Encyclopedia of **Vogue Dolls**, Izen/Stover	$29.95
5904	Collector's Guide to **Celebrity Dolls**, Spurgeon	$24.95
5599	Collector's Guide to **Dolls of the 1960s and 1970s**, Sabulis	$24.95
6030	Collector's Guide to **Horsman Dolls**, Jensen	$29.95
6025	**Doll Values**, Antique to Modern, 6th Ed., Moyer	$12.95
6032	**Madame Alexander** Collector's Dolls Price Guide #27, Crowsey	$12.95
6033	**Modern Collectible Dolls**, Volume VI, Moyer	$24.95
5689	**Nippon Dolls** & Playthings, Van Patten/Lau	$29.95
5365	**Peanuts Collectibles**, Podley/Bang	$24.95
6026	**Small Dolls of the 40s & 50s**, Stover	$29.95
5253	Story of **Barbie**, 2nd Ed., Westenhouser	$24.95
5277	**Talking Toys** of the 20th Century, Lewis	$15.95
2084	**Teddy Bears, Annalee's & Steiff** Animals, 3rd Series, Mandel	$19.95
5371	**Teddy Bear** Treasury, Yenke	$19.95
1808	Wonder of **Barbie**, Manos	$9.95
1430	World of **Barbie** Dolls, Manos	$9.95
4880	World of **Raggedy Ann** Collectibles, Avery	$24.95

TOYS & MARBLES

2333	Antique & Collectible **Marbles**, 3rd Ed., Grist	$9.95
4559	Collectible **Action Figures**, 2nd Ed., Manos	$17.95
2338	Collector's Encyclopedia of **Disneyana**, Longest, Stern	$24.95
5900	Collector's Guide to **Battery Toys**, 2nd Edition, Hultzman	$24.95
4566	Collector's Guide to **Tootsietoys**, 2nd Ed., Richter	$19.95
5169	Collector's Guide to **TV Toys** & Memorabilia, 2nd Ed., Davis/Morgan	$24.95
5360	**Fisher-Price Toys**, Cassity	$19.95
5593	Grist's Big Book of **Marbles**, 2nd Ed.	$24.95
3970	Grist's Machine-Made & Contemporary **Marbles**, 2nd Ed.	$9.95
5267	**Matchbox Toys**, 1947 to 1998, 3rd Ed., Johnson	$19.95
5830	**McDonald's** Collectibles, 2nd Edition, Henriques/DuVall	$24.95
5673	Modern **Candy Containers** & Novelties, Brush/Miller	$19.95
1540	Modern **Toys** 1930–1980, Baker	$19.95
5920	**Schroeder's Collectible Toys**, Antique to Modern Price Guide, 8th Ed.	$17.95
5908	**Toy Car** Collector's Guide, Johnson	$19.95

FURNITURE

3716	American **Oak** Furniture, Book II, McNerney	$12.95
1118	Antique **Oak** Furniture, Hill	$7.95
3720	Collector's Encyclopedia of **American** Furniture, Vol. III, Swedberg	$24.95
5359	Early **American** Furniture, Obbard	$12.95
1755	Furniture of the **Depression Era**, Swedberg	$19.95
3906	**Heywood-Wakefield** Modern Furniture, Rouland	$18.95
1885	**Victorian** Furniture, Our American Heritage, McNerney	$9.95
3829	**Victorian** Furniture, Our American Heritage, Book II, McNerney	$9.95

JEWELRY, HATPINS, WATCHES & PURSES

4704	Antique & Collectible **Buttons**, Wisniewski	$19.95
1748	Antique **Purses**, Revised Second Ed., Holiner	$19.95
4850	Collectible **Costume Jewelry**, Simonds	$24.95
5675	Collectible **Silver Jewelry**, Rezazadeh	$24.95
3722	Collector's Ency. of **Compacts**, Carryalls & Face Powder Boxes, Mueller	$24.95
4940	**Costume Jewelry**, A Practical Handbook & Value Guide, Rezazadeh	$24.95
5812	Fifty Years of Collectible **Fashion Jewelry**, 1925–1975, Baker	$24.95

1424	**Hatpins** & Hatpin Holders, Baker	$9.95
5695	**Ladies' Vintage Accessories**, Bruton	$24.95
1181	100 Years of Collectible **Jewelry**, 1850–1950, Baker	$9.95
4729	**Sewing Tools** & Trinkets, Thompson	$24.95
6038	**Sewing Tools** & Trinkets, Volume 2, Thompson	$24.95
6039	Signed Beauties of **Costume Jewelry**, Brown	$24.95
5620	Unsigned Beauties of **Costume Jewelry**, Brown	$24.95
4878	Vintage & Contemporary **Purse Accessories**, Gerson	$24.95
5696	Vintage & Vogue Ladies' **Compacts**, 2nd Edition, Gerson	$29.95
5923	**Vintage Jewelry** for Investment & Casual Wear, Edeen	$24.95

INDIANS, GUNS, KNIVES, TOOLS, PRIMITIVES

1868	Antique **Tools**, Our American Heritage, McNerney	$9.95
5616	Big Book of **Pocket Knives**, Stewart	$19.95
4943	Field Guide to Flint **Arrowheads & Knives** of the North American Indian	$9.95
2279	**Indian Artifacts** of the Midwest, Book I, Hothem	$14.95
3885	**Indian Artifacts** of the Midwest, Book II, Hothem	$16.95
4870	**Indian Artifacts** of the Midwest, Book III, Hothem	$18.95
5685	**Indian Artifacts** of the Midwest, Book IV, Hothem	$19.95
6132	**Modern Guns**, Identification & Values, 14th Ed., Quertermous	$14.95
2164	**Primitives**, Our American Heritage, McNerney	$9.95
1759	**Primitives**, Our American Heritage, 2nd Series, McNerney	$14.95
6031	Standard **Knife** Collector's Guide, 4th Ed., Ritchie & Stewart	$14.95
5999	**Wilderness** Survivor's Guide, Hamper	$12.95

PAPER COLLECTIBLES & BOOKS

4633	**Big Little Books**, Jacobs	$18.95
5902	**Boys' & Girls' Book** Series	$19.95
4710	Collector's Guide to **Children's Books**, 1850 to 1950, Volume I, Jones	$18.95
5153	Collector's Guide to **Chidren's Books**, 1850 to 1950, Volume II, Jones	$19.95
5596	Collector's Guide to **Children's Books**, 1950 to 1975, Volume III, Jones	$19.95
1441	Collector's Guide to **Post Cards**, Wood	$9.95
2081	Guide to Collecting **Cookbooks**, Allen	$14.95
5825	Huxford's **Old Book** Value Guide, 13th Ed.	$19.95
2080	Price Guide to **Cookbooks** & Recipe Leaflets, Dickinson	$9.95
3973	**Sheet Music** Reference & Price Guide, 2nd Ed., Pafik & Guiheen	$19.95
6041	Vintage **Postcards for the Holidays**, Reed	$24.95
4733	**Whitman Juvenile Books**, Brown	$17.95

GLASSWARE

5602	Anchor Hocking's **Fire-King** & More, 2nd Ed.	$24.95
4561	Collectible **Drinking Glasses**, Chase & Kelly	$17.95
5823	Collectible **Glass Shoes**, 2nd Edition, Wheatley	$24.95
5897	Coll. **Glassware** from the 40s, 50s & 60s, 6th Ed., Florence	$19.95
1810	Collector's Encyclopedia of **American Art Glass**, Shuman	$29.95
5907	Collector's Encyclopedia of **Depression Glass**, 15th Ed., Florence	$19.95
1961	Collector's Encyclopedia of **Fry Glassware**, Fry Glass Society	$24.95
1664	Collector's Encyclopedia of **Heisey Glass**, 1925–1938, Bredehoft	$24.95
3905	Collector's Encyclopedia of **Milk Glass**, Newbound	$24.95
4936	Collector's Guide to **Candy Containers**, Dezso/Poirier	$19.95
5820	Collector's Guide to **Glass Banks**, Reynolds	$24.95
4564	**Crackle Glass**, Weitman	$19.95
4941	**Crackle Glass**, Book II, Weitman	$19.95
4714	**Czechoslovakian Glass** and Collectibles, Book II, Barta/Rose	$16.95
5528	Early American **Pattern Glass**, Metz	$17.95
6125	**Elegant Glassware** of the Depression Era, 10th Ed., Florence	$24.95
3981	Evers' Standard **Cut Glass** Value Guide	$12.95
5614	Field Guide to **Pattern Glass**, McCain	$17.95
5615	Florence's **Glassware** Pattern Identification Guide, Vol. II	$19.95
4719	**Fostoria**, Etched, Carved & Cut Designs, Vol. II, Kerr	$24.95
3883	**Fostoria** Stemware, The Crystal for America, Long/Seate	$24.95
5261	**Fostoria** Tableware, 1924 – 1943, Long/Seate	$24.95
5361	**Fostoria** Tableware, 1944 – 1986, Long/Seate	$24.95

cb
COLLECTOR BOOKS
Informing Today's Collector

5604	**Fostoria**, Useful & Ornamental, Long/Seate	$29.95
5899	**Glass & Ceramic Baskets**, White	$19.95
4644	**Imperial Carnival Glass**, Burns	$18.95
5827	**Kitchen Glassware** of the Depression Years, 6th Ed., Florence	$24.95
5600	Much More Early American **Pattern Glass**, Metz	$17.95
5915	**Northwood Carnival Glass**, 1908 – 1925, Burns	$19.95
6136	Pocket Guide to **Depression Glass**, 13th Ed., Florence	$12.95
6023	Standard Encyclopedia of **Carnival Glass**, 8th Ed., Edwards/Carwile	$29.95
6024	Standard **Carnival Glass** Price Guide, 13th Ed., Edwards/Carwile	$9.95
6035	Standard Encyclopedia of **Opalescent Glass**, 4th Ed., Edwards/Carwile	$24.95
4732	**Very Rare Glassware** of the Depression Years, 5th Series, Florence	$24.95
4656	**Westmoreland Glass**, Wilson	$24.95

POTTERY

4927	**ABC Plates & Mugs**, Lindsay	$24.95
4929	**American Art Pottery**, Sigafoose	$24.95
4630	**American Limoges**, Limoges	$24.95
1312	**Blue & White Stoneware**, McNerney	$9.95
1959	**Blue Willow**, 2nd Ed., Gaston	$14.95
4851	Collectible **Cups & Saucers**, Harran	$18.95
5901	Collecting **Blue Willow**, Harman	$19.95
1373	Collector's Encyclopedia of **American Dinnerware**, Cunningham	$24.95
4931	Collector's Encyclopedia of **Bauer Pottery**, Chipman	$24.95
4658	Collector's Encyclopedia of **Brush-McCoy Pottery**, Huxford	$24.95
5034	Collector's Encyclopedia of **California Pottery**, 2nd Ed., Chipman	$24.95
3723	Collector's Encyclopedia of **Cookie Jars**, Book II, Roerig	$24.95
4939	Collector's Encyclopedia of **Cookie Jars**, Book III, Roerig	$24.95
5748	Collector's Encyclopedia of **Fiesta**, 9th Ed., Huxford	$24.95
3961	Collector's Encyclopedia of **Early Noritake**, Alden	$24.95
3812	Collector's Encyclopedia of **Flow Blue China**, 2nd Ed., Gaston	$24.95
3431	Collector's Encyclopedia of **Homer Laughlin China**, Jasper	$24.95
1276	Collector's Encyclopedia of **Hull Pottery**, Roberts	$19.95
3962	Collector's Encyclopedia of **Lefton China**, DeLozier	$19.95
4855	Collector's Encyclopedia of **Lefton China**, Book II, DeLozier	$19.95
5609	Collector's Encyclopedia of **Limoges Porcelain**, 3rd Ed., Gaston	$29.95
2334	Collector's Encyclopedia of **Majolica Pottery**, Katz-Marks	$19.95
1358	Collector's Encyclopedia of **McCoy Pottery**, Huxford	$19.95
5677	Collector's Encyclopedia of **Niloak**, 2nd Edition, Gifford	$29.95
3837	Collector's Encyclopedia of **Nippon Porcelain**, Van Patten	$24.95
1665	Collector's Ency. of **Nippon Porcelain**, 3rd Series, Van Patten	$24.95
5053	Collector's Ency. of **Nippon Porcelain**, 5th Series, Van Patten	$24.95
5678	Collector's Ency. of **Nippon Porcelain**, 6th Series, Van Patten	$29.95
1447	Collector's Encyclopedia of **Noritake**, Van Patten	$19.95
4951	Collector's Encyclopedia of **Old Ivory China**, Hillman	$24.95
5564	Collector's Encyclopedia of **Pickard China**, Reed	$29.95
3877	Collector's Encyclopedia of **R.S. Prussia**, 4th Series, Gaston	$24.95
5679	Collector's Encyclopedia of **Red Wing Art Pottery**, Dollen	$24.95
5618	Collector's Encyclopedia of **Rosemeade Pottery**, Dommel	$24.95
5841	Collector's Encyclopedia of **Roseville Pottery**, Revised, Huxford/Nickel	$24.95
5842	Collector's Encyclopedia of **Roseville Pottery**, 2nd Series, Huxford/Nickel	$24.95
5917	Collector's Encyclopedia of **Russel Wright**, 3rd Editon, Kerr	$29.95
4713	Collector's Encyclopedia of **Salt Glaze Stoneware**, Taylor/Lowrance	$24.95
5370	Collector's Encyclopedia of **Stangl Dinnerware**, Runge	$24.95
5921	Collector's Encyclopedia of **Stangl Artware**, Lamps, and Birds, RUnge	$29.95
3314	Collector's Encyclopedia of **Van Briggle Art Pottery**, Sasicki	$24.95
4563	Collector's Encyclopedia of **Wall Pockets**, Newbound	$19.95
2111	Collector's Encyclopedia of **Weller Pottery**, Huxford	$29.95
5680	Collector's Guide to **Feather Edge Ware**, McAllister	$19.95
3876	Collector's Guide to **Lu-Ray Pastels**, Meehan	$18.95
3814	Collector's Guide to **Made in Japan Ceramics**, White	$18.95
4646	Collector's Guide to **Made in Japan Ceramics**, Book II, White	$18.95
2339	Collector's Guide to **Shawnee Pottery**, Vanderbilt	$19.95
1425	**Cookie Jars**, Westfall	$9.95
3440	**Cookie Jars**, Book II, Westfall	$19.95
5909	**Dresden Porcelain** Studios, Harran	$29.95

5918	Florence's Big Book of **Salt & Pepper Shakers**	$24.95
2379	Lehner's Ency. of **U.S. Marks** on Pottery, Porcelain & China	$24.95
4722	**McCoy Pottery**, Collector's Reference & Value Guide, Hanson/Nissen	$19.95
5913	**McCoy Pottery**, Volume III, Hanson & Nissen	$29.95
5691	**Post86 Fiesta**, Identification & Value Guide, Racheter	$19.95
1670	**Red Wing Collectibles**, DePasquale	$9.95
1440	**Red Wing Stoneware**, DePasquale	$9.95
6037	**Rookwood Pottery**, Nicholson & Thomas	$24.95
1632	**Salt & Pepper Shakers**, Guarnaccia	$9.95
5091	**Salt & Pepper Shakers** II, Guarnaccia	$18.95
3443	**Salt & Pepper Shakers** IV, Guarnaccia	$18.95
3738	**Shawnee Pottery**, Mangus	$24.95
4629	Turn of the Century **American Dinnerware**, 1880s–1920s, Jasper	$24.95
3327	**Watt Pottery** – Identification & Value Guide, Morris	$19.95
5924	**Zanesville Stoneware** Company, Rans, Ralston & Russell	$24.95

OTHER COLLECTIBLES

5916	Advertising **Paperweights**, Holiner & Kammerman	$24.95
5838	Advertising **Thermometers**, Merritt	$16.95
5898	Antique & Contemporary **Advertising Memorabilia**, Summers	$24.95
5814	Antique **Brass & Copper** Collectibles, Gaston	$24.95
1880	Antique **Iron**, McNerney	$9.95
3872	Antique **Tins**, Dodge	$24.95
4845	Antique **Typewriters & Office Collectibles**, Rehr	$19.95
5607	Antiquing and Collecting on the **Internet**, Parry	$12.95
1128	**Bottle** Pricing Guide, 3rd Ed., Cleveland	$7.95
3718	Collectible **Aluminum**, Grist	$16.95
4560	Collectible **Cats**, An Identification & Value Guide, Book II, Fyke	$19.95
5060	Collectible **Souvenir Spoons**, Bednersh	$19.95
5676	Collectible **Souvenir Spoons**, Book II, Bednersh	$29.95
5666	Collector's Encyclopedia of **Granite Ware**, Book 2, Greguire	$29.95
5836	Collector's Guide to **Antique Radios**, 5th Ed., Bunis	$19.95
3966	Collector's Guide to **Inkwells**, Identification & Values, Badders	$18.95
4947	Collector's Guide to **Inkwells**, Book II, Badders	$19.95
5681	Collector's Guide to **Lunchboxes**, White	$19.95
5621	Collector's Guide to **Online Auctions**, Hix	$12.95
4652	Collector's Guide to **Transistor Radios**, 2nd Ed., Bunis	$16.95
4864	Collector's Guide to **Wallace Nutting Pictures**, Ivankovich	$18.95
1629	**Doorstops**, Identification & Values, Bertoia	$9.95
5683	**Fishing Lure** Collectibles, 2nd Ed., Murphy/Edmisten	$29.95
5911	**Flea Market Trader**, 13th Ed., Huxford	$9.95
4945	**G-Men and FBI Toys** and Collectibles, Whitworth	$18.95
6029	**Garage Sale & Flea Market Annual**, 10th Ed.	$19.95
3819	**General Store** Collectibles, Wilson	$24.95
5912	The **Heddon** Legacy, A Century of Classic **Lures**, Roberts & Pavey	$29.95
2216	**Kitchen Antiques**, 1790–1940, McNerney	$14.95
5991	**Lighting Devices** & Accessories of the 17th – 19th Centuries, Hamper	$9.95
5686	**Lighting Fixtures** of the Depression Era, Book I, Thomas	$24.95
4950	The **Lone Ranger**, Collector's Reference & Value Guide, Felbinger	$18.95
6028	Modern **Fishing Lure** Collectibles, Lewis	$24.95
2026	**Railroad** Collectibles, 4th Ed., Baker	$14.95
5619	**Roy Rogers and Dale Evans** Toys & Memorabilia, Coyle	$24.95
5919	**Schroeder's Antiques Price Guide**, 20th Ed., Huxford	$14.95
5007	**Silverplated Flatware**, Revised 4th Edition, Hagan	$18.95
6040	**Star Wars** Super Collector's Wish Book, Carlton	$29.95
6139	Summers' Guide to **Coca-Cola**, 4th Ed.	$24.95
5905	Summers' Pocket Guide to **Coca-Cola**, 3rd Ed.	$12.95
3892	**Toy & Miniature Sewing Machines**, Thomas	$18.95
4876	**Toy & Miniature Sewing Machines**, Book II, Thomas	$24.95
3977	Value Guide to **Gas Station Memorabilia**, Summers & Priddy	$24.95
4877	Vintage **Bar Ware**, Visakay	$24.95
5925	The Vintage Era of **Golf Club Collectibles**, John	$29.95
6010	The Vintage Era of **Golf Club Collectibles** Collector's Log, John	$9.95
6036	Vintage **Quilts**, Aug, Newman & Roy	$24.95
4935	The W.F. Cody **Buffalo Bill** Collector's Guide with Values	$24.95

This is only a partial listing of the books on antiques that are available from Collector Books. All books are well illustrated and contain current values. Most of these books are available from your local bookseller, antique dealer, or public library. If you are unable to locate certain titles in your area, you may order by mail from COLLECTOR BOOKS, P.O. Box 3009, Paducah, KY 42002-3009. Customers with Visa, Discover or MasterCard may phone in orders from 7:00–5:00 CST, Monday–Friday, Toll Free 1-800-626-5420, or online at www.collectorbooks.com. Add $3.00 for postage for the first book ordered and 50¢ for each additional book. Include item number, title, and price when ordering. Allow 14 to 21 days for delivery.

Schroeder's ANTIQUES Price Guide

OUR #1 BEST-SELLER!

...is the #1 bestselling antiques & collectibles value guide on the market today, and here's why...

• More than 450 advisors, well-known dealers, and top-notch collectors work together with our editors to bring you accurate information regarding pricing and identification.

• More than 50,000 items in over 600 categories are listed along with hundreds of sharp original photos that illustrate not only the rare and unusual, but the common, popular collectibles as well.

• Each large close-up shot shows important details clearly. Every subject is represented with histories and background information, a feature not found in any of our competitors' publications.

• Our editors keep abreast of newly developing trends, often adding several new categories a year as the need arises.

Schroeder's ANTIQUES Price Guide

OUR #1 BEST-SELLER!

Identification & Values of Over 50,000 Antiques & Collectibles

8½" x 11"
608 pages
$14.95

If it merits the interest of today's collector, you'll find it in *Schroeder's*. And you can feel confident that the information we publish is up-to-date and accurate. Our advisors thoroughly check each category to spot inconsistencies, listings that may not be entirely reflective of market dealings, and lines too vague to be of merit. Only the best of the lot remains for publication.

Without doubt, you'll find
Schroeder's Antiques Price Guide
the only one to buy for reliable information and values.

cb

COLLECTOR BOOKS
P.O. Box 3009 • Paducah, KY 42002–3009
www.collectorbooks.com